"In *My Salvation Is Close at Hand*, Benjamin Giffone provides the tools necessary for preachers in our present generation to engage responsibly with the closing section of the book of Isaiah. These chapters, from what is often considered the 'fifth gospel,' are rarely broached in Christian circles, even though Jesus began his ministry by reading from their very core in Isaiah 61. Take this opportunity to read and preach the full context of Christ's missional text with attention to its message to a community reeling from the exile which provides perspective for all of us bringing the gospel into alienating circumstances."

—MARK J. BODA, professor of Old Testament, McMaster Divinity College, Hamilton, Ontario, Canada

"Benjamin Giffone is inclined to think that the last part of the book of Isaiah (maybe the least-read part) is especially significant for our age. It's a day when the people of God are down-sized and down-hearted. We need God to encourage us and challenge us, and that's what God does for the people of God in Isaiah 56–66. So read Benjamin Giffone's exposition of these chapters!"

—JOHN GOLDINGAY, senior professor of Old Testament, Fuller Seminary

"In *My Salvation Is Close at Hand*, Benjamin Giffone offers an accessible yet rich look at Trito-Isaiah (Isa 56–66), highlighting how its original message to a post-exilic community living in the unique political tensions of the Persian Period offers an analogy for thinking through our Christian message and witness within in the post-Christian West."

—JOHN DUNNE, associate professor of New Testament, Bethel Seminary, St. Paul, Minnesota

"In this useful volume, *My Salvation Is Close at Hand*, Benjamin Giffone provides Christians around the world with the resources they need to interact with the last stratum (chapters 56–66) of the book of Isaiah in a masterful manner. The profound messages of Isaiah 56–66 will be better understood and appreciated by preachers, pastors and lay readers in the face of the challenges and the opportunities of our post-Christian societies. Giffone offers insightful interpretations of the most significant passages from the book of Isaiah engaging his own existential experiences with the issues such as immigration, diaspora, family, gender, alienation, scar, and much more."

—JOHANNES UNSOK RO, professor of Old Testament studies, International Christian University

"Dr. Benjamin D. Giffone has written an engaging, relevant, and thought-provoking work on Isaiah 56–66. Attending to the details of the biblical text, he considers how these passages connect to our culture, society, church, and individual lives. His reflections and prayers suggest practical implications for living and encourage modern readers to continue to learn from the Old Testament."

—BRIAN G. TOEWS, professor, Center for University Studies, Cairn University

"In this wonderfully accessible guide to Isaiah 56–66, Giffone provides rich and helpful content that makes one of the most important prophetic texts approachable and understandable, helping students, pastors, and laypeople hone their reading and interpretive skills so that the message of these chapters can be applied in incisive ways for our complex, modern context."

—SEULGI L. BYUN, chair, Department of Biblical and Religious Studies and Philosophy, Grove City College

My Salvation Is Close at Hand

My Salvation Is Close at Hand

Isaiah 56–66 for the Church After Christendom

BENJAMIN D. GIFFONE

WIPF & STOCK · Eugene, Oregon

MY SALVATION IS CLOSE AT HAND
Isaiah 56–66 for the Church After Christendom

Copyright © 2025 Benjamin D. Giffone. All rights reserved. Except for brief quotations in critical publications or reviews, no part of this book may be reproduced in any manner without prior written permission from the publisher. Write: Permissions, Wipf and Stock Publishers, 199 W. 8th Ave., Suite 3, Eugene, OR 97401.

Wipf & Stock
An Imprint of Wipf and Stock Publishers
199 W. 8th Ave., Suite 3
Eugene, OR 97401

www.wipfandstock.com

PAPERBACK ISBN: 979-8-3852-3448-6
HARDCOVER ISBN: 979-8-3852-3449-3
EBOOK ISBN: 979-8-3852-3450-9

02/24/25

Unless otherwise noted, scripture quotations are from the ESV® Bible (The Holy Bible, English Standard Version®), © 2001 by Crossway, a publishing ministry of Good News Publishers. Used by permission. All rights reserved. The ESV text may not be quoted in any publication made available to the public by a Creative Commons license. The ESV may not be translated in whole or in part into any other language.

For those who have labored for God's glory in smallness, obscurity, persecution, and suffering:

"Behold, this is our God;
we have waited for him, that he might save us.
This is the LORD; we have waited for him;
let us be glad and rejoice in his salvation."
(Isa 25:9)

Contents

Preface		ix
Acknowledgments		xi
List of Abbreviations		xiii
1	Why Struggle with Isaiah?	1
2	How Does the Old Testament Speak to Christians?	8
3	How Does the Book of Isaiah Work?	24
4	Give Careful Thought to Your Ways: The Persian Period and the Church after Christendom	48
5	No Dry Trees (Isa 56:1–8)	64
6	Blind Watchmen and the Sorceress's Children (Isa 56:9—57:13)	78
7	I Have Seen Their Ways, but I Will Heal Them (Isa 57:14–21)	89
8	Then You Will Find Your Joy in YHWH (Isa 58)	99
9	His Own Arm Worked Salvation for Him (Isa 59:1–21; 63:1–6)	112
10	Nations Shall Come to Your Light (Isa 60)	126
11	He Has Clothed Me in Robes of Righteousness (Isa 61)	138
12	A New Name That the Mouth of YHWH Will Bestow (Isa 62)	149
13	No One Strives to Take Hold of You (Isa 63:7—64:12)	160
14	I Stretched Out My Hands All Day Long (Isa 65:1–15; 66:1–6)	171
15	Rejoice Forever in That Which I Create (Isa 65:16–25; 66:7–24)	183
16	Isaiah 56–66 for Believers After Christendom	196
Bibliography		207
Subject Index		211
Scripture Index		213

Preface

The challenge of writing about a book or portion of the Bible is to sufficiently consult commentaries so that one avoids missing an important point, but not so much as to lose one's own voice in presenting insights from the biblical text. This is not a technical commentary, but I have cited sources for key insights at important junctures.

In addition to those works explicitly cited, certain works have been useful to me over quite a few years of teaching and preaching Isaiah. John Goldingay has written or cowritten many commentaries on Isaiah, including: *Isaiah* (Understanding the Bible Commentary Series); *The Theology of the Book of Isaiah*; *A Critical and Exegetical Commentary on Isaiah 56–66* (ICC); and with David Payne, *A Critical and Exegetical Commentary on Isaiah 40–55* in two volumes (ICC). I have appreciated Brevard S. Childs's work on biblical theology—the most relevant works for this study being: *Isaiah* (Old Testament Library); and *The Struggle to Understand Isaiah as Christian Scripture*. Another evangelical scholar of the Old Testament prophets, J. Gordon McConville, has recently published an important commentary that I have made use of in this book: *Isaiah* (BCOT).

A number of scholars have written about the use of Isaiah in the New Testament. Particularly influential for me have been Ben Witherington III's, *Isaiah Old and New: Exegesis, Intertextuality, and Hermeneutics*; and Rikki E. Watts's, *Isaiah's New Exodus in Mark*. Those who wish to explore intertextuality between Isa 56–66 and other Old Testament texts should consult Gary E. Schnittjer's *Old Testament Use of Old Testament*.

Also, I have been influenced by the works of N. T. Wright and Richard B. Hays on the New Testament's use of the Jewish Scriptures. Both scholars are quite prolific, and any number of their books would be a great place to start—but these in particular could serve as a point of entry for anyone wishing to study more: *The Climax of the Covenant: Christ and the Law in Pauline Theology* and *The New Testament and the People of God* by N. T. Wright; and *Echoes of Scripture in the Letters of Paul* and *Echoes of Scripture in the Gospels* by Richard B. Hays.

Acknowledgments

Even though I have only started writing about Isaiah more recently in my teaching career, I have had the privilege of teaching the book of Isaiah since 2011 when I was still in graduate school, and now at institutions in four different countries. These experiences have honed my thinking on this majestic book of Scripture. I am thankful for those opportunities for deep study and preparation and for conversations shared with my students at Cairn University (USA), LCC International University (Lithuania), Zaporizhzhia Bible Seminary (Ukraine), and Hindustan Bible Institute & College (India).

Of all my students, I especially thank Sage Wile, one of my LCC students, who wrote such a good paper for my course that we developed it together into a now-published article. I have integrated many of those insights into the chapters of this book that cover Isa 63–66.

This book is the fruit of years of preaching Isaiah in the pulpits of various churches in the USA and abroad, including congregations of Laisvųjų Krikščionių Bažnyčia (Free Christian Church) in Klaipėda and Kaunas (Lithuania), and especially Center Church (EPC) in Grove City, Pennsylvania, USA.

I am grateful to my family for their support and encouragement through the writing of this book and through the ups and downs of ministry and mission in which this book was conceived and gestated. My mother, Susan Soesbe, taught me to love the Bible from a very young age; my father, Ralph Giffone, got me started in studying biblical Hebrew—I've simply continued on the path they set for me. My mom also took the time to comment on portions of this book—I am grateful for her dedication and expertise.

My wife, Corrie, and my children, Daniel and Elizabeth, have been beside me all the way. Five-year-old Daniel rejected "children's Bibles," asking, "Why can't we just read *the Bible*?" Since then, he has never let me skip a chapter as we've read through nearly the whole Bible. Many of these reflections on Isa 56–66 have been inspired from our family devotions. We have now gone all the way through Isaiah together, twice—and then they have also heard me preach Isa 56–66. I am grateful to my kids for always keeping me accountable to read the Bible and pray from what it says. (When you turn thirty, you have my permission to read the parts we skipped when you were little: Ezek 16 and 23, and the Song of Songs!)

This book is dedicated to all who labor in small churches, especially in difficult situations where fruit seems difficult to come by. Your faithful service will be rewarded: "Behold, this is our God; we have waited for him!" (Isa 25:9).

Benjamin Giffone
Grove City, Pennsylvania, USA
Spring 2025

List of Abbreviations

1QIsaª	Great Isaiah Scroll
ANET	Pritchard, James B., ed. *Ancient Near Eastern Texts Relating to the Old Testament*. 3rd ed. Princeton: Princeton University Press, 1969.
BBET	Beiträge zur biblischen Exegese und Theologie
BCOT	Baker Commentary on the Old Testament
BSac	*Bibliotheca Sacra*
FAT	Forschungen zum Alten Testament
ICC	International Critical Commentary
LCL	Loeb Classical Library
LSTS	The Library of Second Temple Studies
LXX	Septuagint
MT	Masoretic Text
Neot	*Neotestamentica*
OBT	Overtures to Biblical Theology
SBL	Society of Biblical Literature
SBLDS	Society of Biblical Literature Dissertation Series

1

Why Struggle with Isaiah?

THE STRUGGLE IS REAL!

Why Is It So Hard to Read the Bible?

Most Christians have a sense that they should read the Bible—it's God's word, after all. And yet many are convicted by the feeling that they don't read the Bible enough, or don't get enough out of it when they read it. Why is it so hard to read the Bible?

First of all, one is struck by the sheer length of the Bible itself. By word count in most English translations, the Bible is nearly five times the length of the Qur'an. Even a lengthy novel, such as *The Order of the Phoenix* in the Harry Potter series, is only a third of the length of the Bible.

And then there is the real feeling that the Bible belongs to a different place and time. This is true—in fact, the Bible was written in many times and in various places, over the course of centuries. There are unfamiliar places, people, cultures, and practices mentioned in the Bible. As a result, the Bible can feel irrelevant to our lives. This can lead to frustration or a defeatist attitude, more so than when reading a novel or a history text; as believers we know that the Bible is relevant to our lives somehow, but when we can't see how it is relevant, we get discouraged and avoid it.

This sense of alienation from the Bible is fueled, I believe, by warring powers in the spiritual realm. Evil spiritual forces don't want us to read

God's word and receive his revelation. Moreover, our own sinful natures resist having God's light shined upon our lives that don't measure up to him—so even though there is good news of forgiveness and redemption, we also face spiritual obstacles to reading the Bible. We don't face the same external and internal resistance as we do when we're trying to get through *Great Expectations* or *War and Peace*.

Why Is It So Hard to Read the Old Testament?

The Old Testament in particular is hard for many Christians to read. Of the Bible's immense length already mentioned, three-quarters of it constitutes the Old Testament. Whereas the New Testament books were written within a few decades of one another and the events they describe, the Old Testament texts were written over centuries, sometimes centuries after the events and contexts they describe. In terms of unfamiliar places, people, cultures, and practices, many more of them are in the Old Testament than in the New.

The New Testament also feels easier for us (minus the book of Revelation) because it consists of letters written to fellow Christian believers and stories about Jesus and his followers. The instructions in the letters seem like they can be applied more easily to our own lives, as do Jesus's teachings. By comparison, much of the Old Testament is not "hortatory" (commands or teaching), and the parts that are hortatory are directed at people and situations that seem to be so different from us and our lives that they appear to be irrelevant.

This feeling is compounded by influences in our contemporary culture that tell us that the Bible is violent, racist, misogynist, backward, etc. Unfortunately, many Christian leaders' handling of the Old Testament does little to controvert those messages. Many more sermons are preached on the New Testament than on the Old Testament, even though, as noted, the Old Testament comprises three-quarters of God's words.

Occasionally, when reading the New Testament, we find passages that seem dependent on Old Testament words, stories, ideas, or concepts. But then, if we investigate the original context of the Old Testament text or idea, it isn't always obvious why the New Testament brings it into play. And what about the vast majority of the Old Testament that *isn't* quoted or alluded to in the New Testament—is it irrelevant?

Why Is It So Hard to Read Isaiah?

The book of Isaiah within the Old Testament presents its own unique challenges. It is one of the longest books within the Old Testament, so it is easy to miss the forest when among the trees. Isaiah's scope covers several historical contexts (as we will see), meaning that in some cases specific background information is necessary to understand what is being said.

Much of the book of Isaiah is written as poetry, as is more than half of the Old Testament (depending on how it is defined). Poetry is characterized by elevated style and subject matter, terseness (fewer words), and rarer vocabulary—making it more difficult to interpret. When something is difficult to read, we tend to shy away from it and look for what seems like greener pastures.

Much of the poetry in the Old Testament is found in the so-called prophetic books, and Isaiah also belongs in this category. Classifying Isaiah as "prophecy" or "prophetic," however, conjures for many readers the idea of a repository of predictions that are supposedly fulfilled by Jesus in the New Testament. Armed with this very narrow definition of "prophecy," readers are then surprised to find very few predictions in a prophetic book like Isaiah, most of them vague imagery.

It is certainly true that the New Testament contains many quotations from and allusions to the book of Isaiah. But then, what is the connection—if any—between the quotations as part of the original book of Isaiah and their occurrences in the New Testament texts? What about instances in which the New Testament authors appear to have adapted the quotations or images of Isaiah to mean something different from the original meaning? In short, does the book of Isaiah have coherent meaning and message on its own, apart from the New Testament authors' use of it—and can those meanings be reconciled?[1]

How Does This Book Help?

It might be helpful to start out with what this book is *not*. Even though I am a professor, this book is not a scholarly monograph that offers a new

---

1. In a sense, many readers face a challenge that is the inverse of that identified by Brevard Childs in the early church. Whereas Childs wrote of the *Struggle to Understand Isaiah as Christian Scripture*, many lay Christian readers struggle to understand Isaiah as *pre-Christian* Scripture in its original historical context(s). It will become clear through this book that I think both struggles are valid and important.

thesis concerning Isa 56–66 for other academics to read and evaluate. Nor is this a comprehensive verse-by-verse commentary on a section of Isaiah, even though the comments are based on a close reading.

Instead, it is better to think of this book as a guide or apprenticeship to help the text of Isa 56–66 appear less intimidating for the average reader. In order to accomplish this, I have provided some information that contextualizes Isa 56–66 historically: What was going on when it was originally written, read, and heard? I have also sought to contextualize Isa 56–66 literarily and theologically: How does this section contribute to the meaning of the book of Isaiah, and what is its place in the theology of the whole Old Testament and the Bible?

But mainly, this "guide" to Isa 56–66 will help readers see how this section is relevant to our lives and contemporary concerns: how it connects to God's grand story of salvation told in the Bible and to our own lives and places within that story. Specifically, the book has a lot to say to North American churches, as we think about how to live faithfully as the church in a society that was once thoroughly "leavened" with Christian ideas and principles but is now increasingly hostile to Christian beliefs. Many North American churches, like the ones I have served and preached to in rural Pennsylvania, used to be full even as recently as forty or fifty years ago but now have dwindled to consist mainly of a few older members—and they wonder, "What happened? Why aren't things the way they used to be—and can we ever get back to those good old days?"

In this sense, the message of Isa 56–66 lands differently in North America (and perhaps Europe) than it does in other places I've had the privilege to visit and serve (more on my background below). In places such as sub-Saharan Africa—where Christianity is booming—or places such as South Asia—where Christians are a small minority but Christendom was never established like it was in Europe and North America—a guide to Isa 56–66 written specifically for those communities might be shaped differently.

But regardless of where you sit as both a reader of Isa 56–66 and this book, we all live in a global community, in the twenty-first century, shaped by globalization and technology as never before in human history. Many of the challenges faced by North American believers are universal, and Isa 56–66 is God's word for all of us in all times and places—so it is worth reading.

THE BIBLE'S AGENDA VERSUS MODERN QUESTIONS

How is the Bible relevant? Sometimes we come to the Bible with an agenda: we are looking for specific themes or answers to specific questions. There is nothing wrong with this in principle. But the danger is that we might only see what we want to see—I'm not just referring to misinterpreting the Bible (although that is a problem) but also to a limited view of the Bible. If we only read the Bible looking for answers to our own questions, then we might have too narrow a "diet" of truth from God's word.

That's why it's a good idea to read the Bible—whole chapters, sections of books, and entire books—to listen to what God is saying to us, without any agenda or question we're seeking to answer. Even though we always come to the Bible with our own perspective, reading the Bible methodically and thoroughly lets God set the agenda for our listening to him and for our prayers as well.

Moreover, reading the Old Testament thoughtfully through the lens of God's whole revelation helps us to grasp the significance of Israel for a church made up of people from many nations, tribes, and tongues.

That said, I do believe that Isa 56–66 contains a great many teachings that connect to the challenges of modern life. All around us, we see individuals and communities struggling to adjust to rapid change: economic, technological, political and ideological, and theological. Whereas many of our ancestors were used to living their entire lives in small communities surrounded by people who looked like them and thought like them, we are challenged by diversity and plurality of views, experiences, and identities as never before.

We see the effects of changing views of sexuality, gender, and gender identity in the last few decades—we are starting to see people who have been chewed up by the prevailing views and practices in our culture, who are looking for life and healing beyond the "sexual revolution." We see the effects of technology on young people especially, resulting in rising access to information but rising rates of depression, anxiety, and self-harm.

Churches are struggling with generational change—the widening chasm between generations' understandings of God, truth, authority, and the purpose of human existence. We also see churches failing in holiness, evangelism, and cross-cultural mission.

Along with these changes—in fact, reinforcing many of these changes—is the rise of other stories of human purpose and meaning. Some are ideologies like the myth of progress, Marxism, or global capitalism.

Others belong to the realm of fiction and fantasy; it's no coincidence that science fiction, fantasy, and comics dominate film, television, and literary output as never before.

Many of these stories are attempts to provide *re-enchantment* in a world that fell into the trap of mere materialism and secularism in the nineteenth and twentieth centuries. Attempting to suppress the human hunger for transcendence is like trying to keep a large beach ball underwater in the pool—even as you might wrestle to keep the inflated ball entirely submerged, it will shoot out one side or the other in search of the surface. In the supposedly secular West, there are fewer and fewer pure atheists, but many people identify as "spiritual rather than religious" because they remain open to . . . *something* transcendent.

I believe that we can find many resources in Isa 56–66, especially the ways in which the target audience is forced to reassess and reapply old truths in new contexts. The interpretation of older biblical ideas is instructive for us as we face circumstances that are different but have many parallels to earlier experience of faithful believers. This will be the focus of chapters 3 and 4, but throughout the book we will examine parallels between the world of Isa 56–66 and our own.

ABOUT ME

That said, who am I, and what is "my world"? Why would anyone care what I have to say about the Bible? It's always a fair question to consider—both for me as an author and for you as the reader.

I have been blessed to have served in a variety of ministry and academic settings. I have been a pastor in a local church, a hospice chaplain, and a music leader. But my main ministry vocation has been teaching and researching in biblical studies at universities and seminaries. I was trained in seminary in the Philadelphia area and then completed research graduate study in Old Testament while working in a professional field (pharmaceutical research). My family served in academic missions in Eastern Europe for six years before transitioning back to our native USA and into local church ministry.

Even though I am an American, my perspective is shaped by global experiences: I got my PhD in South Africa, taught for six years in Eastern Europe, and lectured at seminaries in Ukraine, India, and Singapore. I am blessed to be in regular contact with friends and former students and colleagues all over the world.

This book is the result of many years of preaching and teaching Isaiah. I regularly taught a semester-long course on the book of Isaiah for undergraduates for several years, beginning in 2011. In 2022, I taught a graduate course on Isaiah for a seminary in Ukraine. More recently, I have been regularly teaching Hebrew exegesis of Isa 40–55 for a seminary in India. Over the years, as I had chances to fill the pulpit in the USA and in Europe, I found myself preaching from Isa 56–66 on occasion. So in early 2023 when embarking on a new pastoral call, I preached my first sermon series for our rural church on Isa 56–66, for reasons I'll explain below.

Much of my work as a professor consists of writing articles and books for other scholars and students to read. My scholarship has focused on the narrative literature of the Old Testament and on the Persian period; I have also written about Hebrew poetry and the prophetic literature.

Early in my research, particularly in graduate studies, I focused on the "weirder" texts, the books of the Bible that Christian readers often overlook, such as Lamentations, Numbers, and Chronicles. One book I never thought I would write about was Isaiah! It is difficult to feel "qualified" to write about a book as majestic as the one that John F. A. Sawyer has rightly dubbed "The Fifth Gospel."[2] Moreover, after many centuries of Jewish and Christian reflection on this book, and many books and commentaries, what is left to say about it?

Even though this is my first book aimed at a popular audience, I've always had a passion for sharing the Bible and biblical scholarship (which are not the same thing!) with people of various backgrounds and levels of training. My perspective is informed by an interest in and extensive "lay" reading of economics, political economy, and media ecology.

This integrated, global perspective is one that I bring to the text of Isa 56–66. I am passionate about worship and helping people understand God's word. I also relish helping people who struggle with faith to keep and strengthen their faith in the triune God. The Bible contains many things that are hard to understand and other things that are easy to understand but hard to embrace and do. My hope is that this guide can make that struggle to understand Isa 56–66 slightly easier and more rewarding.

---

2. Sawyer, *Fifth Gospel*.

2

How Does the Old Testament Speak to Christians?

HOW DO WE LOOK TO THE BIBLE FOR GUIDANCE?

A close friend of mine from college used to joke that he discovered his "life verse" when he was considering whether to propose to his girlfriend. He opened up his Bible at random, put his finger down on the page without looking, and read these words from Matt 1:20: "Do not fear to take Mary as your wife." Thankfully, his girlfriend's name was Mary, so this settled the matter for him.

The other, darker joke is about a man who was looking for guidance in this random-verse fashion and was "led" in succession to the following verses: "[Judas] went and hanged himself" (Matt 27:5); "You go, and do likewise" (Luke 10:37); "What you are going to do, do quickly" (John 13:27).

Some may chuckle at this method of seeking guidance from biblical verses extracted from their context. And yet, many Christians read the Bible in ways that are only slightly less thoughtful: taking isolated verses and applying them directly to their lives. How many graduation addresses have you heard from Jer 29:11, "For I know the plans I have for you, declares the LORD"? Somehow, those "promised" plans for graduates never include living in slavery and exile for seventy years.

THE BIBLICAL STORY IS OUR STORY, TOO

When we look at the Old Testament—especially passages that contain many criticisms of ancient Israel or instructions that seem direct and specific to Israel or to ancient culture—it's helpful to take a step back and ask a couple questions: *Why* do we look to the Old Testament for guidance, as individuals and as a congregation? And *how* do we look to the Old Testament for guidance?

Looking back into history, it's always been a tricky issue that the church has had to navigate. Even when we go back to the earliest debates in the church that we find in the book of Acts, or in Galatians and the other letters from the apostles in the New Testament, some of the most important issues they struggled with were whether non-Jews needed to follow the provisions of the Mosaic law in order to follow the Jewish Messiah, Jesus. If not, then which aspects of the law are restated as important for believers in Jesus to follow? Why not treat the Old Testament as altogether obsolete, as the ancient heretic Marcion suggested (and as, sadly, some well-known Christian leaders are saying today)?[1]

One example from the New Testament (among many) is particularly instructive, pointing us to why the Old Testament—Israel's laws, Israel's stories, Israel's wisdom, Israel's prophetic messages—is still important for us.

In 1 Cor 10, Paul, a Jewish apostle, is speaking to a mostly gentile audience: the Jesus-follower community in Corinth. He starts out, "For I do not want you to be unaware, brothers, that our fathers were all under the cloud, and all passed through the sea" (10:1). Here is a Jewish Pharisee saying to these gentiles that the ancient Israelites who were called out of Egypt are "our fathers"—as we read down the passage, it's clear he's not talking about "us Jewish people"; he means in verse 11, "[us] on whom the end of the ages has come," so he means those who believe in Jesus, Jew and gentile together. He says that "Christ" was the rock that followed the Israelites in the wilderness, giving them water. And he says in verse 6, again, that the things that happened to *our* predecessors, the Israelites, serve as "patterns" or "examples" (Greek *typoi*) for us. The ancient Israelites are *our* ancestors, and we can learn from them because their story is *our* story.

---

1. Prominent pastor and author Andy Stanley of North Point Community Church (Georgia) has written of the need for Christians to "unhitch our faith" from the Old Testament; Stanley, *Irresistible*, 72, 158. Many preachers pay lip service to the importance of the Old Testament but rarely preach on it, or only preach from it in an "exemplarist" fashion.

FIVE HERMENEUTICAL LENSES FOR THE OLD TESTAMENT

One of the reasons why Christian readers avoid the Old Testament is that we struggle to find its relevance to our lives. The people to whom the books of the Old Testament were originally written lived very different lives from ours in the twenty-first century, especially those of us in the WEIRD (Western, Educated, Industrialized, Rich, and Democratic) world. Before we undertake our journey through Isa 56–66, we need to be armed with different *hermeneutics* for reading the Old Testament. *Hermeneutic*, from the Greek word for "translate," is not about translating from one language into another but about translating the *meaning* of a text and applying it in a new context. This is exactly what we are always doing when we read a text like the Bible: we have to understand what the words meant in the place and time in which they were written (original context) and then consider how those meanings can be useful for us in our contexts.

There have been at least five sorts of ways that Christians have read the Old Testament—I will call them *lenses*. Each of these lenses has advantages and disadvantages, and often we read through two or more lenses without even realizing it.[2] I will briefly outline these approaches to the Old Testament; then, we will apply them to a sample text: Isa 7:14–16.

Exemplary Approach

Our first, most natural instinct when reading an Old Testament passage is to try to find some example or direct teaching that is applicable to our lives. This *exemplary* lens is based on the assumption that there is something universal about human identity and experience, so if something was good or true for an ancient Israelite person, then it should be good or true for me, as well. This lens is generally a good place to start, but it gets us off-track quickly when we come across characters whose situations seem so utterly different from ours—how is this relevant? There are also problems when we attempt to apply commands to the Israelite nation (such as killing Canaanites) in our individual lives, or when we come across the ceremonial laws. How are these directly relevant to our lives, if at all?

---

2. Here I am indebted to my former professor, Vern S. Poythress, who has written about these five lenses or approaches in several works over decades, most recently in *Biblical Typology: How the Old Testament Points to Christ, His Church, and the Consummation*.

Prediction and Fulfillment

A second lens for interpreting the Old Testament is one of *prediction and fulfillment*. With this lens, we look for corresponding fulfillments of Old Testament direct predictions in the New Testament (or sometimes in the Old Testament, as the case may be). This lens works well for texts that make specific predictions. Believing readers of the Bible understand that the Creator God inspired biblical authors and gave them insight into future events that he would bring to pass.

There are severe limits on this approach, however. Most texts of the Old Testament are not predictive, and even those that do contain predictions—such as the book of Isaiah—tend to do so in very general terms and imagery that is open to interpretation. When we read texts in the books of the Prophets, sometimes it's unclear whether they are speaking about the future, the present, or the past.[3] For example, when Hosea writes, "When Israel was a child, I loved him, and out of Egypt I called my son" (Hos 11:1), is he speaking of Israel's exodus from Egypt in the ancient past, or about Jesus in the future—or both? The text seems plainly to be speaking about the past, but Matt 2:15 says that this prophecy is "fulfilled" when Jesus, Mary and Joseph live in Egypt for a time to escape Herod's decree—a "future" fulfillment from the standpoint of Hosea in the eighth century BC.

The problem remains that most Old Testament texts are not predictive, and those that are predictive are vague.

Typology

Often, when New Testament writers say, "This happened to fulfill what was written," they actually mean *typology*, which is our third lens. A *type* in the literary sense, from the Greek *typos*, means an image, a pattern, or

---

3. Some of the ambiguity is due to the grammar of Hebrew poetry. Hebrew verb forms often represent *aspect* rather than *time*. *Time* refers to *when* something happens (i.e., past, present, or future), whereas *aspect* refers to *how* it happens (continuous, completed, imperfect, punctiliar, iterative). For example, "I threw the baseball at the window in order to get his attention" could be *past* with *completed* or *punctiliar* aspect; and "I would throw the baseball with Bret at the field for hours each day when I was in high school" is *past* with *iterative* or *continuous* aspect. Conversely, a verb that only indicates *imperfect* aspect without reference to time, like some Hebrew verb forms, could technically indicate past ("darkness *was covering* the earth"; Isa 60:2), present ("darkness *covers/is covering* the earth"), or future ("darkness *will cover* the earth"). Context usually determines, but sometimes the text is vague (perhaps intentionally).

a sign of something else. The "something else" to which the type points is called the *antitype*.[4] A type is not an exact copy but gives a pattern of or a pointer to the antitype which is understood to be in some sense greater than the type.

Because an individual type is a pattern, it can point to more than one antitype. For example, Boaz is described as a "mighty man of strength" (*gibbôr ḥayil*) from the tribe of Judah who uses his position and influence to protect the poor and downtrodden in his town (Ruth 2:1). His great-grandson, David, is also described as a *gibbôr ḥayil* (1 Sam 16:18), but David's actions in battle (and later, as king) to protect the poor and the downtrodden of all Israel from the Philistines go far beyond what his great-grandfather accomplished, both in terms of their bravery and in the scope of those they saved. But then David's (and Boaz's) descendant, Jesus the Messiah, in his death and resurrection for the sake of all peoples, goes far beyond what even David did on behalf of Israel only. Therefore, we can say that Boaz is a type of both David and Jesus.

Additionally, more than one type can point to the same antitype. Just as David and Boaz are both types of Jesus in his role as savior and king, Moses is a type of Jesus as prophet and law-giver—consider how Jesus sat on a mountaintop and instructed the people in God's ways (Matt 5–7) just as Moses brought God's law down from Mount Sinai (Exod 32–34). Just as Jesus was a greater savior and king than David, Jesus was a greater lawgiver than Moses ("The crowds were astonished at his teaching, for he was teaching them as one who had authority, and not as their scribes"; Matt 7:28b–29; cf. Deut 18:18–20).

This way of understanding Old Testament persons and events as types or *shadows* is explicitly commended to us in the New Testament—sometimes the world *typos* ("pattern") is even used in this figurative sense. For example, Paul describes Adam as a "type" of Jesus who was to come (Rom 5:14). The author of Hebrews describes Moses and the priests who serve in the Jerusalem temple as pointing ahead to a greater revelation and a greater priesthood: Jesus (Heb 3:1–6; 4:14–5:10; 8:1–6).

There is a joke about a Sunday school teacher who walked into her class of first graders on Sunday morning and asked, "Kids: what has fur, a bushy tail, lives in trees and eats nuts?" One honest boy raised his hand and said, "Teacher, I know the answer is 'Jesus,' but it sure sounds like a squirrel to me!" So also with Old Testament typology, the answer is not

---

4. In this English word, the borrowed Greek prefix *anti-* does not mean "against," but rather "corresponding to."

always "Jesus"! In the New Testament, the antitype of the Old Testament types and shadows is not always "Jesus" but sometimes "the church." In Rom 4, Paul uses Abraham as an example (or type) of those who would become part of God's people by faith, not by birth (because Abraham was justified by faith before he received circumcision, the sign of covenant-belonging). As we saw previously, in 1 Cor 10:1–13, Paul describes the events that happened to Old Testament Israel in the wilderness as *typoi* (plural of *typos*) of what could happen to members of the church who disregard God's revelation and disrespect his table (the Lord's Supper). So just as individual figures can be types of Jesus, individuals and groups can be types of the new covenant people of God.

The advantage of typological reading of the Old Testament is that it is thoroughly Christ-centered. Typology relies not solely on the imagination or perception of the New Testament authors reading symbolism *back* into the Old Testament, but on the sovereignty of the divine Author of the story of Scripture. Typology helps us to see the unity of the plan of salvation across both Testaments and all of redemptive history.

There are dangers in typological readings, mainly when we take them too far or use them to the exclusion of other valid readings. Merely observing a typological relationship does not provide us with any *application* or hortatory content from the Old Testament. As with prediction and fulfillment, typology can obscure the uniqueness of the Old Testament story/figure because we immediately jump to the antitype in our interpretive process. There is also the trap of "hypertyping": seeing parallels where no organic relationship exists. A classic example from the Patristic period is Justin Martyr's *Dialogue with Trypho the Jew* in which he judges nearly every mention of wood in the Old Testament to be a prefiguration of the cross. While the salvation accomplished through the wooden cross is perhaps represented typologically by Noah's ark made out of wood,[5] it makes less sense of the stick that Elisha threw into the water to make an iron ax-head float.[6] This miracle recorded in 2 Kgs 6:1–7 seems to serve the purpose merely of validating Elisha's prophetic authority, and no more.

Typology is distinct from *allegory*. An allegorical reading uses a narrative as a springboard to focus on a moral or spiritual ideal—that is, something *other* (from the Greek *allos*, meaning "another") than what the

---

5. Justin Martyr, *Dial.* 138.2.
6. Justin Martyr, *Dial.* 86.6.

text appears on the surface to be saying. Whereas *typology* sees an organic spiritual connection between type and antitype, allegory is untethered from the original historical context and meaning. Allegorical readings were popular in the Hellenistic Jewish milieu and in the early Christian church, but some stretch the bounds of reason and overshadow the original contextual meaning of the Old Testament story.[7]

God's-Character Approach

The *God's-character* approach might also be described as a systematic theology approach. It asks: What does this passage reveal about the character of God, and more broadly, what can we learn about the nature of humanity (God's image) and the world (God's creation)?

This approach maintains a thoroughly God-centered stance toward the text. If we believe that God is "the same yesterday and today and forever" (Heb 13:8), then we should be able to learn about his consistent character from Old and New Testament texts alike. When practiced in a contextually-sensitive way, the God's-character approach can help us to see the consistency of God's truth across the witness of the Old and New Testaments.

The challenge with this approach is that, if practiced without sensitivity to narrative and context, it can treat the Old Testament as a mere repository of facts about God, rather than a set of propositions *and* narratives about God's dealings with the world. The very fact that systematic theologians disagree about theological conclusions based on the same set of Scriptures should indicate to us that the situation is more complex. Attempts to build a comprehensive "theology" on the Bible but distinct

---

7. Examples from Jewish and Christian interpreters could be multiplied. Philo (c. 20 BC–c. AD 50), a Jewish writer from Alexandria in Egypt, sanitizes the unsavory story of Tamar and Judah in Gen 38. He interprets Tamar veiling herself like a prostitute and offering herself to her (unwitting) father-in-law, Judah, as representing virtue and wisdom that make themselves available to anyone who would stop and examine them (*Prelim. Studies* 124). Philo may have in mind the image of Lady Wisdom in Prov 1:20–33, crying out in the streets, offering herself to any man who would unite himself to her.

Hippolytus (c. AD 170–c. 235), like nearly all Christian interpreters until the 1950s, interprets the Song of Songs allegorically as referring to Christ and the church. His allegorizing extends so far as to designate the sachet of myrrh between the woman's breasts (Song 1:13) as Christ, while the breasts represent the Old and New Testaments (LXX Song 1:2). See the translation and commentary offered by Smith, *Mystery of Anointing*, 8, 269, 363.

from the Bible will always be provisional and cannot be authoritative in the same way that the Bible itself is authoritative.

This is not to say, as some of my fellow Old Testament scholars might, that the project of systematic theology is fruitless. But our human-made systems—however elegant and internally consistent they may be—should not be allowed to override the plain meaning of a biblical text.

Preparation Approach

The *preparation approach*, which is sometimes called the redemptive-historical approach, asks concerning a specific Old Testament passage: How did God work forward his story of redemption? How was this text/event leading historically and narratively toward the birth, life, death, and resurrection of Jesus?

The advantage of this approach is that it requires us to contextualize Old Testament texts. We can see its usefulness in passages that present bad or evil events, or events that don't have any apparent moral lesson (exemplary approach) or symbolic value (typology). Such texts may simply be telling us that God was moving the story forward—we don't have to squeeze them for some moral meaning or "shoehorn" them into some systematic theology or typology.

The downside of the preparation approach is that it can communicate that an Old Testament text is distant from our context and mostly irrelevant for our lives—there may in fact be a lesson to learn (exemplary approach). Ironically, the preparation approach can also untether Old Testament passages from Christ that might otherwise be connected typologically. To pick up on an earlier example, it is true that David's victory over the Philistines results in the establishment of the Israelite monarchy, which leads eventually to Jesus's birth. But David himself also serves as a type of Jesus, in a way that his less-faithful descendants (also Jesus's ancestors) do not. A reader using only the preparation approach might miss this connection.

The preparation approach in practice can also be repetitive. If the only meanings we take from, say, the middle chapters of Judges are that 1) people are sinful and that 2) God is moving the story forward from the Conquest era to the monarchy, then the nuances of the individual stories in Judges are lost or overshadowed.

Testing Our Hermeneutics: Isaiah 7:14–16

I hope you've gotten the impression thus far that none of these five hermeneutical lenses is sufficient on its own. Rather, we should read Old Testament texts through multiple lenses. In order to demonstrate how this can be done, I will give us a brief interpretation of perhaps the most well-known but also widely-misunderstood verse in the book of Isaiah: Isa 7:14. This is not intended to be comprehensive but to highlight some distinctions in interpretive approaches, especially the difference between "prediction and fulfillment" and "typology," which can be challenging to grasp.

Isaiah 7–8 is a narrative, set in Jerusalem, in the midst of a crisis: King Rezin of Aram (also called Syria) and King Pekah of Israel (sometimes called Ephraim, after the largest of the Northern Israelite tribes) have attacked the kingdom of Judah, which was led by King Ahaz (7:1–2). They have besieged Jerusalem, the capital of Judah; Ahaz's officials have gone out to inspect the water supply, and YHWH[8] instructs the prophet Isaiah to meet them there with a message of hope for Ahaz (7:3–9).

To provide Ahaz with assurance, YHWH tells Ahaz to ask for a sign that before long the threat from Aram and Israel will be averted (7:10–11). However, Ahaz refuses to ask for a sign (7:12). His wording, "I will not put [YHWH] to the test," sounds like pious adherence to Deut 6:16, but the rest of the passage indicates a more cynical motive: Ahaz wanted public and elite support to ask the Assyrian empire for assistance against Aram and Israel (7:17–20; 8:7–8). A sign from YHWH might erode public support for an alliance with Assyria. Ahaz trusts more in the Assyrian power than in YHWH.

In response, YHWH gives Ahaz a sign anyway:

> Therefore the Lord himself will give you a sign. Behold, the virgin shall conceive and bear a son, and shall call his name Immanuel. He shall eat curds and honey when he knows how to

---

8. I prefer to write out and to say out loud the name of the God of Israel, YHWH, which is represented by the all-caps word "LORD" in most English Bibles. There's a complicated story behind how that tradition of rendering God's name as "LORD" developed. But I think we have freedom in this matter, as long as we don't invoke God's name in vain or frivolously. I like to be called "Benjamin" or "Benj," and I think God likes to be called by his name (or the shortened form "-YH," the final part of many Hebrew names such as "Isaiah," meaning "Salvation of YH[WH],") as well. In this book, I mostly use "LORD" when quoting translations, such as the ESV, but "YHWH" otherwise.

refuse the evil and choose the good. For before the boy knows how to refuse the evil and choose the good, the land whose two kings you dread will be deserted. (Isa 7:14–16)

When we approach this text with an *exemplarist* lens, we can see in Ahaz an example of what *not* to do. Ahaz was given a promise from YHWH and then was offered a chance to have his faith (and the faith of his beleaguered people) strengthened with a miraculous sign. But Ahaz preferred to trust in the horses and chariots of Assyria rather than in YHWH. Moreover, he misapplied Scripture in service of his own agenda—not unlike the devil when he tempted Jesus (Matt 4:1–11).

When we approach this text with our God's-character lens, we see that YHWH is loyal to his people. In this crisis, he determines to save them—regardless of Ahaz's response—and he keeps his word. He compassionately offers his people the assurance of a sign in the meantime. However, we also see that he will later judge their unbelief by bringing the Assyrians upon them—he is holy (Isa 6), and his association with this people is put to the test by their pervasive unholiness (Isa 1; 3; 5–6). But he ultimately will preserve a sanctified remnant of his people (7:3) so that he and they can enjoy holy fellowship, and he can receive his rightful glory.

What about the *prediction* in 7:14 and its *fulfillment*?

Most Christians who are familiar with the birth story of Jesus found in the Gospel of Matthew are aware of the supposed fulfillment of Isa 7:14 in Matt 1:22–23: "All this took place to fulfill what the Lord had spoken by the prophet: 'Behold, the virgin shall conceive and bear a son, and they shall call his name Immanuel' (which means, God with us)."

However, when we read the Isaiah prediction in its original context, it seems to be referring to a son who will be born very soon—and before he "graduates" from toddler to little boy, the threat of the kings of Aram and Israel will be averted. One interpretation from the immediate context is that Isaiah's own son, Maher-shalal-hash-baz, with Isaiah's own wife (who also seems to be a prophet—'birds of a feather'), fulfills this prophecy:

> Then the LORD said to me, "Take a large tablet and write on it in common characters, 'Belonging to Maher-shalal-hash-baz.' And I will get reliable witnesses, Uriah the priest and Zechariah the son of Jeberechiah, to attest for me." And I went to the prophetess, and she conceived and bore a son. Then the LORD said to me, "Call his name Maher-shalal-hash-baz; for before the boy knows how to cry 'My father' or 'My mother,' the wealth of

Damascus and the spoil of Samaria will be carried away before the king of Assyria." (Isa 8:1–4)

Later, the child (or Isaiah—it's not entirely clear) seems to be referred to by YHWH as "Immanuel" (8:8).

On the surface, the problem with this interpretation is that Maher-shalal-hash-baz is not born of a virgin but through normal marital relations between Isaiah and his wife. However, the difficulty becomes more complex when we observe that the Hebrew text of Isa 7:14 does *not* use the word that technically means "virgin," a woman who has not had intercourse (*bᵉtûlâ*), but rather *'almâ*, which means "a young woman of marriageable age."[9] Isaiah's wife would be an *'almâ*, but not a *bᵉtûlâ* (certainly not by the time she gives birth to Isaiah's second son!).

So where does Matthew come up with the idea that a child born of a virgin would "fulfill" the Immanuel prophecy? The more commonly-used version of the Jewish Scriptures in the first century (LXX) renders the Hebrew *'almâ* as *parthenos*, which does mean "virgin"—a woman who has not had intercourse.[10] Should we conclude from this that Matthew was incorrect, or basing his statement on an incorrect translation?

Here is where our distinction between *prediction and fulfillment* approach and *typology* can help us understand both Isa 7–8 and Matt 1. On one level, this prediction offered in Isa 7:14, as transmitted to us in the original Hebrew in which it was spoken, was fulfilled in the few years following this moment of crisis faced by Ahaz, the siege of Jerusalem. Nine months after Isaiah "went to the prophetess" his wife (8:3), she gave birth to a son; before that son was weaned or could speak basic words, the siege was lifted and the threat was averted. This Immanuel-child, named Maher-shalal-hash-baz, was a visible sign to Ahaz and all of Judah that YHWH was with them and would protect them (despite Ahaz's lack of faith). A child born over seven hundred years in the future would not provide much assurance to Ahaz of YHWH's presence and protection. Thus, the prediction of 7:14 was "fulfilled" within a few years of its utterance.

But in another, deeper sense—the level of *typology*—Jesus's birth by the Virgin Mary fulfills the Isa 7:14 prophecy, also. Isaiah's son,

---

9. The Great Isaiah Scroll (1QIsa^a) found at Qumran (i.e., among the so-called Dead Sea Scrolls) confirms this reading as *'almâ*.

10. The other great Greek versions of the Jewish Scriptures / Old Testament—Aquila, Symmachus, and Theodotion, sometimes together called "the three"—translate *'almâ* with *neanis*, which means "young woman" without indicating virginal status.

Maher-shalal-hash-baz, is himself a type of Jesus. Both babies were promised by God and born under special circumstances. Both babies were designated as "Immanuel" ("God-with-us") but were called by other names. Both births were signs of YHWH's presence with his people: Maher-shalal-hash-baz in a symbolic sense, but Jesus as God incarnate (the antitype greater than the type). Both baby boys represented God's coming judgment: Maher-shalal-hash-baz represented the judgment upon Israel and Aram (and later, on Judah) by means of Assyria; Jesus represents the offer of punishment or pardon based on whether one believes.

In serving as a type of Jesus, Isaiah's second son is like his first son, Shear-jashub (Isa 7:3), whose name means "a remnant will return." Built into God's promise of future judgment upon unbelief was a promise of forgiveness and restoration, which would come to its fullest manifestation through God's own son, Jesus.

As we have seen in the earlier example of Matthew's application of the Hos 11:1 text to Jesus, the New Testament authors sometimes use the word "fulfill" (Greek *plēroō*) in the *typological* sense of "filling-out" an earlier figure or event. They even apply "fulfillment" to Old Testament texts that are not plainly understood as predictions of future events. Typology, as we see it discovered and presented to us in the New Testament, gives us an important key to understanding the Old Testament, especially Isa 56–66.

Coming back around to the preparation approach, we can see that, through the events of Isa 7–8, YHWH moved redemptive history forward to save the kingdom of Judah, thereby preserving the line of the Messiah.

All of these lenses are useful when reading Isa 7:14, and none of them individually can fully account for the meaning and significance of this text. Let's keep this in mind as we study Isa 56–66: we will do our best to situate it in historical context, but we will always be seeing ways that the New Testament "fills out" our understanding of the Old Testament passages and the Old Testament as a whole.

STARTING OUT IN SEASON 5? (OR, HOW TO BINGE-WATCH THE BIBLICAL STORY)

We have seen a few examples, but there are countless other instances, of the apostles and the New Testament authors indicating that Jesus's identity and mission are inextricably linked to the story of Israel—both through the use of typology and redemptive history.

Anyone who reads the New Testament after reading the Old, or who simply glances at the marginal cross-references in a study Bible version of the New Testament, can't help but notice how many parallels and citations there are from the Old Testament. It certainly seems that knowledge of the Old Testament would be helpful in understanding the New. And yet, knowing Jesus through the witness of the Gospels is usually where seekers and new believers start out in their journey to know and trust the God of the Bible. Just how important is it to go back and study the Old Testament carefully? Wouldn't it be better to focus mainly on the New Testament in order to be a follower of Jesus?

As a fan of television more than of film, I've sometimes used this (imperfect) analogy in my own teaching about the relationship between the Old and New Testaments. Reading the New Testament as non-Jews, and embracing and believing in what it says about Jesus, and following Jesus, is like joining in watching a popular TV series that your friends (in this analogy, representing Jewish believers in Jesus, such as the apostles) have been watching from the beginning. Let's say the show is currently in season 5, and your friends have been saying, "You *really* should check out this show!" So you watch one episode from the current season—and you're hooked! It's life-changing!

What do you do for the moment, amid the current season? Well, you'll continue watching season 5, of course, so that you can talk with your friends about it (and avoid spoilers!). If the writing is good, season 5 will make sense on its own terms, even for those who haven't watched seasons 1–4. But eventually, once season 5 is over (and even before the next season is released), you will want to go back and watch seasons 1–4. As you start from the beginning with knowledge of season 5, you will be able to make better sense of the characters—what makes them tick, their back-stories, their development. You'll understand the running jokes and motifs, the grand storylines. Then, you'll rewatch season 5 (and continue on in the series)—and everything will make even more sense.

So also, readers of the New Testament will find themselves drawn to reading the Old Testament—that is, the earlier seasons. If the story of Jesus in the Gospels is "season 5," then the period of the biblical story to which Isa 56–66 belongs is "season 4": the period of the Persian empire (c. 539–332 BC). Maybe season 1 is Genesis: the story of how the world came to be (Gen 1–11) and how Israel's ancestors (Abraham, Isaac, Jacob,

Judah, Joseph) came to meet and follow the God YHWH (Gen 12–50). After a four-hundred-year hiatus (slavery in Egypt), season 2 would be like the show coming into its own: Israel's period of answering only to their God, YHWH—the period of Moses, of Joshua, the judges (up until about 1030 BC). Later season 2 could include the independent monarchy under kings Saul, David, and Solomon (c. 1030–930 BC). This might be thought of as the "heyday," the golden age of God's people. (Of course, it's a lot more complicated than that, but it was definitely better than living under oppressive pagan empires!)

Then, maybe season 3 would be the time of decline from that golden age. Israel's kings got weaker and often made protection deals to submit to stronger empires to the north and the southwest. The polity itself actually split (c. 930 BC) into two kingdoms: Northern Israel, with Samaria as its capital, and Southern Judah, led by the descendants of King David from Jerusalem. The society became less interested in following the good laws that YHWH had given through Moses, and they often worshiped YHWH in improper ways, and they worshiped other gods as well. This decline and weakening eventually led to the Assyrians taking over Israel (722 BC) and then the Babylonians taking over Judah (605–539 BC), the destruction of the Jerusalem temple (587 BC), and the replacement of the kings descended from David with governors. This is the period described at the end of the book of Kings and in the books of the prophets Jeremiah and Ezekiel.

The Persian period, 539–332 BC, has a different tone. Even though things are better and freer than under the Babylonians, there are still lots of challenges. The heyday of the Israelite kingdom, season 2, is long past—really, it's just something that their grandparents told them about, and it's hard to believe it was ever true. They wondered: *Was YHWH really that good to his people in times past?*

Isaiah 56–66 speaks into this situation and addresses many of these questions, as we will see. In the next chapters, we will consider the background, structure, and movement of the book of Isaiah, and we'll set the scene of season 4, the Persian period in the province of Yehud, in more detail.

In order to make sense of this "season 4" text, we must sometimes look backward to the earlier stories of Israel (seasons 1–3). Isaiah 56–66 also points us ahead to "season 5" and beyond: the return of YHWH in the person of Jesus the Messiah and the establishment of the church under the guidance of the Holy Spirit.

EXCURSUS: JUDAHITES, YEHUDIANS, JEWS?

At this juncture, it is necessary to define certain terms referring to peoples and places that are central to the biblical story. Names such as "Hebrews," "Israelites," and "Jews," apply to related peoples but connote different time periods.

"Hebrews" or "Hebrew people" is derived from the name "Eber," the ancient ancestor of Abraham (Gen 10:21, 24-25; 11:14-17; cf. Num 24:24). "Hebrew people" is a more ancient designation, used mainly in Genesis to refer to Abraham and in Exodus to refer to the slaves in Egypt. "Hebrew" is not used in the book of Isaiah.

"Israel" is another name given to Jacob (Gen 32:28; 35:10), meaning "strives with God." "Israel" subsequently, and in Isaiah, often means the people descended from Jacob's twelve sons. Sometimes it connotes the twelve tribes together, or the idea of "the people belonging to YHWH" regardless of tribe. After 1 Kgs 12 in the biblical story, "Israel" can refer to the Northern Kingdom of ten tribes of which Samaria was the capital; when I refer to this smaller Israel, I will use "Northern Israel" or "Samarians."[11] Isaiah sometimes uses "Israel" in this way (e.g., Isa 7:1; 8:14; 17:3), but more frequently uses "Ephraim" (a leading Northern tribe) or "Samaria" to refer to the North (e.g., 7:9; 8:4; 9:9).

"Jew," "Judaism," "Yehud," and "Judah" are all derived from the name of Jacob's fourth son, $y^eh\hat{u}d\hat{a}$ (Gen 29:35), usually translated in English as "Judah," meaning something like "praiseworthy." Later, "Judah" became one of the leading tribes in twelve-tribe Israel. The "Kingdom of Judah" refers to the Southern Kingdom headquartered in Jerusalem, which existed independently after the 1 Kgs 12 split-off of Northern Israel.

"Yehud" is a more phonetic rendering of the name of the province under the Babylonian and Persian empires that roughly corresponded to the former Kingdom of Judah.

In this book, I use "Judahites" to refer to the persons who lived in the kingdom of Judah (until the Babylonian conquest), or to persons identified with the tribe of Judah (in any era). "Yehudians" refers to inhabitants

---

11. As a matter of historical curiosity, it is an underappreciated fact that, long after "Israel" ceased to be a twelve-tribe entity and Northern "Israel" ceased to be an independent kingdom, the "Judah"-associated scribes who preserved the texts of the Hebrew Bible nevertheless continued to regard "Israel" as an important identification for themselves and their heritage. Several of the Prophets regarded the reconstitution of "Israel" including the Northern Israelite tribes as an important dimension of their eschatological vision. See the intriguing historical study of Fleming, *Legacy of Israel*.

of Yehud province (after the Babylonian conquest), regardless of tribal identification (Judahite, Benjaminite, Levite, etc.)

"Jews" / "Jewish people" refers to all the cultural, ethnic, or religious descendants of the former Kingdom of Judah, regardless of tribe (Judah, Benjamin, Levi) or location (Mesopotamia, Persia, Egypt, Yehud/Palestine, or later throughout the Hellenistic or Roman empires), down to the present.

3

How Does the Book of Isaiah Work?

Before we study closely the section of Isa 56–66, we have to think about how the book of Isaiah works and how prophecy works, generally. Maybe the idea that different biblical books "work" in different ways is a new one for you.

Some books of the Bible are short, self-contained discourses or literary units—for example, the book of Ruth: four chapters that together tell a single, continuous story.

Other books of the Bible are longer narratives (or are part of longer narratives that span several books), that have a main plotline but also side-stories. A great example would be the narrative that runs through Joshua, Judges, Samuel, and Kings (the Former Prophets in the terminology of the Hebrew Bible). The main storyline is the political development of the polity called Israel. But there are other side-stories, such as the establishment of different peoples and places, that don't seem that relevant to the main story. Later, the main storyline splits into two, as 1 Kgs 11 through 2 Kgs 17 bounces back and forth between the Samaria-centered Northern Israel and the Jerusalem-centered Southern Judah (with other side stories along the way).

Books of poetry, on the other hand, often do not have a chronological or linear focus with chapters or sections building upon one another. It is possible to read individual psalms, and individual verses from the book of Proverbs, without any reference to what comes before or after—each small unit could stand on its own, or the units could be arranged in the book differently without significantly affecting the meaning.

Isaiah, like most of the "Prophetic Books," is mostly poetic oracles. However, this doesn't mean it has no flow or continuity. In this chapter, we will consider first how prophecy tends to work in the Old Testament; how the book of Isaiah is structured; and how we might contextualize Isa 56–66 within the overall book.

HOW DOES PROPHECY WORK?

There are many excellent books that explain carefully and helpfully the features and functions of biblical prophecy. As a good starting point, I recommend D. Brent Sandy, *Plowshares and Pruning Hooks*, and J. Gordon McConville, *A Guide to the Prophets*.[1] In this section, I choose to highlight a few points that are relevant for our study of the book of Isaiah, especially chapters 56–66.

Poetry as Prophecy

We noted in the beginning that the "struggle" to read parts of the Bible involves wrestling with the complexities of poetry. Much of the prophetic literature, and most of the book of Isaiah (including nearly all of Isa 56–66), would be classified as poetry. Some readers find poetry challenging or annoying, but poetry can sometimes communicate meanings that mere prose cannot. What are some features of poetry, and how do we approach it?

The features of poetry, as contrasted with *prose* and other kinds of writing, vary across languages. In some languages, poetry rhymes or has specific meter or rhythm—in others, not as much. There are some common elements, however. We know poetry when it uses an elevated style: vocabulary and imagery that are lofty and may not be typical of common speech or writing. Poetry often uses imagery and metaphor, and may use them to express universal themes, ideas, and feelings. If an author were to describe her trip to the grocery store in poetic style (I'm not going to attempt this!), we might interpret the poem as getting at something of the specialness of even mundane actions, or perhaps despair and sadness

---

1. Sandy, *Plowshares and Pruning Hooks*; McConville, *Guide to the Prophets*, xi–xxviii.

over the smallness of the poet's world—but probably not merely an account of a trip to the store.

Poetry is often characterized by terseness (using fewer words) and vagueness. This is part of how poetry connects to broader ideas and sentiments. But it means that it can leave a lot of room for interpretation, which can frustrate us when we are reading the word of God in poetry—we might want it to say more, more clearly.

Hebrew poetry is different from English-language poetry. It does not emphasize rhythm or rhyme. Instead, Hebrew poetry in particular is characterized by *parallelism*, which is usually two lines that complement one another in some way. Sometimes the B-line restates what we see in the A-line (synonymous parallelism); sometimes it introduces a contrast (antithetical parallelism). In other instances, the relationship between the two is difficult to determine, but we know they're connected somehow because the poet put them together (synthetic parallelism). Let's look at how this works in Isa 60:1–2. It begins, speaking to Zion (the feminine personification of Jerusalem):

> 1a Arise! Shine, for your-light has-come | 1b And the glory of YHWH on-you has-risen ||
> 2a For behold, darkness will cover the earth | 2b And thick-darkness the peoples ||
> 2c But on-you YHWH will-rise | 2d and his-glory on you will-appear.[2]

Lines 1a and 1b together equate Zion's light with YHWH's glory. Lines 2a and 2b also seem to parallel one another, drawing attention to the earth and its peoples, and the darkness upon both. Lines 2a–b seem to be a contrast with 1a–b (light vs. darkness). But then together, 2c and 2d come back to some of the same terms as 1a and 1b, this time equating YHWH himself rising over Zion with YHWH's glory and Zion's light. Here, we have synonymous and antithetical parallelisms.

What does all this mean? It means for Zion that her children (the people of Jerusalem and Judah) will return to the land (60:4, 9). But notice that the precise cause-and-effect relationship between the "rising of glory and light" and the return of the people is not stated. Does the "rising of glory and light" cause the people to return? Or, does "the rising of glory and light" itself *mean* the return of the people? We must read further to see.

---

2. Translation mine.

Reading poetry is a skill that can be learned and refined. If the whole Old Testament is the inspired word of God (2 Tim 3:16), and half of the Old Testament is poetry, then learning to read poetry well is a necessary task for those who wish to be faithful readers of the Bible.

Prophecy in Performance

Prophets were public figures, not just private authors in their "offices" writing with pens on scrolls. Prophets would come and go before kings, priests (some were priests themselves), and other officials, and would also make pronouncements in public places for people of all classes to hear.

It's difficult in our day to conceive of a religious leader who would have such political influence—coming and going before kings and wealthy people, as well as preaching to the man on the street. But we have to remember that our modern separation of religious and political life was unknown in the ancient world. After all, if the gods (or the one true God) are sovereign over all areas of life, every political, social, or economic decision would either please or displease heaven—and you did not want to displease the gods! As the direct connection to the gods, prophets influenced all spheres of life.

Along with speeches, prophets sometimes performed strange acts as "public service announcements" on YHWH's behalf. In Isa 20, Isaiah walks around with his robe untied so his rear end is uncovered. In Jer 19, Jeremiah purchases a clay pot, takes it to a public place outside Jerusalem, and smashes it before the elders of the city. In Ezek 3-4, Ezekiel makes a little "Lincoln Logs" model of Jerusalem in the town square, shaves his beard, burns part of the hair, and stuffs the rest in his pants.

For these public acts they were subject to misunderstanding, ridicule, persecution, and even execution. You can imagine that prophets were frequently unpopular because of their messages. Kings and wealthy people don't like being told what to do—come to think of it, no one likes being told what to do!

Prophecy: From Performance to Writing

Did prophets always speak in poetry? Did they do other things, as well? How did their public utterances come to us in written form? Again, many thoughtful books have been written about each of those questions, and I commend another book, co-authored by Sandy with John Walton, about how we have received written Scripture from an oral culture such as ancient Israel.[3] I would highlight a few things to consider as we jump into study of Isaiah.

First of all, the prophetic books themselves clue us into the fact that the prophets employed scribes (e.g., Baruch the scribe of Jeremiah: 36:4–32; 45:1–5). Most people could not write; reading, writing, and copying literary texts was a specialized skill.[4] Often the most trusted scribes were those who were the prophet's own disciples (Isa 8:16).

As disciples, and as professionals, scribes seem to have enjoyed some freedom or even the responsibility of preserving the prophets' messages in compelling written form—which may have included editing, smoothing out, and even supplementing the words of the prophets. Thus, what the scribes wrote might have differed somewhat from what the prophets had performed. Because Scripture is inspired by the Holy Spirit, we can understand that this inspiration process would have included the prophets' disciples and scribes who preserved the prophets' messages for us. The scribes also made choices about the order in which to present oracles, which may have been performed multiple times in various places (just as Jesus would probably tell the same parable dozens of times in different towns). This accounts for the two versions of Jeremiah that have similar content but in a different order.[5]

Speaking of the arrangement of the books, we see that prophetic oracles presented in poetic form in the book of Isaiah are generally paired with a relevant prose narrative. Isaiah's prophetic call recorded in chapter 6 follows the alternating oracles of judgment and blessing in chapters 1–5. The Aram-Israel invasion of Judah, narrated in chapters 7–8, is the backdrop for chapters 9–12. Amidst the so-called "Burdens/Oracles Concerning the Nations" in Isa 13–27, chapter 20 records the sign act performed by Isaiah (mentioned earlier). Isaiah 28–35 is set against the backdrop of the Assyrian threat and the temptation to appeal to Egypt for help. Isaiah 36–39 is then drawn mostly verbatim from 2 Kgs

---

3. Walton and Sandy, *Lost World of Scripture*.

4. Van der Toorn discusses the different kinds of literacy in the ancient Levant, and what might have been the rates of so-called "high literacy," the ability to read literary texts; see Van der Toorn, *Scribal Culture*, 10–16.

5. For a discussion of the significance of two versions of Jeremiah for evangelical doctrines of Scripture, see Hays, "Jeremiah," 133–49; Giffone, "Theological Interpretation," 153–78.

18:13—20:19.[6] Isaiah 39, which describes Hezekiah's failure of faith that leads to the eventual Babylonian conquest and exile of Judah, provides a narrative springboard to Isa 40–55. Interestingly, there are no prophetic sign acts or prose-narratives in 40–66. We will discuss the provenance and focus of this section below.

The point I'm making is that when we read poetic oracles found in the book of Isaiah, we are receiving the result of a process of inspired performance by the prophets, inspired writing and refining by their scribes and disciples, and inspired editing/arranging—perhaps by other scribes.

Prophecy as Teaching, Warning, or Prediction?

It's important to distinguish between two types of prophetic intent: *fore*-telling and *forth*-telling. Foretelling is prediction in the plainest sense: describing things that will (or might) happen in the future. *Forth*-telling explains how things are and why they need to be reformed—it is essentially a teaching or a confronting. These two intents overlap: a prophetic oracle might foretell a future consequence of present behavior, as a way of trying to get the audience to change.

When considering the nature of prophecies that seem to contain predictions and warnings, we can further divide foretelling—describing the future—into *warnings* and *true predictions*. Sometimes, the prophets' predictions are of things that will happen only if the audience doesn't change their course—it's not fixed in stone. These could be classified as warnings; the majority of prophetic predictions of judgment fall into this category.

There is another concept closely related to prophecy, sometimes categorized as a subset of prophecy: *apocalyptic*, from the Greek word meaning "revelation" or "unveiling." Apocalyptic texts, which are found in some of the biblical Prophets and then reach their full flowering in the apocalypses of Dan 7–12, 1 Enoch, and the New Testament book of Revelation (*Apokalypsis* in Greek), provide a window into the spiritual battles in the unseen realm that have consequences in the visible realm.

---

6. The idea that Isa 36–39 is adapted/copied from the book of Kings is a widely-held view among scholars, to which I have added my own case from a literary point of view. However, some scholars hold the very plausible position that the Isaiah material is original and the author/editor of Kings later adapted these stories into his work. Another plausible option is that both Kings and Isaiah are drawing this material from a common source that we do not have. See Giffone, "Toward a Better 'Hezekiah,'" 473–74.

Apocalyptic texts use vivid imagery and tend to focus on final solutions of judgment and re-creation. Within the book of Isaiah, chapters 24–27 and 34–35 are understood to exhibit apocalyptic features.[7]

In prophecy (classically understood), the judgments warned of can be averted if the people change their ways from wicked to righteous. The wicked will be punished and the righteous delivered, but it is still possible for the wicked to turn from their ways and be righteous. In apocalyptic writings, the judgment is baked in and cannot be averted—the only path for the righteous is to hunker down, endure the suffering, and trust that God will break into history to judge the wicked and usher in his righteous kingdom and gracious healing. In a sense, both are warnings, but different responses are expected / hoped for.

An example of this distinction between prophetic warnings and apocalyptic predictions that I sometimes present in my classes is a short video clip from the 2012–14 television series, *The Newsroom*. In this fictional series about a network news show, the anchor invites a climate scientist on his show to talk about the dangers of climate change.[8] The scientist presents a litany of deeply disturbing facts about CO_2 levels and rising seas, as the anchor and producers expected.

But then the moment comes when the anchor asks if there is any policy that could reverse the catastrophic effects of climate change. "There's a lot we could have done twenty years ago," the scientist says, "Or even ten years ago. But now—no." The anchor and his team are stunned. "You sound like you're saying it's hopeless. . . . Let's see if we can't find a better spin—people are starting their weekends." The anchor begins fishing for some hopeful fact or feasible policy path forward that could avert the coming ecological disaster. The scientist has no hope to offer: "Those would have been great—twenty years ago."

All scientific issues aside, this bit of television demonstrates the difference between prophecy and apocalyptic. The TV anchor and his producers were looking for a climate *prophet* to share an urgent message: someone who would warn the people what would happen if they didn't change course. But what they got instead was a climate *apocalypticist*: an expert saying that there is nothing to be done but weather the storm (literally). This is not what the government agency who employs the scientist or the TV producers want, because then there is no hortatory

---

7. Sandy, *Plowshares and Pruning Hooks*, 106–11.
8. Poul, "Main Justice."

value, no actions to be taken by their voting audience or policy makers. "Are you going to get in trouble for saying this publicly?" the anchor asks, in exasperation. "Who cares?" the scientist responds.

The difference between climate apocalypticism and biblical apocalyptic writing is that the biblical texts provide hope that God is in control and will bring about re-creation after the intense trouble. We find this in Isa 26–27, 35, and 65–66.

One more word to say about predictive prophecy. In the last chapter, we talked about hermeneutics and distinguished between *prediction-and-fulfillment* and typology. We saw that in use, these can overlap. We also saw that one type can refer to two or more antitypes. This is also the case with prophetic and apocalyptic imagery describing the future. In some cases, God gave a prophet a single image as a picture of two or more future fulfillments. One analogy might be when we see a two-dimensional image, not realizing that there is depth and distance. If you look at a painting of a foregrounded object with mountains in the background, you can see the mountains off in the distance. But it's difficult to tell just how far away they are without perspective—some might be close and others might be really far behind the nearer ones, but you can't tell. So it is with some prophetic visions What the prophet might have foreseen as one future moment of both comfort and vengeance, God in his sovereign plan had destined for two moments in history: a moment of comfort and forgiveness in Jesus's death and resurrection, and a moment of future judgment when Jesus returns. This is especially useful when we look at Isa 56–66, which intertwines both judgment and forgiveness. The New Testament's use of Isa 56–66 in particular shows us that Jesus and the apostles were viewing these two moments as related but distinct fulfillments of these prophecies.

Summary

As we have seen in this section, prophecy is a complex phenomenon in the Old Testament, involving poetry, performances, sign acts, warnings, and predictions of both bad and good things to come.

At the beginning of this section, we talked about how books of the Old Testament "work" in terms of communication (rhetoric and genre would be the fancy words), and I suggested a spectrum between Kings on the one hand and the Psalter on the other hand. The longer books that are sometimes called "Major Prophets," which are designated "Latter Prophets" in the Hebrew Bible, fall somewhere in the middle. For example, even though the book of Ezekiel is not a narrative, Ezekiel's oracles are structured nearly entirely chronologically (only one exceptional case), and the chronology helps to build toward a meaning. Jeremiah's oracles are all "out of order" chronologically, but there is still a literary structure that holds the book together and a theological argument that develops across the book. Both of these books contain poetry, narrative, and apocalyptic.

In these respects, Isaiah as a book fits right in the middle of the spectrum between Jeremiah and Ezekiel—some apparent chronological arrangement, some pieces "out of order." It also combines poetic oracles with narratives, even adopting [nearly] verbatim material from 2 Kgs 18–20. Apocalyptic is woven in with classical prophecy; there are judgment sections and hopeful sections. In our next section, we turn to see how the book of Isaiah develops, and the common ideas and themes that hold it together—reaching their culmination in Isa 56–66.

STRUCTURE OF THE BOOK OF ISAIAH

There are many excellent commentaries on the whole of Isaiah; I have mentioned several in the preface to this book. There are various opinions about the substructures and literary seams within the book—debates about whether this or that chapter is more closely associated with the one before it or the one after it. We do not need to go deep into those debates; what I present here is a very general literary outline of Isaiah that would be broadly agreeable to most Isaiah scholars. Table 1 connects these big chunks of the book of Isaiah to different time periods and describes some features that hold each chunk together.

Table 1: The Book of Isaiah—Speaking into Various Contexts

	Isa 1–12	Alternating condemnation and hope (1–5)
		Commissioning (6)
Part I		Aram-Israel crisis; Assyria on the rise (7–10)
c. 740–680 BC	Isa 13–27	Ten oracles/burdens concerning the nations
	Isa 28–35	Aram-Israel crisis; Assyria on the rise
	Isa 36–39 // 2 Kgs 18–20	c. 715–701 Sennacherib (Assyria) crisis

Babylonian Period (598–539 BC)		
Part II c. 550–540 BC	Isa 40–55 (links backward to 35, 39)	Babylonian conquest has happened; New Exodus on the horizon
		Audacious hope in YHWH, not idols (41–44)
		Cyrus of Persia rising (45)
		Inclusion of the gentiles (42; 45; 49; 52; 55)
		The Servant of YHWH (41–45; 48–50; 53)
		The (re)marriage of YHWH and Zion (49; 51–52; 54)
Part III c. 530–500 BC	Isa 56–66	Return from exile is disappointing
		Hopes fully "eschatologized"
		Inclusion of the gentiles

Starting from the Middle: Isaiah 36–39

Isaiah 36–39 might be described as a hinge or a turning point in the book of Isaiah. These chapters consist of prose narratives (stories) that are mostly identical to 2 Kgs 18:13—20:19 (with a few subtractions and additions). Three stories are told about King Hezekiah of Judah and the ministry of the prophet Isaiah in Hezekiah's court. First, there is the invasion of King Sennacherib of Assyria in which he besieges Jerusalem (Isa 36–37), which occurs around 701 BC. This is a fascinating instance in which we have an event described in the Bible for which there is an account from another perspective: Sennacherib's own annals describe this invasion with some of the same details but a very different emphasis.[9] Second, Isa 38 tells us about Hezekiah's recovery from a dire illness, which is miraculously signified by the sundial shadow going in reverse. This episode seems to happen prior to Sennacherib's invasion (predicted in 38:6). Isaiah 38 contains a celebratory praise poem of Hezekiah to YHWH that is not included in 2 Kgs 20 (Isa 38:9–20).

The third episode is one in which Hezekiah shows his treasury and armory to the envoy from Merodach-baladan, King of Babylon, apparently

9. Sennacherib's annals report: "As to Hezekiah, the Jew, he did not submit to my yoke.... Himself I made a prisoner in Jerusalem, his royal residence, like a bird in a cage." Pritchard, *ANET*, 287–88. Sennacherib understandably makes no mention of his failure to capture Jerusalem, or of the massacre of his army by the angel of YHWH (Isa 37:36).

in an effort to forge an alliance with Babylon against Assyria (Isa 39)—also apparently preceding the events of chapters 36 and 37. This episode will have catastrophic consequences for the kingdom of Judah, which will be exiled to Babylon—though not in Hezekiah's days (39:8). It exhibits faith in foreign rulers and armies rather than in "YHWH of Armies" (the LORD of Hosts), which is a recurring theme of Isa 1–33 and 36–37. I have written elsewhere about how this tragic failure of Hezekiah is presented in the book of Isaiah in such away that the reader's hopes might be raised that Hezekiah could be the fulfillment of the messianic prophecies of Isa 4:2–4; 9:2–7; and 11—but then those hopes are dashed, and the reader comes to understand that the great Davidic king is still in the future.[10]

Chapter 39 is followed, without any new introduction or narrative transition, to a situation in chapters 40–55 in which the anticipated exile to Babylon has already happened (see below). Chapter 40 links up with certain imagery and themes from chapter 35, which anticipate the return from exile in Babylon through the wilderness. Thus, these narrative chapters, Isa 36–39, provide a conclusion to the first part of Isaiah (1–39) and a transition to what comes after.

Three Panels: Isaiah 1–35

Isaiah 1–39 is recognized to be divided into three main segments: chapters 1–12, chapters 13–27, and chapters 28–39 (see table 1). These three "panels" or sections are not identical but share some common elements. In this first part of the book, oracles of warning and condemnation alternate with oracles of hope. The nations will be used to judge first Israel and then Judah, but those nations will also be judged. In each section there is a major imperial threat to Judah and a possible partner in an alliance that Isaiah warns against (see table 2).

Table 2: Imperial Threats in Isaiah 1–39

Major threat to Judah	Possible foreign help	Major threat is punished
Aram and Israel (5; 7–8)	Assyria (7:15–20; 8:4–8)	Aram and Israel (7–8)
Assyria (10; 19–20; 30–31; 36)	Egypt (20; 30:1–5, 16–17; 31:1–3; 36:6, 9)	Assyria (10; 37)
Assyria (39)	Babylon	Assyria (37)
Babylon (13–14; 21:9; 23:13)	(None)	Babylon (14; 21:9; 24–25)

---

10. This is the central argument in Giffone, "Toward a Better 'Hezekiah.'"

Many important themes are introduced in Isa 1–12, which are then reiterated in 13–39 and continue throughout the book. We see that YHWH is called by the heavenly beings in 6:3, "Holy, holy, holy" and also designated "the Holy One of Israel" (1:4; 5:19, 24; 10:20; 12:6).[11]

We see paired together the ideas of justice (*mišpāṭ*) and righteousness (*ṣedeq/ṣᵉdāqâ*), which are characteristics of a holy God and what he expects from / wants for his people, too (1:21, 26–27; 5:7, 16; 9:7; 11:4).[12]

The idea of a remnant, a subset of YHWH's people left over after a purifying trial (4:3; 10:19–22; 11:11, 16), is also introduced in Isa 1–12, including in the name of Isaiah's own son, Shear-jashub (7:3).[13] In another important passage the idea of "remnant" is present though the word is not used. The conclusion of the prophecy in Isa 6:9–13 (which is quoted several times in the New Testament) is that after a judgment only "a tenth will remain in the land," and that "the holy seed" will be a stump. But after the judgment, a remnant will return, and "a shoot will spring from the stump of Jesse"—that is the anointed king from the line of David. The idea of a holy remnant becomes very important in Isa 40–66, especially the fact that non-Israelites/non-Jews will be added to the Jewish remnant (a prefiguration of the church).

Each panel concludes with two poems that celebrate the deliverance that YHWH has given to his people: 12:1–3 and 4–6; 26:1–6 and 27:1–5; 37:22b–29 and 38:9–20.

Comfort, Comfort My People: Isaiah 40–55

Isaiah 1–39 warned that disaster was coming (first for Northern Israel, then for Southern Judah) if the people did not return to following YHWH and his law. Ultimately this judgment did indeed fall upon Israel at the hands of the Assyrians (722 BC) and upon Judah at the hands of the Babylonians (605–587 BC). The second part of the book, Isa 40–55,

---

11. This epithet continues throughout the rest of Isaiah: 17:7; 29:19; 30:11–12, 15; 31:1; 37:23; 41:14, 16, 20; 43:3, 14; 45:11; 47:4; 48:17; 49:7; 54:5; 55:5; 60:9, 14.

12. This pairing also continues throughout the rest of the book: 16:5; 26:9; 28:17; 32:1, 16; 33:5; 43:26; 50:8; 51:5; 54:17; 56:1; 58:2; 59:4, 9, 14.

13. Uses of the "remnant" word *šᵉʾār/šᵉʾērit* include: 14:22, 30; 15:9; 16:14; 17:3, 6; 21:17; 24:6, 12; 28:5; 37:4, 31–32; 44:17; 46:3; 49:21. Similarly, and used in an overlapping fashion, are *pᵉlêṭîm*, "survivors" (4:2; 5:29; 10:20; 15:9; 37:31–32; 45:20; 66:19) and *yṯr*, "leftovers" (1:8–9; 4:3; 7:22; 30:17; 39:6).

speaks into a situation in the middle of the sixth century, when this judgment through Babylon has occurred. These chapters speak hope and forgiveness for YHWH's people after they have been repaid "double for all their sins" (40:2; compare to Jer 16:16–18).

The bold message of Isa 40–55 is that the destruction of the temple and the exile of the people did *not* mean that Marduk was more powerful than YHWH—rather, YHWH has caused all this to happen and will rescue his people very soon, using King Cyrus and the Persians as his instrument. YHWH is the one who "creates" (*bārāʾ*) as in Gen 1, and "forms/fashions" (*yāṣar*) as in Gen 2:7. He creates and fashions the heavens and earth and everything in them (40:26–28; 42:5; 45:18). He creates and fashions human beings as his images for flourishing as they give glory to him (45:11–12). He creates and fashions his particular people (Israel, Jacob, the prophet, Cyrus, the Servant) for roles to play in his sovereign story (41:25; 43:1, 7, 15, 21; 44:2, 21, 24; 46:11; 49:5). He creates and fashions events, i.e., the course of history, both good and bad (41:20; 45:7–9; 48:7). And he is capable of creating a "new thing": a new exodus, providing water in the wilderness and a smooth way in the desert for the remnant to return to Zion (40:3; 41:18–19; 43:19–20; 50:2; 51:3, 11).

Isaiah 40–55 also has a lot to say about the pathetic enterprise of people trying to form/fashion their own gods. In these so-called "idol polemic" passages (40:18–20; 41:6–7; 41:21–29; 42:17; 44:9–20; 46:1–7), the message is that YHWH is far superior to other gods and their idols, who cannot "help" (41:6–7) or "save" (43:11–13; 44:17, 20; 45:20; 46:4, 7) those who worship them. YHWH is compared also to those who form/fashion the gods—the idol-makers.[14] YHWH gives breath and spirit to people (42:5; 45:11–12), but people who fabricate and worship unresponsive images become just like the images (42:16–20; 43:8–9), who know nothing (44:18–20).

In Isa 40–55, YHWH interacts with two representative figures of Israel/Judah/Jerusalem—one feminine, one masculine. The feminine figure is Daughter Zion, who is the mother of the people of Judah and the "wife" of YHWH. This imagery is also found in the book of Lamentations,[15] the Psalms, and other prophetic books such as Hosea and Ezekiel. Daughter

---

14. Holter, *Second Isaiah's Idol-Fabrication Passages*, 30, 239.

15. The poets of Lamentations repeatedly ask of Daughter Zion, "Who can console (*niḥam*) you?" (Lam 1:2, 9, 16, 17, 21; 2:13; cf. Isa 51:19). Isaiah 40–55 insists that God is the consoler (*mᵉnaḥēm*) of Israel (Isa 40:1, 49:13, 51:3, 12; 52:9; 54:11). See Mintz, *Hurban*, 45; Tull Willey, *Remember the Former Things*, 132.

Zion has been an unfaithful wife to YHWH—that is, the leaders and people of Judah have committed spiritual adultery with other gods (49:14-26; 50:1-3; 51:17—52:3; 54). Daughter Zion has "drunk from the hand of [YHWH] the cup of his wrath ... drunk to the dregs ... the cup of staggering" (51:17). When drunk, unspeakably bad things have happened to her (52:1) and to her children—she thought she'd lost them all (51:18-20). But YHWH is determined to find Daughter Zion, redeem her from whatever slavery she's sold herself into (50:1-3; 52:3-5), see her cleaned up and adorned as on their wedding day (49:18; 52:1), and remarry her (54). In fact, they were never divorced (50:1; 54:6-8), so it's just a celebration of their fresh start. And the children she thought she'd lost will be restored to her (49:19-22; 54:1-3). Those who tormented Daughter Zion will be shamed and punished like what she experienced (47; 51:22-23).

The masculine representative figure, the Servant, is one that evolves a bit over the course of Isa 40-55. If Christian readers of the Bible are familiar with any passage from Isaiah (other than the Immanuel verse, 7:14), it will likely be the Suffering Servant described in 52:13—53:12. It is easy to see how this Servant figure is fulfilled in Jesus.

However, other figures in Isa 40-55 are described as "servants of YHWH," but not all have been very suitable to the role. Israel/Jacob (41:8-10; 42:19-20; 43:8-10; 48:20; 49:1-7) has not been a good servant to YHWH—the people are rebellious, deaf, and blind (42:19-20; cf. 6:9-10). Other figures have been faithful servants in their specific roles, such as Cyrus (45:4) and the prophet himself, who has suffered for the message he preaches (50:4-11).

But there is a lingering sense that not even these faithful servants can adequately fulfill the image-bearing and redeeming task that YHWH has for the Servant. I have likened this development to a director watching various actors audition for a lead role in his film: as he watches their audition tapes, he realizes not only that these portrayals don't do justice to the role—the character itself is even more important and complex than he originally conceived of it in the script. So it is with "the Servant of YHWH," which begins to demand a figure greater than Israel, Cyrus, or the prophet—someone in the future (42:1-4; 44:1-2, 21-26). This culminates in the Servant who would suffer not just ridicule and scorn but death on behalf of YHWH's people—and receive eternal life and honor for his sacrifice (52:13—53:12).[16]

Isaiah 55 concludes the section hopefully with statements of YHWH's provision ("Come, everyone who thirsts"; 55:1-2), his faithfulness (55:3-5), and a call to repentance (55:6-7). YHWH's sovereignty over world events for the good of his people is reaffirmed ("For my thoughts are not your thoughts"; 55:8-11). The going-out from exile, a new exodus, will trigger the renewal and rejoicing of the natural world (55:12-13) that reverses the curse from Gen 3:17-19.

A More Glorious Future: Isaiah 56–66

If the book of Isaiah consisted only of chapters 1–55, then one might think that the return from exile in Babylon would have ushered in the renewal of the cosmos. Isaiah 56–66 makes clear that YHWH's full restorative plan does not conclude with the return from Babylonian exile but has an even more glorious future in mind. The renewal promises of Isa 1–55 are "fully eschatologized" (Greek *eschata*, "last things"), meaning that they will be fulfilled at the end of time and on a much grander scale than the partial restoration of the Persian period.

This is apparent when we review the history of this period and find that the situation in Judah (now called the Persian province of Yehud) and in the diaspora is underwhelming. Many of the exiles have returned, but others remain scattered in Babylonia and Persia to the east, and in Egypt to the southwest. This is when characters such as Zerubbabel, Ezra, Nehemiah, and Esther would have lived. The Jerusalem temple was rebuilt in the last part of the sixth century—we will see in the next chapter, from the books of Haggai and Ezra, that the work started, then stopped for a few years, and then resumed as a result of Haggai and Zechariah's messages from YHWH. But we don't see any evidence of a glorious return of YHWH's presence to the temple (as predicted in Ezek 43–45). The book of Malachi, written later in this Persian period, says, "The Lord whom you seek *will suddenly come* to his temple" (3:1, emphasis mine)—implying that he hasn't been there.[17] There is also no independent kingship in Judah, only governors appointed by the Persian emperor.

---

16. See the excellent exposition offered by Goldingay, "Isaiah 53," 147–53.

17. On the idea of the "continuing exile" even to the New Testament period, see Wright, *People of God*, 268–71.

Despite the purifying trial of the exile, the people of Israel and Judah continue to be . . . morally disappointing. The people cannot remain consistently faithful about following the law of Moses. Nehemiah has to try to whip the people into shape in the middle of the fifth century![18] They're not keeping laws even as basic as the Sabbath requirement.

And so, this text is characterized in part by disappointment: disappointment over all that the people brought upon themselves, and disappointment that YHWH's promises of forgiveness and restoration in Isa 40–55 haven't panned out. In Neh 9, the leaders of the people confess: "We remain slaves to this day, in the land that you gave us." The impassioned plea of Isa 63:15–19 captures this ongoing alienation from YHWH: "Where are your zeal and your might? The stirring of your inner parts and your compassion are held back from me. . . . You, O LORD, are our Father, our Redeemer from of old is your name. . . . Why do you make us wander from your ways and harden our heart, so that we fear you not? . . . Our adversaries have trampled down your sanctuary. We have become like those over whom you have never ruled."

And so, the section looks ahead to a fuller restoration of YHWH, his land, his city, and his people—but the "twist" is that people from many nations, languages and tongues will be part of his renewed, restored world. In another "twist," the kingship in the line of David disappears nearly completely—instead, YHWH himself acts as a warrior on behalf of his people (59:15b–21), and the Spirit of YHWH comes upon the Servant, who makes an appearance in 61:1–3. These two figures together fulfill the role that the Davidic king/messiah was supposed to fulfill in Isa 1–39.[19]

Isaiah 56–66 is recognized as having a chiastic (concentric) structure—here is an adaptation of Goldingay's outline (table 3).[20]

---

18. See Schnittjer, "Ezra-Nehemiah," 32–56.

19. In Isa 40–55, David is only mentioned once (55:3), and only Cyrus of Persia is called the "anointed one" (*māšîaḥ*; 45:1).

20. Goldingay, *Book of Isaiah*, 133.

Table 3: Chiastic Structure of Isa 56–66

- 56:1–8 Preface (inclusion of foreigners)
- 56:9—59:8 Challenges about Israel's life
- 59:9–15a Prayer for forgiveness and restoration
- 59:15b–21 Vision of YHWH in judgment
- 60:1—62:12 Visions of Jerusalem restored
- 63:1–6 Vision of YHWH in judgment
- 63:7—64:12 Prayer for forgiveness and restoration
- 65:1—66:16 Challenges about Israel's life
- 66:17–24 Postscript (inclusion of foreigners)

A Note on Authorship and Time of Writing

I have chosen to write about Isa 56–66 as if it were written mainly in the Persian period. This may be surprising to some readers who are accustomed to reading the entire book as if it were written by Isaiah ben Amoz in the eighth and seventh centuries BC. While this is a traditional view, many scholars who believe in the inspiration of the Bible nevertheless hold that Isa 40–66 was written not by Isaiah, but by one or more prophets writing in the tradition and style of Isaiah, building on his theology in the period of the Babylonian exile (c. 587–539 BC) and/or the Persian period (539–332 BC). Scholars call these portions of the book "Second Isaiah" (or Deutero-Isaiah) and "Third Isaiah" (or Trito-Isaiah). Sometimes they will use those terms to describe the putative authors of those sections (Isa 40–55 and 56–66, respectively), because those prophets did not add their names to these works.

Some scholars adopt this "multiple-authorship" view because they believe that predictive prophecy is not possible, and so the prophet Isaiah *could not* have known about details like Cyrus of Persia (45:1). I reject this modernist contention that God could *not* have inspired the prophet Isaiah before the exile to write about later events of the sixth century.

Other scholars and most traditional readers of the Bible contend that, in order for the book of Isaiah to be inspired and infallible, it must have been substantially the work of Isaiah ben Amoz (and scribes/disciples writing down his prophecies, within his lifetime). Some also argue for single-authorship by Isaiah ben Amoz on the basis that the New Testament authors introduce their references to passages from Isa 40–66 with "Isaiah" or "Isaiah the prophet" (e.g., Matt 3:3 and Isa 40:3; Matt 8:17, Acts 8, and Isa 53; Rom 10:20–21 and Isa 65:1–2) and that this indicates that the NT authors believed these passages were written by Isaiah himself.

While I appreciate these arguments and what they are trying to preserve about the integrity of the Bible, I disagree with the contention that the entire book called "Isaiah" *must* have been substantially the work of Isaiah ben Amoz in order for the book to have been inspired by God. This neglects the role of the Holy Spirit as the divine superintending Author of all of Scripture, who could have allowed that scribes and later disciples writing in an "Isaiah tradition/school" could have written inspired Scripture and simply not regarded their names as worthy of being added to the Isaiah scroll.

Furthermore, the New Testament authors' citations of Old Testament Scriptures should be regarded as affirmations of the Old Testament as authoritative Scripture, but not necessarily as statements about human authorship of individual passages. After all, Matt 27:9 says, "Then was fulfilled what had been spoken by the prophet Jeremiah," but then the Evangelist quotes from Zech 11:13. In 1 Cor 14:21, Paul says, "In the Law it is written," but then he quotes from Isa 28:11, which is part of the Prophets, not the Law.

I do think that Isa 40–55 makes the most sense if understood as having been written in the Babylonian period by an anonymous prophet. Those who wish to engage this evangelical perspective in more detail, I refer to the commentaries of Goldingay and McConville,[21] among others. In my view, predictive prophecy is actually maintained and strengthened by multiple authorship over several eras—we can see predictions made and fulfilled. In Isa 41:21–29, for example, the idols of Judah and Babylon are summoned by YHWH to a showdown: "Who declared [these events] from the beginning?" The answer to this rhetorical question is "YHWH"—whereas the idols had proven unable to predict what would happen to Judah. This would make little sense and have no rhetorical effect if it were written by Isaiah ben Amoz over a century before Babylon conquered Judah, because YHWH had not yet been proven right in his judgment warnings. Isaiah 41:21–29 *does* make sense if it is spoken to the

---

21. Goldingay, *Book of Isaiah*, 14–16; Goldingay, *Isaiah*, 3–5; McConville, *Isaiah*, 6–9.

Judahite exiles in Babylon in the 540s, and it demonstrates that the exiles can trust YHWH's prediction that he will soon rescue them by means of Cyrus of Persia (45:1–13). The prediction of Cyrus would be of little interest to Isaiah ben Amoz's eighth- and seventh-century audiences before the exile but would be reassuring to the exiles in the sixth century (and also a test of their faith).

Likewise, I think that Isa 56–66 makes the most sense if understood as having been written in the Persian period (see table 4). The Babylonian conquest leading to the exile (605–587 BC, in several stages) appears to have happened already (63:15—64:12). Yet there are references to "walls" of the temple (56:5) and of the city of Jerusalem (62:6).[22] The Second Temple was built sometime between 520 and 515 BC (see Ezra 1–6; Hag 1–2), and the walls of Jerusalem were rebuilt by Nehemiah sometime after 458 BC (see Neh 2–7). The next chapter will paint a fuller picture of the historical backdrop of this period. I acknowledge that these passages *could* have been written in a predictive fashion by Isaiah ben Amoz—but rhetorically, they are not predictive but hortatory. The true predictions of Isa 56–66 point to a future beyond the Persian period.

Therefore, in this book, I have chosen to refer to "the prophet," in order to avoid specificity and unnecessary distraction from the main themes of the text. Readers who believe that Isaiah ben Amoz is the author of the entire book that bears his name can still acknowledge that Isa 56–66 appears to *speak into* a time (which is yet future in Isaiah's day) of partial restoration and blessing after exile—namely, the Persian period.

---

22. But in 60:10, foreigners *will* build up Zion's walls.

Table 4: Dates Relevant to the Book of Isaiah

Chronology of Isaiah ben Amoz

- Isaiah likely knew the work of earlier prophets such as Amos and Micah
- 745: Tiglath-Pileser III of Assyria rises to power
- 740/39: Death of Uzziah (Azariah) of Judah (Isa 6:1)
- 735: Syro-Ephraimite crisis. Syria and Northern Israel try to recruit Ahaz to fight with them against Assyria (Isa 7–10)
- 722: Fall of Northern Israel to Assyria
- 705: Death of Sargon II of Assyria
- 701: Hezekiah rebels, but Sennacherib invades all Judah except Jerusalem (Isa 36–37)

Later relevant dates

- 612–609: Defeat of Assyria by Babylon
- 598: Babylon prevails in Judah
- 587: Zedekiah rebels, temple destroyed, exile to Babylon
- 539: Cyrus II (the Great) of Persia defeats Babylon (Isa 44–45)
- c. 520–515: Second Temple built
- 332: Alexander the Great conquers Persian Empire

Threads Connecting the Book of Isaiah

Whatever you believe about how many prophets the Holy Spirit used to write the inspired book of Isaiah, it is easy to see that he caused the human author(s) to write using common themes and motifs across the book. These threads connect the three sections of the book of Isaiah. In this section we will highlight just a few,[23] but in my main chapters on Isa 56–66 I will often show how that section picks up on ideas and images from Isa 1–55:

---

23. See especially the helpful presentation by Goldingay, *Book of Isaiah*, 19–87.

- *YHWH, the Holy One of Israel*—The phrase "the Holy One of Israel" appears twenty-five times in the book of Isaiah, in every major section of the book.[24] We saw earlier the significance in Isa 6 of YHWH being called "holy, holy, holy" by the *seraphim*.

- *YHWH as Savior and Redeemer*—YHWH is mainly called *gōʾēl* (Redeemer) in Isa 40–66. He saves his people to display his greatness to the nations (Isa 49:25–26; 52:7–10). He saves his people because he is their father (Isa 1:2; 45:11; 63:16). Just as YHWH redeemed Israel from Egypt, so he will redeem them from bondage in Babylon. They were sold for nothing, so they will be redeemed without money (Isa 52:3).

- *Remnant*—As we saw earlier, the preservation and sanctification of a remnant is how YHWH remains faithful to his holiness and his word (Isa 10:20–22; 11:11, 16; 28:5; 37:4, 31–32; 46:3; 65:8, grapes left in the cluster).

- *The Spirit of YHWH*—From the beginning, the Spirit (*rûaḥ*) of God was involved in creation (Gen 1:2). In Isaiah, the Spirit is involved in re-creation out of chaos (32:15; 34:16—35:2; 59:21—60:2; 63:10–14). Out of moral chaos, the Spirit brings order and justice (28:6, 42:1, 44:3). The Spirit is upon the Davidic king, giving wisdom and understanding (11:2), and upon the Servant (42:1, 61:1), proclaiming the good news of YHWH's salvation (61:1). The Spirit makes possible the announcement of the purposes of YHWH (Isa 48:16).

- *YHWH's sovereignty over history*—In Isa 1–39, YHWH strongly asserts sovereignty over the nations, who move at his bidding (10:15). Isaiah 40–66 exults in the prophecies regarding the nations being fulfilled. YHWH's rule is in contrast with the Mesopotamian gods, who lied, schemed, seduced, deceived, made war on each other—they were essentially understood as glorified human beings. The God of Isaiah is sharply different: he faces no contingency or surprise—he speaks, and things happen.

- *Reliance on YHWH rather than on temporal powers*—This is a significant component of the message of Isa 7–8; 19–20; 28–33; 36; 39; 45; and 59.

---

24. Isa 1:4; 5:19, 24; 10:20; 12:6; 17:7; 29:19; 30:11–12, 15; 31:1; 37:23; 41:14, 16, 20; 43:3, 14; 45:11; 47:4; 48:17; 49:7; 54:5; 55:5; 60:9, 14.

HOW DOES THE BOOK OF ISAIAH WORK? 45

- *Polemics against the nations*—Each section of Isaiah contains major passages that are critical of the nations who worship other gods and are antagonistic to YHWH's people (10; 13–23; 46; 47; 59).
- *The inclusion of the nations*—But also, each section of Isaiah anticipates that some from among the nations will become part of YHWH's people through loyalty to him (2:2–4; 11:10; 42:1–9; 56:1–8; 60; 65–66).
- *"Don't be afraid" versus the fear of YHWH*—YHWH's people and prophets are told "Do not be afraid" of the circumstance or their enemies.[25] Instead, YHWH is the only one who should be feared.[26] As the saying goes: if you fear God, you will fear nothing else—if you don't fear God, you will fear everything else!
- *Imagery (trees, water, potter/clay, light/darkness, etc.)*—Certain imagery develops and continues across the book: YHWH as the potter and humans as clay in his hands (29:16; 45:9–10; 64:8); or a highway/road in the wilderness for YHWH's people, with water and plants flourishing along the way (11:16; 26:7; 35; 40:1–9; 42:16; 43:16; 49:11; 57:14; 62:10). In 9:2a we find this promise, "The people who walked in darkness have seen a great light"; 42:16b likewise promises, "I will turn the darkness before them into light"—but these have not been fulfilled by the time we get to 59:9b: "We hope for light, and behold, darkness, and for brightness, but we walk in gloom."

One final thread links us back to the beginning of our chapter: how does prophecy itself *work*. Prophets are commissioned to provide verbal (spoken and written) warnings to those who face judgment if they don't change their ways—but the warnings may or may not be heard or heeded. This interplay between responsibilities of the prophet and the people, and the failure or success of the prophetic ministry, progresses over the course of the book.

After the warnings of Isa 1–5, Isaiah is commissioned as a prophet—but his messages will fall on deaf ears, blind eyes, and hard hearts (6:8–13). In 8:16–18, the testimony against Judah is to be "bound up" and "sealed" among Isaiah's disciples—the prophetic inspiration is hidden. It remains sealed or unreadable to the people in 29:11–14. They will hear threatening words spoken in a foreign language, which they will

---

25. Isa 7:4; 8:12; 10:24; 35:4; 37:6; 40:9; 41:10–14; 43:1, 5; 44:2; 51:7, 12; 54:4, 14.
26. Isa 11:2–3; 29:13; 33:6; 50:10; 57:11; 59:19; 63:17.

be unable to understand (28:9–13)—their failure to comply with their overlords' orders will result in suffering.

But after this period of warnings not being heard or understood—and the punishment of exile—the prophet overhears YHWH commissioning the comforters of Jerusalem: "Cry to her that her warfare is ended, that her iniquity is pardoned, that she has received from the LORD's hand double for all her sins" (40:2b). A prophet is again commissioned: "Cry!" "What shall I cry?" (40:6) The prophet will be a good-news-messenger (40:9; 52:7).

Still later, we read of another prophetic commissioning by YHWH: "Cry aloud; do not hold back; lift up your voice like a trumpet; declare to my people their transgression, to the house of Jacob their sins" (58:1). The people were not remaining obedient to the covenant, so they needed more prophecy/exhortation. But the Servant also picks up the prophetic vocation and proclaims both amnesty and judgment (Isa 61:1–3).

If we regard each section of Isaiah as written by a different prophet, we could regard each "Isaiah" as picking up the ministry or prophetic mantle of the previous one.[27] When we get to Luke 4:16–21, we find Jesus reading Isa 61:1–2 and picking up the prophetic mantle/ministry of all three (we will look at this more in chapter 11). This demonstrates the uniqueness of Jesus' ministry *and* the ongoing ministry of the prophets.

SUMMARY: HOW DOES THE BOOK OF ISAIAH SPEAK TO US TODAY?

Back in chapter 1, I asked: Why is it so hard for us to read the Old Testament? Why is it so hard for us to read the book of Isaiah? I hope that chapters 2 and 3 have provided some help that will make our journey through Isa 56–66 less intimidating and more interesting.

The Bible is not a single unit—various books and sections within the Bible build upon others, and the Bible has a story arc. In chapter 2, we looked at how the New Testament builds upon the Old Testament, and how followers of Jesus (whom we meet in the New Testament) can actually read the Old Testament forward as Scripture. Saint Augustine, the North African Bishop (AD 354–430), famously wrote, "The New

---

27. Goldingay, *Book of Isaiah*, 77–78.

Testament is in the Old concealed; the Old Testament is in the New revealed" (In case you're wondering, it rhymes in the original Latin, too!).[28]

Even though we ourselves have not seen the prophet Isaiah performing in front of the kings of Judah, speaking in Hebrew, the book of Isaiah nevertheless speaks prophetically to us in the twenty-first century. We have seen that, in God's providence, the words of Isaiah have been recorded and presented in writing, then picked up by later prophets who strengthened and re-presented those messages of warning and salvation. This prophetic ministry continues down through Jesus and the apostles, even after Jesus's death and resurrection. We will come back to this in the epilogue of this book.

Isaiah 56–66 in particular has something important to say to us in the Western world, where Christendom has existed but has now receded (or is even completely eclipsed, such as in Europe). We ourselves, people in our churches and our communities and societies in general, have heard God's word over and over again for centuries, and yet, today, God's prophetic word is not having the impact that we expect or want. Is it possible for us to pick up God's powerful word, recover its strength, and discover new ways that old truths can be proclaimed and applied in our time? Just as Isa 56–66 picks up the earlier ministry and prophetic word of Isa 1–55, these eleven chapters can be a guide for us as we seek to be faithful to God. If we follow these Scriptures, let us not be surprised if God does in our midst "awesome things that we did not look for" (64:3).

---

28. "Novum Testamentum in Vetere latet, Vetus in Novo patet." Augustine, *Quaest. Hept.* 2.73, as quoted in Schaff, *History*, 605n2.

4

Give Careful Thought to Your Ways
The Persian Period and the Church After Christendom

THE CHURCH PUZZLE

Let me tell you about a church in my area. It's a small congregation, mostly consisting of older people who have served in the church for a long time.

This church has been around for a long time. Back in the 1970s, it was often full when services were held. Speaking of which, services used to be held on Sunday morning and Sunday night, and then there was Wednesday night prayer meeting. There were events for women and retirees during the day and Bible studies and youth group in the evenings. They raised money for overseas missionaries, who would occasionally visit and report to a packed church, equipped with slide presentations about their ministries.

But now, attendance is sparse with plenty of unused pews during their lone Sunday service. Most of the older members' adult children and their grandchildren don't attend. Some of them have moved away and attend church somewhere else, but many don't attend church at all for various reasons that their parents don't understand.

Because the number of attendees has decreased, and many are older and on a fixed income, tithing is down. The church has had to lay off staff or not replace them when they retire or move on. Now, they have only a part-time pastor, who is himself ready to retire soon. They still give the same percentages to local ministries and international missions, but the pie is a lot smaller than it used to be.

The folks at this church have tried different activities to bring people into the church, like cultural and outdoor activities, vacation Bible school, and fun events for young people. But fewer and fewer people come, and most who come are already connected at another church. Children and teens these days are busy with school; sports and other activities are now scheduled on Sundays, making church attendance difficult. The older members are losing energy and motivation to keep up outreach endeavors that aren't working.

Twenty years ago, the church tried switching from hymns led by a piano, to a praise band with guitars and drums. There was some grumbling, but eventually the older folks accepted it. But now, no younger people are stepping up to lead the praise band or play guitar—it's the same folks who led twenty years ago, who are now in their sixties. The church has tried to make its online outreach more sophisticated: a more helpful website, social media accounts, and even an app. They even invested in streaming equipment to "keep things going" during COVID. But the church keeps shrinking, and no one knows why.

There have been some divisive moments in this church over the years—some over important matters of doctrine, some over silly, nonessential matters. Each of those divisions and mass exoduses left a scar, but those people are "out of sight and out of mind"—except to those who remember. Some people have switched to attending this church because they were disgruntled or hurt by another church—they bring their own scars and foibles. But it's been a long time since someone joined the church who wasn't already Christian or previously involved in another church.

Looking around at the world, the members of this church are concerned. When they were younger, society's values were shaped by Christianity, regardless of what people believed in their hearts. But now, openly affirming Christian belief or values in school or the workplace could get someone written off as weird, backward, sexist, foolish, and bigoted.

In sum, the church is dying, and no one knows what to do, except more of the same. How could it be that this is happening? The people of the church acknowledge that they haven't been perfect, but it feels like they should be getting *some* return for their efforts on God's behalf.

How much of this sounds familiar to you? Probably a lot, though the details might be different depending on what part of North America or Europe you live in and whether your setting is urban, suburban, or rural. What I've described is actually an amalgam of several churches that I've served in Western Pennsylvania, but it overlaps with the profile of many churches in America and in Europe where I used to live.

It's more urgent than ever for us to be looking to God's word for guidance. I remain hopeful because Christ has made promises to his universal church, of which our local congregations are just individual local expressions. But what parts of the Bible should we look to? Is there anything in the Old Testament that is relevant for this situation?

Christian readers who are familiar with the Old Testament tend to remember the stories that tell of ancient Israel in its heyday: Abraham, Isaac, Jacob, and Joseph in Genesis; the exodus from Egypt and the time of Moses's leadership; the time of Israel's judges and kings in the land of Canaan. We tend to romanticize these times—we see examples of YHWH, Israel's God, continually adding to their understanding of who he is, through his laws and his actions. And there are characters that are exciting and serve as examples for us of what to do (or not do!).

But there are great resources from the Old Testament that were generated in times of crisis—both in the midst of crisis, and picking up the pieces afterward. Isaiah 56–66 has particular lessons for the North American church, and local congregations like the ones I've served, in the time and the place where we find ourselves as the first quarter of the twenty-first century comes to a close. The struggles experienced by small, declining congregations are not unique—there are surprising parallels in the struggles of Persian period Jews.

PERSIAN PERIOD

As a way into studying Isa 56–66, we'll take a close look at some texts that set the scene. In this chapter, we will be looking at passages from two other prophets: Haggai and Zechariah. Haggai and Zechariah were writing their prophecies at roughly the same time for/in which Isa 56–66 was written.

We sometimes forget that the "heyday" of Israel didn't last: after many years of moral and political decline, the separate polities of Israel and Judah lost their independence to the Assyrian Empire and the

Babylonian Empire, as we saw in chapter 3. YHWH had done amazing things for Israel: political liberation, placing them in a homeland, setting a righteous king, David, over them, and giving them a sanctuary in Jerusalem in which they could worship him. But the exile reversed and destroyed all that good. The prophets before the exile had warned Israel and Judah to change their hearts and their ways, or else YHWH would discipline them.

And yet, the memories of Israel's "glory days" continued to be part of Israel's community memory, in the songs that they sang (many of the psalms), the stories they told, and the texts that they wrote. Even though they had seemingly lost everything, they held onto the past—not just out of national pride, but out of a hope that YHWH might still reverse their situation and bless them again.

In due time, YHWH did bless them again—to a degree. When Cyrus the Great of Persia conquered the Babylonians, he permitted the exiles from Judah to return to their homeland, the province of Yehud. They were permitted a certain freedom to worship as they wished. But the Judean "liberation" under Persian rule never turned out to be as complete as things had been in the days of David and Solomon, and certainly not as glorious as the Prophets had predicted.

Imagine you were a child of the exile, born in the 540s, around the time of Second Isaiah. Your great-grandparents had been taken captive by Nebuchadnezzar, but they had obeyed the words of the prophet Jeremiah: they had put down roots in Babylon, gotten married, had kids, and sought to advance the welfare of that city (Jer 29:1–14).

Now, under the Persians, your family returned to Jerusalem, in the hopes of rebuilding the temple. Your parents and grandparents had told you stories of Israel's glorious past and its tragic fall. As you grew, you expected to see the renewal and rebuilding that Jer 30–33 and Ezek 40–48 had predicted.

But as the years passed, no such renewal happened. In fact, everything around you still seemed disjointed and displaced. Regarding YHWH worship: compared to the situation your ancestors faced, in which YHWH held the privileged position (for example, under King Josiah in the late seventh century), things are more difficult. In Mesopotamia, YHWH was just the god of a people defeated by the people of Marduk (Bel), but the hope was that, with the Persian defeat of Babylon, YHWH worship could then be revived in Judah (now Yehud province). But YHWH no longer holds a privileged position in Yehudian society—he's just one god among many options: gods from Mesopotamia in the east, gods indigenous to Canaan, and gods from Egypt.

There's the question of where and how YHWH should be worshiped. Should we rebuild the Jerusalem temple, or can we worship at other places like Bethel, Mount Gerizim, or Elephantine in Egypt?[1]

There's conflict and territorialism: returnees from the east to Judea ("children of the exile," like you and your family) wanted their grandparents' land back. But those descended from the Judahites left behind (see 2 Kgs 24:14) have continued living on and cultivating that land for several generations already—they don't want to give it up. There's conflict between the tribal identities of Israel: Judah, Benjamin, Levi, and the remnants of several other affiliations. Is it permissible to intermarry with people outside the community? How open should we be to the "outside world"? What is our God going to do for us, now that the pagans are in charge?

So the Jewish communities, now living in Judea and in the Egyptian and Mesopotamian diasporas, looked to their past traditions, and to YHWH and his prophets, to understand how to live in these less-than-ideal times. What role should the glorious past play in our present and our future? Can we find a path forward to more obedience and more blessing? Or will we be permanently hobbled, trying to solve today's problems with yesterday's solutions?

SCRIPTURE: HAGGAI 1:1-11

It is into this moment that Haggai arises as a prophet. The people in his day are wondering: what do we do now? Has YHWH truly forgiven us of our sins and rebellion? If so, why aren't things better than they are? Will we get punished again? Is YHWH ever going to come back and live in our midst again? The book of Haggai is short and has some sharp warnings, but also hope!

> In the second year of Darius the king, in the sixth month, on the first day of the month, the word of the LORD came by the hand of Haggai the prophet to Zerubbabel the son of Shealtiel, governor of Judah, and to Joshua the son of Jehozadak, the high priest: "Thus says the LORD of hosts: These people say the time

---

1. These were the likely competitors to Jerusalem for the worship of YHWH in the Persian period; see the summary in Giffone, *Storymaking*, 106–19.

has not yet come to rebuild the house of the LORD." Then the word of the LORD came by the hand of Haggai the prophet, "Is it a time for you yourselves to dwell in your paneled houses, while this house lies in ruins? Now, therefore, thus says the LORD of hosts: Consider your ways. You have sown much, and harvested little. You eat, but you never have enough; you drink, but you never have your fill. You clothe yourselves, but no one is warm. And he who earns wages does so to put them into a bag with holes.

"Thus says the LORD of hosts: Consider your ways. Go up to the hills and bring wood and build the house, that I may take pleasure in it and that I may be glorified, says the LORD. You looked for much, and behold, it came to little. And when you brought it home, I blew it away. Why? declares the LORD of hosts. Because of my house that lies in ruins, while each of you busies himself with his own house. Therefore the heavens above you have withheld the dew, and the earth has withheld its produce. And I have called for a drought on the land and the hills, on the grain, the new wine, the oil, on what the ground brings forth, on man and beast, and on all their labors." (Hag 1:1–11)

This prophecy is dated to the 2nd year of one of the Persian kings called Darius, and this seems to be roughly 520 BC. This is eighteen years after the earlier Persian king, Cyrus, issued a decree that the Judahites were permitted to return from the east to their land in Palestine. An initial wave of returnees, led by Sheshbazzar, brought back the temple tools and articles. Then there seems to have been other groups of returnees, led by Joshua the priest and Zerubbabel the governor, who rebuilt an altar on the site of the destroyed temple. This was supposed to be the first steps in the rebuilding of this sacred site, where YHWH could once again live among his people, and they could honor him!

But, by the time Haggai receives this message, the people had stopped building, and this is what prompts this passage. What is the holdup? It's a few things.

It says in verses 4 and 9 that instead of building the temple, the people were busy with their own houses. Now, if it were just building basic shelter for themselves, we could understand that. So, maybe their excuse is: we *have* to have safe and dry houses to live in while we're building the house for YHWH! But we know that's not what's going on, because he says, "You are living in paneled houses"—paneling that would be a luxury for the inside of the house, not part of the structure. So, YHWH is accusing the people of having misaligned priorities: they're focused on enhancing their own lives, rather than honoring him.

There's also probably a fear component, here, too. In Ezra 4–5, the returnees were threatened by opponents in the land, who bullied them into stopping the temple construction and even wrote lies about them to the Persian king so he would make them stop. While this was a real threat and a danger, their stopping the building has shown that they fear man more than they fear YHWH.

So, they have given in to apathy, greed, and fear. In a sense, they've become the exact inverse of ancient King David. David said, "See now, I dwell in a house of cedar, but the ark of God dwells in a tent" (2 Sam 7:2), and then made plans to build a temple. YHWH responded to David's zeal by declaring that David's son, not David, would eventually build a house for YHWH (7:5–7)—but that YHWH would in the meantime build a house for David (7:11).

Moving on to verses 5–11, YHWH says twice: Consider, give careful thought to your ways. Check yourselves, guys, before you wreck yourselves! He says: You are putting in effort, but not getting out of your work what you expected. You are consuming, but never being satisfied. You're earning money, but then it burns a hole in your pocket! Because of your priorities, YHWH has withheld the produce of the land from you.

Why is all this happening? Well, we've already seen why: Because you haven't built YHWH's house! And here, it's important to remember *why* the temple of YHWH was so important. He says, build my house, "so that I may take pleasure in it." On the surface, it might sound like YHWH just wants the fancy house, the "smells and bells" of incense, and priests in fancy robes! But, that's not the main thing. In Isa 1, YHWH said two hundred years prior: I don't care about your festivals and your sacrifices, if your hearts aren't devoted to me, and to compassion and justice! In Ps 50:12–15, YHWH says sarcastically (my paraphrase): "If I were hungry, why would I bother to ask *you* guys to give me some meat? The whole earth is mine! What—do you think I eat raw bull meat and drink goat-blood? No, guys—I want you to honor me, fellowship with me, follow my instruction, care about justice and the things that I care about!" That is what YHWH means when he says through Haggai, "that I may take pleasure in it and"—what else does he say?—"be glorified" (Hag 1:8). It's not just that they haven't built the house, it's that they haven't cared enough about God to know him and spend time with him and to care about his glory and the things he cares about!

It's interesting, though, that YHWH doesn't construe this as *punishing* them for this lackluster effort on their part. He doesn't threaten to send them back to exile in Babylon, to bring catastrophe on them (he promised not to do that again, in Isa 54:7–10). They had been punished in the past—but now, redeemed, and forgiven. But they are not living fully into the blessed life that God wanted for them, because they weren't wholeheartedly pursuing God's glory.

Now, you could envision the people getting angry and defensive about this and further blaming God. But in fact, their hearts *do* turn toward him, and they follow Haggai's words! (Incidentally, Haggai seems to be the only of the writing prophets whose prophetic warnings are actually *all* heeded! Maybe that's because the book is so short—he was one-for-one, "batting a thousand," so he quit while he was ahead!)

In Hag 1:12 and following, and in Ezra 5:2, we read that the work resumes under Zerubbabel and Joshua! The leaders of the returnees show courage and reordered priorities. And the result is, in Ezra 6:13–22, the Second Temple is finished. YHWH receives glory at this important moment: it's seen as a good thing in the eyes of the pagan emperor, and the Passover is celebrated in the new temple, celebrating the ancient rescue from slavery in Egypt. Some divisions that had emerged in the community, which had hobbled them in the past, are overcome, and there is unity! And, even some gentiles from outside the community are incorporated by faith (Ezra 6:21).

A CHURCH IN DECLINE?

New Temple, New Stones

As we look at this episode from Haggai, how is it relevant for us as the church? The Old Testament often gives us pictures of how we are to live as people of God in the new covenant. The apostle Paul says in Eph 2:11–22 that the "temple" for us as believers in Jesus is *the church*, made up of believers from every ethnic background, built on the foundation of the apostles and prophets (and their writings, which is the Bible), with Christ as the cornerstone. *That* is the place where the Holy Spirit dwells: in the church!

If we take the message in Haggai to heart for us as the church, we're not just talking about building facilities in which to worship—those are not essential, and we already have plenty of those. Building YHWH's house means evangelism, telling others about the good news—adding stones to God's temple, the church—and discipleship—regathering and strengthening and smoothing the stones that are already part of the temple.

Rebuilding with Old Stones?

Let's go back to the scenario I started out this chapter with. Again, the congregations I served in rural Western Pennsylvania have been in decline for a while, by several ways of measuring such things. Like many churches, there was a long period of struggle even before COVID, and then the pandemic response accelerated existing trends.

There have been tough situations: some confusion, some conflict, and some disagreement and divisions. When we looked at the budget, thankfully, there were some funds in savings, but our congregation was spending more than it was receiving in tithes. Looking at things on paper and speaking according to human wisdom, there would be only a few years to turn this ship around, or this congregation would be forced to close. Maybe your church is in a similar situation.

Our Lord Jesus promised that his church *as a whole* will always continue, but he doesn't promise that any one congregation will continue forever. I asked the congregation: Why should this particular congregation continue to exist, when there are other Bible-believing churches—even other churches in our Reformed tradition and in our denomination—in the area, within a fifteen-minute drive? Why shouldn't we convert our building into a non-profit historical site, or a community center, and just join other churches in town?

Given the situation and the trajectory, the answer for such churches cannot simply be, "Just give more to the church so that we can continue doing what we're doing!" Rather, we have to consider our purpose and our mission.

I think there are parallels between the challenges of the Judean community that Haggai is speaking to and the challenges faced by long-standing congregations. First of all, such churches have a blessing: a historic legacy of being a place where the Holy Spirit dwells and has been at work in a community. Some members have been part of one congregation most or all of their lives! There is a lot of "spiritual capital." By contrast, in the country in Eastern Europe where my wife and I served as missionaries, our small congregation had a lot of younger people, but because the denomination was so young, there were not many older and spiritually mature Christians from Soviet times to model what it means to be a follower of Christ over decades and a lifetime. So, this is a blessing that many American churches have.

But our past can get in the way of us recognizing how things have changed around us. It's not 1801 (the founding year of one of the congregations I served), or 1901, or even 2001 anymore. Western culture has become hostile to Christianity; people's frameworks for ideas like God, sin, morality, the family, human dignity, etc., are not based on the Bible. Our area happens to still be quite "Christian," with many churches, Christian schools, a couple of Christian colleges, and some Christian ministries headquartered nearby. But in parts of the country where a majority of Americans live—including colleges and universities where our young people go to be prepared (in theory) for their vocations—being marked as a Christian is a social liability.[2] The elites of society have already turned in some very dark directions, and those are going to trickle down to the institutions and culture.

This can lead us to respond in fear, like the Judeans in Haggai's time, and we could become insular, closed off from the world. Or, like the Judeans in Haggai's day, it can be easy to become apathetic about God's house; we have our sense of what God and church means for us and our lives, and we don't much care if it becomes more than what it is. We go to church, we sing some songs that we've always sung that make us feel good, we hear a pep talk from the pastor, we go home and watch football. Then, during the week, we pray and hope God will make us better and make our lives better. But maybe we're not fully "sold out" in doing what it takes to build God's kingdom, building God's temple for him to dwell among us.

A Foundation for New Building Stones

Let's imagine that your congregation undertook some outreach effort that was massively successful, and you suddenly had 50 percent more people walk into your church on Sunday for worship! And let's say that those people don't know much about Christ at all, but the Holy Spirit has drawn them there. They're coming with varying degrees and kinds of struggle in their personal lives: difficult family relationships; finances that are less

---

2. Renn, *Life in the Negative World*.

stable or less blessed than many of us can claim; people with disabilities, addiction, and depression. They'll have basic questions about the Christian faith; they'll be praying and reading the Bible for the first time.

It takes time and resources, and emotional energy, and spiritual and biblical wisdom, as well as love and compassion, to come alongside people like this and help them as they begin or continue their walk as followers of Christ. Maybe each of us only has "room" in our lives to help *one* teenager who's struggling with self-harm, or *one* single mom with two kids.

I would guess that a sudden arrival of that many needy people would feel like *too much* for your church or mine to handle, according to human wisdom! But what about when we've rejected apathy and fear, and prepared ourselves in faith to receive and disciple the individuals and families that God might draw to our doors? As we ourselves seek to become better followers of Jesus, we should be building our capacity to proclaim the gospel and to help and encourage the dear people that God brings to us. As God says through Malachi, another prophet from this period: "Put me to the test, says the LORD of hosts, if I will not open the windows of heaven for you and pour down for you a blessing until there is no more need" (Mal 3:10).

Fewer Stones, Fewer Builders

I think we will need to do this amidst circumstances that are going to get tougher—both in terms of our economic resources, and for us as Christians in North American society. When my wife and I left "the mission field," we didn't feel like we were coming back to "safety," or to "serious Christian land" in the USA. We actually prayed about whether God wanted us to go to a part of the world where Christianity is on the upswing—maybe in sub-Saharan Africa (where I studied for my doctorate), or India or Singapore, places where I've served as a visiting professor. Coming back to the USA felt honestly like being called deeper into the heart of the empire! Someone needs to be teaching pastors in Uganda or India—pastors whose children and grandchildren will be sent as missionaries to re-evangelize North America in the decades to come.

These increasingly adverse circumstances are a chance to rediscover our dependence on God, rather than on our safe circumstances and comfortable rhythms. This starts with recovering orthodoxy: we need to get straight in our own hearts and minds the basic truths of historic

Christianity, based in the Bible and articulated in ecumenical creeds and historic confessions.[3] Historic Christianity teaches us our dependence upon God, in contrast to moralism ("Just do the right thing," without the Holy Spirit's power) or therapeutic deism ("God's there to make me feel better").

Once we ourselves are clear on what God actually says in his word, we need to recommit ourselves to God and to the church. This has to involve retooling ourselves to be effective disciple-makers in this new post-Christian society in which we find ourselves! This involves proclaiming the truth clearly, with wisdom, but also asking that God would give us love and compassion for those who have been harmed by the lies of the enemy. (That's something we'll tackle in the next chapter, on Isa 56:1–8.)

Building Together

And—here's a final parallel—*even if* we refocus on building YHWH's house, we will not succeed in this mission if we are divided over things that are non-essential. This is something we'll see in Isa 56–66, addressing the divisions that were in the Persian-period community.

Sadly, the congregation I served when we returned to the USA was a casualty of church division. After several months of things going quite well (so I thought), there was a serious disagreement about strategy and direction between me and a majority of the elders. The disagreement reached an impasse, such that I announced after only six months that I had to resign as their pastor.

What I discovered was that the congregation was deeply divided before I arrived. The matter that brought the divisions to the surface was ultimately a rather ridiculous one, which I don't want to elaborate on here (a proposed facilities enhancement). While a vocal minority campaigned vigorously for the project, roughly one-third of the church said that the project was a waste of money and the last straw for them after many years of feeling that their voices were not heard.

After my own research and talking to other pastors in town, I concluded that the project was not a good idea on the merits. But even more concerning to me was the prospect of splitting the church over something

---

3. As Second Isaiah says in the midst of crisis, "Look to the rock from which you were hewn" (Isa 51:1).

that is not an essential of our faith. I tried to convince the elders not to move forward in this direction, that it would split the church. I eventually told the elders that if they voted to move forward with the project, I would interpret that as a vote of "no confidence" in my leadership, and, like a prime minister who had lost the support of his party, I would be compelled to resign. But a slim majority (four to two) decided to move forward anyway, so I resigned.

In the end, more than half of the members departed, including one of the elders who agreed with me. As I write this, a year on from the split, it doesn't seem that the church can support a full-time pastor.

This is an example of avoidable conflict and division that crippled (and probably fatally wounded) one congregation. But I'm sure your church has divisions, too—not just present differences (mild or severe), but scars of past conflict. If we don't learn to prioritize "building God's house" (the community of individuals) above everything else, then we are just going to be scattering and breaking away temple stones as fast as we are adding other temple stones—two steps forward, three steps backward.

ZECHARIAH 3: HOPE, AND A CLEAN TURBAN

The second passage I wanted to share offers us hope, and a clean slate, by God's grace. Probably about five months after Haggai's prophecy, we have Zechariah's vision in chapter 3. The book of Zechariah is longer, and it has stark, startling visions of what YHWH's judgment will look like, and what is in store for Israel and the nations.

> 1 Then he showed me Joshua the high priest standing before the angel of the LORD, and Satan standing at his right hand to accuse him. 2 And the LORD said to Satan, "The LORD rebuke you, O Satan! The LORD who has chosen Jerusalem rebuke you! Is not this a brand plucked from the fire?" 3 Now Joshua was standing before the angel, clothed with filthy garments. 4 And the angel said to those who were standing before him, "Remove the filthy garments from him." And to him he said, "Behold, I have taken your iniquity away from you, and I will clothe you with pure vestments." 5 And I said, "Let them put a clean turban on his head." So they put a clean turban on his head and clothed him with garments. And the angel of the LORD was standing by. 6 And the angel of the LORD solemnly assured Joshua, 7 "Thus says the LORD of hosts: If you will walk in my ways and keep my charge, then you shall rule my house and have charge of my

courts, and I will give you the right of access among those who are standing here. 8 Hear now, O Joshua the high priest, you and your friends who sit before you, for they are men who are a sign: behold, I will bring my servant the Branch. 9 For behold, on the stone that I have set before Joshua, on a single stone with seven eyes, I will engrave its inscription, declares the LORD of hosts, and I will remove the iniquity of this land in a single day. 10 In that day, declares the LORD of hosts, every one of you will invite his neighbor to come under his vine and under his fig tree." (Zech 3:1–10)

This scene takes place in the heavenly courts. The high priest, Joshua, who represents the people, is standing before YHWH, the judge; also there is an adversary, the divine prosecutor there to accuse him. Joshua's dirty clothes represent the sin of the people and of their leaders, the priests. But instead of justly condemning Joshua for these sins, YHWH rebukes the prosecutor and calls Joshua a flaming stick, pulled out of the fire before it is consumed. This represents the Israelites going through the Babylonian exile: punished for their rebellion, but not fully consumed—instead, they are purified. And in the heavenly court scene, Joshua's dirty clothes and turban are taken away, and he's given clean clothes, instead. And in the remainder of the chapter, he is given a mission, to lead the people in righteousness, and a promise.

Later in the vision, we hear about YHWH's promise to "remove the iniquity of this land in a single day" (v. 9). We can see very clearly that this prophecy reaches its fullest fulfillment in the work of Jesus. He died on the cross to take the penalty for the sins of his people, to remove their sin in a single day. He was raised, ascended into heaven, and serves as our advocate at the right hand of the Father. The Adversary, the Accuser, brings accusations against God's people that are in fact true: we *are* sinners. Each of us personally and as groups, collectively—the church, and our local congregations—fall short of being adequate vessels for God's glory. But because of what Jesus has done on our behalf—he has taken away our dirty clothes, and clothed us in his righteousness—we are considered righteous before the Father. He says to the Father, "These are mine, my holy people!" And the Holy Spirit is at work in our lives to make us holy, conforming us more and more each day to the image of Jesus. Paul says that the Holy Spirit also intercedes for us before the Father. Zechariah 3 provides this beautiful picture of what God would do in Christ, many generations later.

Reflections

So, what does this mean for us today? One important part of it is what we've just seen: the work of Christ in our lives, to cleanse his people from sin and restore that relationship with him. For each of us individually, this passage offers assurance of what God has done and will do for us and through us, despite our sins. This is a truth that we all must treasure!

There is also a dimension of what this vision represents in Zechariah's day, the Persian period, that is directly relevant for us. After the trauma of the exile, the people of Judah were asking themselves: where do we go from here? Is there any hope for us, any future? On the level of groups and communities—families, congregations, towns and cities, denominations, nations—some of us are asking similarly: Is our congregation, our area, our country, in decline? What do we do after COVID,[4] and are we so divided politically that it's beyond repair? Maybe there is repentance that needs to happen, for neglecting faithful preaching and living that would lead to more disciples and the discipleship of the next generation. Is there any hope?

This vision of Zechariah offers us the promise of hope, through Christ, that God gave to Joshua the priest and to "the Branch."[5] This "Branch" is probably Zerubbabel, the governor of Yehud, who was from the former royal family and was an ancestor of Jesus (Matt 1:12–13; Luke 3:27). In the vision, YHWH promises Joshua and Zerubbabel: if you walk in obedience, and keep God's way faithfully, then God will bless the people and be permanently present in your midst (this is what the stone with seven eyes represents). The result is a blessing: peace and fellowship with neighbors, and fruitfulness in the land that God has restored to you. At the end of the book of Zechariah, there is judgment for the enemies of YHWH, salvation for his people, and then the inclusion of a faithful remnant from all the nations. This is the hope that animates us as Christians, and as the church in local congregations, and in global contexts: people of every nation and tongue can receive this restoration (as we will see especially in Isa 56, 60–61, and 65–66). This is the eternal kingdom that Jesus said we should make our only allegiance and highest priority (Matt 6:33).

---

4. My forthcoming book, *A House Divided*, uses insights from the book of Ezekiel to address failures in church leadership during the pandemic.

5. The "Branch" is also a messianic image in Isa 4:2–6; 11:1; Jer 23:5; 33:15.

So, as we seek God's direction as individual believers and as local congregations, let's remember: there is hope for us as individuals in Christ, sinners, saved by grace through faith; there is hope for local congregations seeking renewal and direction; and there is hope for the church within each nation on earth, and a church made up families of every nation, tongue, and people that God has created. The God who gave these prophetic messages to the Judeans in the days of Haggai and Zechariah is the same God who gives us these promises. Let's take God as his word and test him: if we devote ourselves to building his temple, to making disciples—that is, if we honor him with our money, with our time, with our hearts, with our lives—let's see if he won't open the storehouses of heaven and pour out more blessings than we know what to do with!

A Prayer

Father, we thank you for these words of challenge and words of hope through Haggai and Zechariah. We thank you that you haven't chosen to deal with us according to our sins, or to let us remain in constant selfishness and apathy and fear, or in accusation, shame, and sorrow—but you have taken our sins away, and clothed us in Christ's righteousness, and given us a mission: to add stones to your temple. Holy Spirit, we ask that you would guide the leadership of local churches, as they seek direction for faithful living in this era and context. We praise you, Jesus Christ, for this promise that you gave to your global church, that even though at times evil seems to be strong, the gates of hell will not be able to stand against the church—as long as your glorious presence is in our midst. Amen.

5

No Dry Trees (Isa 56:1–8)

As we move on to Isa 56–66, I want to start out on a real positive note—and talk about *despair*. We live in a time of disillusionment and disenchantment, and over time those feelings lead to despair—so I'd like to explore some of its causes.

Try to imagine a feeling of hopelessness caused by things that are beyond your control. Maybe you don't have to *imagine* this feeling—it's something you've experienced. But even if you haven't, put yourself in the shoes of someone you know. Imagine feeling that your life is hopeless because of things you can't change. Maybe it's the circumstances that you were born into or raised in. Maybe it's a very serious mistake you've made in your life that really cannot be undone and has irreversible consequences. Or maybe it's even something that someone else has done *to you* which can't be undone and has consequences that can't be taken back. Whether it's something that was your fault in some way, or something you had no control over—you certainly have no control over it now and no power to undo it.

Whether or not you've ever felt this way, I'm sure you know someone who has arrived at this place of despairing of life. Isaiah 56:1–8 speaks to people who felt like their lives were hopeless, that there was no way forward, nothing redeemable. They felt that there was no way that God would accept them, or have anything fruitful in store for them, because of circumstances that were beyond their control, or because of things they'd done that they couldn't take back. The good news for them, and for us, is that the God of the Bible, the true God, is the Creator, and the God of *new creation*, who is capable of bringing life out of deadness.

Even though I'd read this passage before, it wasn't until just a few years ago that these verses from Isa 56 just struck me as representing something so important, so explosive, so significant for communicating the gospel in our time, in our culture—but really, to all people. Churches in the Western world—North America and Europe—need to be wrestling with what it means to rethink our Christian witness in a time when so many people in our societies are no longer raised with Christian presuppositions or any background in faith.

SCRIPTURE: ISAIAH 56:1-8

1 Thus says the LORD:
"Keep justice, and do righteousness,
for soon my salvation will come,
and my righteousness be revealed.
2 Blessed is the man who does this,
and the son of man who holds it fast,
who keeps the Sabbath, not profaning it,
and keeps his hand from doing any evil."
3 Let not the foreigner who has joined himself to the LORD say,
"The LORD will surely separate me from his people";
and let not the eunuch say,
"Behold, I am a dry tree."
4 For thus says the LORD:
"To the eunuchs who keep my Sabbaths,
who choose the things that please me
and hold fast my covenant,
5 I will give in my house and within my walls
a monument and a name
better than sons and daughters;
I will give them an everlasting name
that shall not be cut off.
6 "And the foreigners who join themselves to the LORD,
to minister to him, to love the name of the LORD,
and to be his servants,
everyone who keeps the Sabbath and does not profane it,
and holds fast my covenant—
7 these I will bring to my holy mountain,
and make them joyful in my house of prayer;

> their burnt offerings and their sacrifices
> will be accepted on my altar;
> for my house shall be called a house of prayer
> for all peoples."
> 8 The Lord GOD,[1]
> who gathers the outcasts of Israel, declares,
> "I will gather yet others to him
> besides those already gathered." (Isa 56:1–8)

SURVEYING FIVE CONCEPTS (FOR LATER)

There is a lot here in this short passage. Especially in the first two verses, there are many important concepts and truths that the prophet brings up here, as he prepares to draw from Isa 1–55, and sets the tone for the entire section that is ahead. What I have in mind in this chapter is twofold. We'll briefly mention a few of the concepts that are present here, but we will not go into too much detail, because we will unpack each of them in connection to other passages ahead of us in the book of Isaiah. Then I will focus on just two important messages that are somewhat unique to this passage.

First, we have these twin ideas of *justice* (*mišpāṭ*) and *righteousness* (*ṣedeq/ṣᵉdāqâ*). In the context of the book of Isaiah, these two words come up many times as the virtues that God himself has and that he wants his people to have. In fact, these two terms are paired together at least twenty times, sprinkled throughout the whole book (see the discussion in chapter 3). This word for "justice" is broader than simply a just verdict in one court case. It has a broader sense of "justice in society," where those who have power and influence ensure that the poor and vulnerable are not taken advantage of but are lifted up and treated with dignity.[2] Think of Boaz in the book of Ruth: he is a wealthy landowner with servants and hired workers, but he ensures that they follow the reaping and gleaning customs to allow the poor, the widows, and the immigrants to gather grain (Ruth 2). We will unpack these more when we come to Isa 57 and 58.

It would be a mistake to think that these are things that the Israelites could do to somehow earn God's favor. The right way to think about this,

---

1. In English translations that render the Hebrew *yhwh* as "LORD," typically "Lord GOD" is used to translate *ᵃdōnoy yhwh*, "Lord/Master YHWH." This is to avoid the awkward English, "Lord LORD." "Lord GOD" appears in this section of Isaiah here and in 61:1, 11; 65:13, 15.

2. Goldingay, *Book of Isaiah*, 20–22.

as we will see, is that these are signs of belief in and loyalty to the God of Israel. I love my wife, and I'm loyal to her. It wouldn't be right to say that I behave lovingly toward her because I'm trying to *earn* her love. But it would also be wrong for me to say to her, "I love you," and then treat her as if I didn't love her or weren't devoted to her.

Next, we have YHWH's salvation, which is said in 56:2 to be "close at hand." Coming up in Isa 59:15b–21 and 63:1–6, we will see that *salvation* is accompanied by *judgment* which are not always ideas that go together in our thinking. But when we look around the world and see that things are not the way they should be, and we pray to our Heavenly Father, "Your kingdom come, and your will be done on earth, just as it is in heaven," we are asking God to rescue and save his people and also to judge evil people and evil spiritual forces in this world. So, judgment and salvation go hand in hand, as we will explore further in chapter 9.

The third concept touched on only briefly here is *ritual impurity* according to the Mosaic law. This is important wherever we see reference to animal sacrifices and offerings, YHWH's altar, profaning or impurifying the altar, and—very important for the section below—two categories of *people* who would have been considered ritually impaired in all circumstances, according to the law. In Isa 64–66, we'll see how Israel's ritual or ceremonial impurity is a picture of their moral impurity before God (further discussion in chapter 14).

Fourth, we have the concept of *covenant*, which is the agreement or arrangement between YHWH and his people, Israel. Among other things, "keeping the Sabbath" and "keeping hands from evil" represent YHWH's whole law, his great covenant with Israel at Mount Sinai. This was a gracious covenant that promised tremendous rewards in exchange for Israel's obedience. God promised that he would live in the midst of the Israelites, if they would keep his covenant. And he promised that he would forgive them and bless them again, after they broke his covenant, if they would only repent and be loyal to him once again.

This is important because "holding fast to the covenant" in chapter 56 is a sign of genuine faith. You can be born into the covenant, but if you don't keep your end of the arrangement (growing up *into* a life of faith), then YHWH may consider you "out" of the covenant. We'll tackle this again in chapter 13, when we come to Isa 63:7–19.

Fifth, related closely to the "covenant," is the *land* that YHWH promised to Israel, and the hope that the people who were scattered from the land will be *regathered* to it. We'll study this more in connection to

Isa 60–62 (chapters 10–12 of this book). YHWH gave Israel the land as an inheritance where they could plant crops and vineyards, and pasture their herds, have children and pass the land on to them, and fulfill in some sense the mission that God gave to Adam and Eve in the garden of Eden. He sent them away from this land because of their faithlessness, but now he's mercifully regathered some of them to the land—but there's still more that need to come back.

FORMERLY EXCLUDED, NOW ACCEPTED

So, from this quick survey of important ideas, we can see in Isa 56:1–8 a message of hope and also a challenge to be faithful. Despite all that has happened with their sins and the punishment of the Babylonian exile, YHWH declares that if they would be loyal to his covenant, he will save them in the coming judgment.

But there is a twist. Two groups that were previously excluded from the fellowship of Israel are now included in this covenant offer.

Foreigners

This passage raises the possibility for foreigners to be included in Israel by faith. Israel, in addition to being a religious community, was also a nation, an extended family. Individuals were born into this family, and males received the mark of covenant membership: circumcision. Foreigners could live among Israel as "second-class citizens," as long as they kept the basic elements of the law of Moses. We learn from Deut 7 and 23 that certain categories of foreigners could only become full members of God's covenant people after several generations of living alongside Israelites—and some groups, like the Canaanites, were permanently excluded.[3]

But in Isa 56, as in numerous places in the Old Testament, the prophet looks ahead to a new covenant reality: people from other nations

---

3. Moabites and Ammonites, considered the distant cousins of Israelites through Abraham's nephew, Lot (Gen 19), are excluded "to the tenth generation" (Deut 23:3–6), which could be understood as "permanently." Edomites, a closer relation, and Egyptians are excluded "to the third generation" (Deut 23:7–8). This could be understood as follows. An Edomite or Egyptian convert to the worship of YHWH would have himself and his sons circumcised as a sign of YHWH's covenant. If his sons are raised in Israel and grow up to circumcise *their* sons (the third generation), then it proves that the original conversion was genuine (Schnittjer, *Torah Story*, 508).

will be fully acceptable to the God of Israel, full members of his people, with an inheritance—as long as they keep his Sabbaths and his covenant. It says they will be "joyful," and their offerings will be accepted on YHWH's altar.

When we lived in Lithuania, one of our favorite places to visit was Vilnius, the capital city. Vilnius has a long history of Jewish culture, which interests me a great deal because my father is Jewish. There had been over a hundred synagogues in Vilnius before World War II, but sadly only one remains. Over this synagogue, called the Choral Synagogue, are written these words in Hebrew from Isa 56:7: "My house shall be called a house of prayer for all peoples." This is an awful irony, given what happened to the Jews in Lithuania and Eastern Europe in the Holocaust. God's intention all along was that Israel would be a light to the nations.

Later, in Isa 66:21, God says that some from these nations will even be priests and Levites, serving before him. This looks ahead to Eph 2:19–22: the new temple made up of stones, Jewish and gentile believers together, one temple in which the Holy Spirit lives.

What Even Is a Eunuch?

What are we to make of these people called "eunuchs"? What even is a "eunuch"? A eunuch is a man who has been castrated, emasculated, and therefore unable to have sexual relations and to conceive children. Because these men were commonly part of a king's palace administration (often overseeing the king's wives), the Hebrew word *sārîs* came sometimes to mean simply "a royal official," without implying this surgery of emasculation. But in Isa 56:3–4, it is clearly referring to a man who cannot have children.

Someone like this could have been born with a birth defect or could have been the victim of an accident. More likely, the men in view here are those who were made eunuchs by conquering empires. This could have happened by force—or these men might voluntarily submit to this procedure in order to get privileged jobs in the royal palace.

To be clear, there is nothing in the Bible that would speak positively about such a procedure. There is no commandment in the Israelite law that would ever require someone to become a eunuch. In fact, eunuchs could not participate fully in the worship of Israel (Deut 23:1). They could not be priests (Lev 21:17–23). Moreover, such men were unable to have children who could receive an inheritance of land. Essentially, they would have been unable to fulfill *biologically* the promise given to Abraham that his descendants would be numerous. This is why a eunuch might say to himself, "I am a dry tree."

To top it all off, if a eunuch had served in the court of a pagan king, he had almost certainly eaten a steady diet of ceremonially unclean foods, and he would have been obligated to participate in the worship rituals of the king's palace. Think about the challenges confronted by Daniel and his three friends in Babylon, to get an idea of the pressures that Jews faced in pagan nations. (I'm not saying that Daniel and his friends were eunuchs; I'm saying that they faced the same temptations to give up following the law of Israel.) A eunuch's whole lifestyle, lived in close connection to the pagan imperial and religious structures, would have been the complete opposite of what the God of Israel would want for his people (or any person).

TWENTY-FIRST CENTURY "EUNUCHS" AND THE SCARS WE ALL BEAR

I know it might be strange, but imagine that you're in the ancient world and you find yourself in the circumstance I've just described. A eunuch is a person who was either assaulted in a terrible way or a person who made a life-altering choice that he can never go back from. He was told he would have a satisfying life by serving the pagan empire and its gods, its customs, its ideology. And now he's found that this path didn't bring satisfaction, only fruitlessness—but there's no going back. Thinking back to the beginning of our chapter, maybe this despair resonates with us now. Some of us have made poor decisions and have become "eunuchs," so to speak, through those choices. Others are "eunuchs" not by our own choices: we bear the scars of life, of illness, or of other people's sins against us—events that were beyond our control.

Scarred by Lies

When I started studying the Old Testament many years ago, I never thought I would see actual eunuchs encouraged and promoted in our Western society. Recently I saw an interview with a young woman, in her early twenties, who is a "detransitioner." When she was a teenager, she felt depressed, uncomfortable in her body (as many teen girls do). When she sought answers and treatment, she was told by people online, by her friends, and even by teachers and *doctors* that she was unhappy because she was actually a man trapped in a woman's body. What she needed, in order to be happy, was to take hormones and have surgery, to appear like a man and to live as a man. She went ahead with this, thinking, "This is what I need to do in order to be happy!"

What she found, however, is that "transitioning" didn't make her less depressed (like most people who attempt this). Thus, after several years of living as a man, she went back to living as a woman. But some of the changes to her body from the hormones and surgery are irreversible. She will always look like a more "masculine" woman. She will have painful infections and other medical problems that will last the rest of her life. She will never be able to have children or experience sexual pleasure.

As this young woman shared her story and began to break down in tears at that last acknowledgment, I found myself filled with anger and sorrow for the irreversible damage that the lies of the culture had done to her body and her soul. Now you might be tempted to write off this person's experience as rare, representing only a tiny minority within North American society. But if you research this phenomenon, you will find that it is much bigger than you think. Because gender transition is being promoted in schools and on social media, it is coming to your community—you likely already have transgender people (and detransitioners) in your community, whether you realize it or not.[4]

Other Scars We Bear

But let's broaden this out a bit. This young woman was a victim of the lies that the culture told her, and now she has scars on her body and on her soul. There are plenty of other lies that the culture tells us, about materialism and fulfillment—but especially, the lies of the sexual revolution. Let's be clear: the Bible teaches us that God's plan for sexuality is that it should be reserved for a man and a woman, within the context of marriage—this protects the husband and the wife and the children that they will hopefully have.

---

4. For further reading on how widespread this phenomenon has become, see Shrier, *Irreversible Damage*.

When we exchange this truth for a lie, then we have to tell ourselves other lies to keep up with the first one. One of the keystone lies of the sexual revolution is that abortion is not always wrong. Legal abortion serves as the backstop for sex without consequences or commitment.

Abortion involves the taking of an innocent human life, and so it's morally wrong. And in addition to destroying a unique life with value and dignity, abortion is a rejection of the fruit that God wants us to bear and to enjoy. This is why women who have had abortions can suffer from post-abortive trauma and depression. Men who have encouraged or paid for an abortion, or who have lost a child that they wanted because their partner had an abortion, also live with the scars of terrible things that can never be undone.

These are only a few examples of the scars with which we and many people around us live. There are other kinds of violence; there are lies that lead us to addictive behaviors that ruin our bodies and our souls, and that alienate us from God and from one another.

Don't get me wrong—I'm not saying that those of us who are victims of the lies of our culture are not also sinners. To be sure, each of us stands before God responsible for the choices we make. But Satan and his allies feed us lies to which he knows we're especially susceptible. These lies become entrenched in a culture and in our hearts such that once we've bought into the lies, we tend to believe (and even *want to believe*) that there's no going back.

Other Kinds of Fruitlessness

We should broaden this out a little bit to include people for whom "despair" is not the right word, but whose lives, for whatever reason, don't quite fit the biblical ideal. The Gen 2 ideal picture is that a man and a woman commit to one another for life, have biological children and raise them together, and (hopefully) live long, harmonious lives. But many people's lives don't fit this picture, for many reasons.

There are people in our society and in our churches who are single, never married. (Some, like the apostle Paul, have chosen to remain single in order to serve God in a special way.) There are single people who are same-sex-attracted and can't imagine ever marrying someone of the opposite sex.

We have couples who can't have children; there are couples who grieve the loss of a child. There are people who are divorced against their will and people who are widows or widowers. We have single parents and blended families from second marriages. There are families who have chosen to integrate children into their families through adoption and fostering.

It might be helpful to think of all these people as encompassed in the meaning of "eunuch," as we apply this text in our own day. Some of us have made poor decisions and have become "eunuchs" through those choices. Others are "eunuchs" not by our own choice: we bear the scars of life, of illness, or of other people's sins against us. How do people in all these family situations pursue the fruitfulness that God wants for our lives?

GOOD NEWS FOR EUNUCHS, GOOD NEWS FOR ALL

Fruitfulness Redefined

Well, the gospel coming from this passage, the good news for all of us, is that we serve a "single" Savior! Jesus never married a human woman, never had biological children. Yet when we read Scripture, we see that his "family" is built differently. According to Isa 53:10, the picture of the "Suffering Servant,"[5] as a reward for his perfect obedience, his Father gave him "offspring" and "prolong[ed] his days"! Jesus showed us that the lasting impact of God's work in our lives is not mainly that we have biological children but that we would have many *spiritual* sons and daughters—people whom we have invited into God's family by faith, and discipled.

Our legacy, our inheritance, "a monument and a name" as Isa 56:5 says, is not measured by biology but by spiritual fruit. Seen in this way, it makes perfect sense to connect foreigners, who were originally excluded from Israel by biology—birth—to eunuchs, who can create a non-biological "dynasty" through faith, obedience, and discipleship.

Thus, we should all be bearing fruit and having *spiritual* children! It's our obligation and our joy to invite all the nations to answer God's call to pray in his house and to join his new covenant by faith, to be part

---

5. See the discussions of prophecy, fulfillment, and typology in chapter 2. The "Servant Songs" of Isa 40–55 can perhaps have several different referents (Israel, the prophet himself, the future Messiah), but Christian tradition has long understood Jesus's sufferings through the lens of Isa 52:13—53:12.

of God's new temple by faith. God's family is his house of prayer for all nations.

Not Defined by Our Scars and Our Sins

This passage redefines what it means to have "fruit" such that foreigners and eunuchs can bear fruit. It also means that if we repent of the lies we've believed and the sins we've committed, and hold fast to the God who reveals himself in the Scripture, then even though we can't *change* the past, we are no longer *defined* by that past. In 1 Cor 6:9–11, Paul says:

> 9 Or do you not know that the unrighteous will not inherit the kingdom of God? Do not be deceived: neither the sexually immoral, nor idolaters, nor adulterers, nor men who practice homosexuality, 10 nor thieves, nor the greedy, nor drunkards, nor revilers, nor swindlers will inherit the kingdom of God. 11 And such *were* some of you. *But* you were washed, you were sanctified, you were justified in the name of the Lord Jesus Christ and by the Spirit of our God. (1 Cor 6:9–11, emphasis mine)

You *were* defined by those sins, and you cannot change the fact that you committed them. Paul had been complicit in violence and murder (Acts 8:1–3; 9:1–2; 1 Tim 1:13), and he would always have those memories on his conscience. *But* because of what God had done in his life to bring him to repentance *out* of despair, he was no longer defined as "murderer"—but instead, forgiven, washed, and set aside for a holy purpose. That promise is for us, too.

REFLECTIONS

Well, so what do we do with these truths that we find growing out of Isa 56?

For Ourselves: Confess and Receive Forgiveness

I think the first thing is that we have to acknowledge our situation before God, confess any sins we've committed, and receive the forgiveness and belonging that he offers.

Because it's sadly common in North America, I want to speak especially to the issue of abortion. If you have been involved in an abortion in the past, and if you have never confessed that sin to God and received forgiveness, then you should absolutely do that today! You need to grieve that sin and that loss, and give it to God—and receive the forgiveness that God offers, and be free! You may find it helpful to say this confession (to God) aloud to someone else—someone that you trust and who will point you to the truth of God's word, such as a pastor, a mentor, or a friend.

Look at the despair of the foreigner and the eunuch in Isa 56. Each one doesn't even bother to address YHWH directly to complain, or to confess, or to ask for acceptance: "The LORD will surely separate me from his people"; "I am a dry tree." Too often, we choose to believe that God would never forgive us or redeem us out of our situation, and so we don't even ask him. "There's no way that God would forgive me for what I've done." "There's no way that God could heal what this person did to me." These are lies! God says instead to the hopeless: there is no sin so great that the Father cannot forgive it, that Christ's sacrifice cannot cover it, and that the Holy Spirit cannot redeem you out of it!

For Our Neighbors: Welcome Everyone, Scars and All

Once we have been honest with ourselves and God about our sins and our scars (however deep), we will be filled with compassion toward those who come into our churches with their own scars. Some people will come into our church with physical "scars of a eunuch" on their bodies, as I described earlier. But many, many more will have scars on their souls.

Is your local Christian congregation a place where people encounter truth *and* love together (Eph 4:15)? Too often, our churches have trouble with one or the other: we preach biblical truth aggressively but without compassion, or we don't talk about what the Bible has to say about serious issues like gender and sexuality—even though withholding the truth is also not compassionate.

Like Paul in 1 Cor 6, will we speak both truth *and* grace to these scarred people? The truth is that those who commit these sins will *not* inherit the kingdom of God—and each one of us belongs in that category—but we were washed, we were sanctified, we were justified in the name of the Lord Jesus Christ and in the spirit of our God. He will do the same for *you* if you hold fast to him. Will your church be a place where that young woman who has detransitioned can find hope in Christ, the promise of abundant life, and the feeling of true belonging in a community of people who love her for who she is, made in the image of God?

And, as we rightly minister to and strengthen nuclear families in our churches, are there ways that we subtly communicate to single people, or divorced people, that they don't quite fit anywhere in this fellowship? While there is a place for ministries that specialize, we have to be careful that we don't impoverish ourselves by separating into groups based on life situation. Maybe we can encourage Bible studies and small groups with people of different life situations so that instead of being defined by a status, each person is a name and an individual whom God loves, and who fits because of identity in Christ, not some other identity.

For Our Young People: Avoiding Scars

A message for younger readers, especially children and teenagers, is that you can save yourself a lot of grief by avoiding these irreversible scars—on your body and on your soul. I was blessed to have grown up in the church and was taught the Bible and its relevance for life from a very young age. Of course, I am not perfect—and there is a kind of pride and smugness that those raised in the church must guard against. But I know that my faithful Christian upbringing preserved me from a lot of bad decisions that I could have made and that many of my friends made—especially sins with respect to the body and sexuality. It's so much better to avoid that grief! Even though God forgives, we should not presume upon God's grace by continuing in sin (Rom 6:1–7) or "put[ting] the LORD [our] God to the test" (Deut 6:16). The Christian life is not a cakewalk, but it is a joyful path! Don't limit your present and future fruitfulness for God by making bad choices now.

For Everyone: Bear Fruit

Once we've confessed our scars and received healing, and become a place where others can do the same, by God's grace—what then? Well, the answer is bear fruit! God wants *you*, and he wants to make good use of you. He gave his only Son to incorporate you into his family. He wants to grow in you and in me, and in all of us, the fruits of the Holy Spirit: fruits in keeping with repentance! He wants to produce through each of us a legacy of many sons and daughters in faith.

Regardless of our family situation, regardless of the circumstances of our lives, God wants us to be about the business of *new creation*, bearing the kind of fruit that Jesus produced in his life—not creating physical offspring but the spiritual rebirth into new life that the Holy Spirit accomplishes in human souls.

For Everyone: Worship

And lastly, we see in Isa 56:7 that the purpose of all of this is *worship*, that we and many spiritual sons and daughters with us would enjoy the presence of God with reverence and joy, without fear, because of what Christ has done. My mind goes to the stunning vision given to St. John in the book of Revelation, a scene in which people of every language and background are gathered around the throne, praising the Lamb who was slain for us:

> 9 And they sang a new song, saying, "Worthy are you to take the scroll and to open its seals, for you were slain, and by your blood you ransomed people for God from every tribe and language and people and nation, 10 and you have made them a kingdom and priests to our God, and they shall reign on the earth." 11 Then I looked, and I heard around the throne and the living creatures and the elders the voice of many angels, numbering myriads of myriads and thousands of thousands, 12 saying with a loud voice, "Worthy is the Lamb who was slain, to receive power and wealth and wisdom and might and honor and glory and blessing!" 13 And I heard every creature in heaven and on earth and under the earth and in the sea, and all that is in them, saying, "To him who sits on the throne and to the Lamb be blessing and honor and glory and might forever and ever!" 14 And the four living creatures said, "Amen!" and the elders fell down and worshiped. (Rev 5:9–14)

A Prayer

God, we thank you that you have been faithful to your covenant, even when your people have been faithless. We thank you for these promises for us, that whether we're born or dragged into seemingly hopeless circumstances, or whether we think we've screwed things up for ourselves, there is always hope because you are the God of new creation. Help us to bear fruit of repentance, in our lives and in the lives of refugees who have had their bodies and souls mangled by the lies of the enemy. Give us wisdom and compassion and a zeal to love in hope. In Christ's name we pray. Amen.

6

Blind Watchmen and the Sorceress's Children (Isa 56:9—57:13)

In the previous chapter, we looked at a hopeful passage from Isa 56 that sets the tone for the rest of the section. We talked about foreigners and eunuchs and saw that whatever we've done, and whatever has happened to us, no person is beyond the reach of God's grace. That's a hopeful message that we need to remember for ourselves each day, and to proclaim to those around us.

But the other part of this truth is that God's grace is for those who have recognized their sin and rebellion, and wish to change, and change direction. The next passage in Isaiah focuses on the shortcomings of the Israelite community in the Persian period (see chapter 4) which end up looking very similar to the sins of their ancestors. We get a picture of individuals and a community that are searching for abundant life and fulfillment but seem intent on exhausting all other possible sources of life before turning to YHWH, the true God.

SCRIPTURE: ISAIAH 56:9—57:13

Even though his name isn't mentioned at all in this passage, Lord YHWH, the God of Israel, the Creator God, is the speaker here—we know this because it's stated in verse 8, and the speech continues without interruption until 57:14.

56:9 All you beasts of the field, come to devour—
all you beasts in the forest.
10 His watchmen are blind;
they are all without knowledge;
they are all silent dogs;
they cannot bark,
dreaming, lying down,
loving to slumber.
11 The dogs have a mighty appetite;
they never have enough.
But they are shepherds who have no understanding;
they have all turned to their own way,
each to his own gain, one and all.
12 "Come," they say, "let me get wine;
let us fill ourselves with strong drink;
and tomorrow will be like this day,
great beyond measure."
57:1 The righteous man perishes,
and no one lays it to heart;
devout men are taken away,
while no one understands.
For the righteous man is taken away from calamity;
2 he enters into peace;
they rest in their beds
who walk in their uprightness.
3 But you, draw near,
sons of the sorceress,
offspring of the adulterer and the loose woman.
4 Whom are you mocking?
Against whom do you open your mouth wide
and stick out your tongue?
Are you not children of transgression,
the offspring of deceit,
5 you who burn with lust among the oaks,
under every green tree,
who slaughter your children in the valleys,
under the clefts of the rocks?
6 Among the smooth stones of the valley is your portion;
they, they, are your lot;
to them you have poured out a drink offering,
you have brought a grain offering.
Shall I relent for these things?
7 On a high and lofty mountain
you have set your bed,

and there you went up to offer sacrifice.
8 Behind the door and the doorpost
you have set up your memorial;
for, deserting me, you have uncovered your bed,
you have gone up to it,
you have made it wide;
and you have made a covenant for yourself with them,
you have loved their bed,
you have looked on nakedness.
9 You journeyed to the king with oil
and multiplied your perfumes;
you sent your envoys far off,
and sent down even to Sheol.
10 You were wearied with the length of your way,
but you did not say, "It is hopeless";
you found new life for your strength,
and so you were not faint.
11 Whom did you dread and fear,
so that you lied,
and did not remember me,
did not lay it to heart?
Have I not held my peace, even for a long time,
and you do not fear me?
12 I will declare your righteousness and your deeds,
but they will not profit you.
13 When you cry out, let your collection of idols deliver you!
The wind will carry them all off,
a breath will take them away.
But he who takes refuge in me shall possess the land
and shall inherit my holy mountain. (Isa 56:9—57:13)

OBSERVATIONS

This section can be divided into three parts. First, 56:9–12 criticizes the leadership of Israel, which could include the political leaders like the governors and elders, the priests and Levites, and the prophets. This is about *why* sin and rebellion has been allowed to flourish. Isaiah 57:3–13 focuses on the nature of the evil itself. Tucked in the middle, there's a two-verse "interlude" at the start of chapter 57, which says essentially: thankfully, the righteous few will not live long to see how evil things are becoming in society—small consolation!

Corruption of Leadership

Let's first look at the corruption of the leadership of Israel in chapter 56. Verse 9 begins with a roundabout jab at the leaders: Israel's watchmen are falling down on the job, so hungry wild beasts are summoned to take advantage of the situation. This sounds a bit like a taunt before battle (see 1 Sam 17:46; Ezek 39:4), and it's clearly hinting that the kings of the nations are like wild beasts ready to attack again if Israel's protection is taken away. The reference in verse 10 to the watchmen reminds us of Ezek 3 and 33: the guard who sees the enemy coming and doesn't raise the alarm has blood on his hands! (This doesn't guarantee that the people will listen to the watchman, but at least he's done his duty if he cries out.) The watchmen are not literal guards on a tower; they are the elites, the prophets, the priests, the governors, the elders—those who should have the insight to perceive threats to the community, and the strength and initiative to take action.

Israel's watchmen are like useless guard dogs, YHWH says; there are at least three different kinds of problems with them. Some of the dogs cannot bark. Maybe these leaders have nothing of value to say to warn the people; they have no voice or are too scared to speak up. Some of the guard dogs are lazy: they'd rather sleep, blissfully ignorant, dreaming of an imaginary world with no threats, rather than doing the hard work of paying attention to the coming danger and communicating to the people. Some of the guard dogs are distracted by their appetites: they're preoccupied with satisfying themselves.[1]

Something else that stands out is that the leaders "lack knowledge" and "lack understanding" (56:10-11), implying that if they possessed knowledge and understanding, they would not seek their own gain but the good of the people. Of course, we have all seen corrupt leaders who are in it for themselves, who are also very intelligent, and know how to use and maintain control. They possess "knowledge and understanding" of a certain kind. But here the prophet is clearly using a biblical, sanctified sense of "knowledge and understanding," for true knowledge and wisdom come from God (for example, Prov 1:2; 2:5-6; 15:14; Isa 11:2) and would lead these leaders back to humility before God, if they possessed them.

---

1. In my forthcoming book, *A House Divided*, I examine the failures of the "watchmen" of God's people, through the lens of leadership in the book of Ezekiel, but also argue that redemption of failed leadership is possible through repentance.

Finally, in 56:12 we see the leaders showing a lack of prudence and foresight—instead of soberly and thoughtfully preparing for the future, they're drinking wine and living only for today. Now this is a common criticism in Isaiah of the leadership of Israel: they are often accused of being addicted to wine and pleasures of the moment.[2] And the problem is not wine *per se*; there are other passages in Isaiah where vineyards and the use of wine in moderation is celebrated as a sign of blessing (25:6; 27:2; 37:30; 55:1; 65:21). But getting drunk is not wise—it leaves you open to being victimized (5:11–12; 29:9; 51:17, 21) and prevents you from protecting and leading those for whom you are responsible.

Overuse of alcohol and other intoxicants is a big problem for many people in our society. But thinking beyond just alcohol and drugs, what are some other pleasures and consumptions that dull our sensitivity and distract us? Think about the constant flow of media and entertainment into our minds, including TV and film, video gaming, and social media. Think about how sexualized much of that entertainment is. Think about the prevalence of gambling, especially online betting on just about anything—it's much more widespread and acceptable than when I was growing up. Back to the watchmen: they should be exercising self-control and prayerfully anticipating threats to their community, but their senses are dulled by all this dopamine.

Interlude: The Righteous Dead

The two-verse interlude at the start of chapter 57 nicely epitomizes the ambiguity of poetry: it may mean something on the surface, but then when you think about it a bit more, it could also be read another way. Here we have a comforting thought: a righteous person is "taken away from calamity" and "enters into peace"—oh, that's nice! But then when you start to think about it, you realize the implication is that the righteous are marginalized and die unnoticed—that generation disappears quietly, going out with more of a whimper than with a bang, so the upcoming generation is even worse.

The way that aging and death are treated in modern Western culture obscures the outrage of this little interlude in which the righteous are not honored or even noticed in death. Unlike just about every culture in history prior to the twentieth century, Western culture is youth-centered,

---

2. Examples include Isa 5:12, 22; 22:13; 24:7–11; 28: 1, 7; 29:9; 49:26; 51:21—52:3.

privileging the priorities and desires of the young over those of wiser elders. As people age, instead of being more respected in the community, they often withdraw from the community—this is partly because people live longer now thanks to modern medicine, even though their quality of life might be diminished.

The result of this is that many elderly now die very quietly, in hospitals or facilities, decades removed from much of their involvement in professional or social circles. Sometimes, if their friends and coworkers are long gone (passed away, or lost touch), their families choose not to have funerals or memorial services. I have observed this myself in my work as a hospice chaplain, and I understand why it happens—no one is "to blame," *per se*. But it means that it is actually quite common for devout and righteous people to die quietly, on a random Tuesday afternoon after years or decades of convalescence, and no one notices.

In ancient times, the intergenerational families living together, and the clan and local social structure, meant that the death of an elder was always tragic and lamented. Here in Isa 57:1–2, the fact that "no one lays it to heart" is not just a real bummer—it's an outrage that reflects a tear in the social fabric.[3]

Spiritual Adultery

Isaiah 57:3–13 is a diatribe against those who worship images. It starts out, "But *you all*," drawing a contrast to the righteous dead in the previous two verses, so what follows is going to describe wicked behavior. One metaphor we see used in this section is something we find quite often in the biblical prophets: adultery as a picture of spiritual unfaithfulness and the worship of idols. (The parallelism between "sorceress" and "loose woman" in 57:3 makes this clearer.) In these prophetic pictures, YHWH is the husband and his people (or, more often, their leaders) are his wife who has been unfaithful by giving her love and honor to other gods. We've seen this before the Babylonian exile, in Hos 1–3, and in Ezek 16 and 23. Interestingly, in the part of Isaiah that is focused on the horrible exile period, Isa 40–55, there are prophecies of forgiveness and

---

3. My own mother and aunt struggled with how to care for my grandmother in the later stages of dementia in a way that showed proper honor to their mother while keeping the family together. My mother tells this story in a moving memoir: Soesbe, *Bringing Mom Home*.

reaffirmation of the marriage relationship between YHWH and Israel—I discussed this as part of chapter 3.

Now, however, in Isa 57, despite the "clean slate" that Israel hoped for when they came back from exile, Israel is still shown to be an unfaithful wife, consorting with other gods. And this is something that she's not even trying to hide at this point—verse 4 says she sticks out her tongue at God, her husband.

Manifestations of Spiritual Unfaithfulness

In 57:5–9, we see how this spiritual unfaithfulness has manifested itself in Israel's life. As we look through this litany of accusations, some of it seems so ancient, so disconnected from our modern life, but I think there are more similarities than we might want to believe there are.

One way of describing Israel's faithlessness is as a perversion of the idea of the divine image. In the biblical worldview, YHWH is the Creator, and he has made human beings in his image to reflect his rule and his presence into the world. So we must worship him, not with handmade idols, but in Spirit and according to the truth that he's given us. And we should honor and revere other human beings because they are made in YHWH's image: neither worshiping other humans, nor treating them as disposable for our use.

But Israel had screwed this all up: they worshiped hand-crafted idols of YHWH and of other gods, and they committed violence and sexual sin. They practiced child sacrifice to Canaanite fertility gods (2 Kgs 17:31; 21:6; Jer 7:30–34; 18–19), doing violence against the weakest members of society for the convenience of the powerful. They practiced ritual sexual behavior, which is described here, and other kinds of sexual sin, treating other people's bodies as objects for enjoyment and consumption.

In our modern age, maybe *our* perversions of the worship of God and our lack of reverence for the divine image don't look exactly the same as in the ancient pagan world, but we certainly are guilty of worshiping images rather than God, of treating people as disposable objects, and of allowing the weak to be victimized and killed. We just have other euphemisms for it; we call it "adult entertainment," "reproductive choice," or "collateral damage of special military operations." I've tried to picture myself in the sandals of a young woman in ancient Canaan who is convinced by her parents and friends to offer her firstborn son up to Moloch, so that Moloch would bless her with long life, many more children, and prosperity. What euphemisms would they have used for "baby killing"? How could I be convinced to burn my own child? Let's not deceive ourselves that we're so modern and enlightened in twenty-first-century North America that we don't do things like this anymore. We're simply better at ignoring or rationalizing.

Next, YHWH accuses Israel of engaging in paganism and the occult, which, among other things, amount to treating the spiritual realm as something we can manipulate. It says that they have "descended to the realm of the dead," which sounds like some sort of attempt to make a pact with the devil against dying—compare it to what we see in 28:14–15. One problem with accessing spiritual powers is that just when they seem controllable, they end up controlling and manipulating you. Only the power of YHWH, the triune Creator God, is enough to overcome death, and his power is not one that we can manipulate, or that manipulates us. Rather, he transforms us, soul and body, so that death is defeated.

Of course, the occult and other forms of spirituality not sanctioned in the Bible are prevalent in our society. Most people at least believe it is possible to connect to spiritual forces or powers—true materialist atheists remain a very small minority. But even beyond vague "spirituality," there are plenty of technologists and innovators who are trying to "defeat death" in other ways. They haven't succeeded yet, but that is a goal for many of them—a quest that is quasi-religious. One common sci-fi trope is the notion of human memories being stored digitally, perhaps edited or fabricated, perhaps copied into a clone body or the body of another. The next step, maybe even more plausible than uploading memories into a meat brain, is a human consciousness that lives and evolves completely inside a processor or cloud. There are a lot of interesting ethical questions surrounding these issues. But we can certainly say that much of this reflects a desire to avoid death by making a pact with the "god" of science.

Maybe we're not that different from ancient people. Maybe when we think more carefully about the appetites, the frailties, and the anxieties that drove the ancient Israelites to all these sins, we find that we are driven by those same motivations—and our resulting sinful patterns in society don't actually look that different from theirs.

Dead Ends

In Isa 57:10–13, we find that all of these paths turned out to be dead ends. The unfaithful Israelites looked for pleasure in life and to avoid death, but it says in verse 10, "you wearied yourself," refusing to admit that these paths were hopeless. Their efforts come across as quite pathetic. In verse 11, we find the motivation for all of this was fear—fear of death, fear of loss, fear of being out of control. And the sad irony is that if they had just feared and honored the all-powerful Creator God, he would have protected them from everything else. The old saying is true: "When you fear God you fear nothing else, whereas if you do not fear God you fear everything else."[4] Over and over again in Isaiah, we see this refrain: "Don't be afraid!" (see chapter 3). But this comfort is only for those who fear YHWH.

Another path they pursued, in 57:12, was righteousness, but this seems to have been a false kind of pious-looking behavior, without true desire to please YHWH. We will see this criticized in Isa 58, compared to the real righteousness that YHWH wants.

How is all this going to turn out for those who rely on idols? Verse 13 says literally "let your collection save you," mocking the inability of handmade things to actually help in a time of trouble. If you want see a really sarcastic take on idols (a true "sick burn" in the Bible!), compare this to Isa 44:9–20. But of course, this can apply to us as well, when we trust anything other than the true God to be our source of strength and safety: money, security systems, guns, doctors, education, whatever. All those idols can be blown away by the wind, just like the princes and the rulers of the earth in Isa 40:24, or the wicked in Ps 1:4–6.

The last part of 57:13 leaves us on a hopeful note, providing a poetic "hinge" on which the passage turns. "My holy mountain" returns our thoughts to 56:7, where the offerings of foreigners and eunuchs will be accepted (echoes also of 2:2; 11:9; and 27:13). All the people's efforts have been directed toward *avoiding* YHWH's presence at his holy mountain. If only they would seek refuge in God! It seems as though the hope is offered as the last resort, after sinful people have tried everything else in pursuit of happiness—when it should have been the first thing they did! But it forms a fitting transition to the next section which speaks about blessings for those who are humble and repentant.

---

4. Chambers, *Quotable Oswald Chambers*, 97.

REFLECTIONS

Let me conclude with a few points that I think are most relevant for us today.

Leadership

The passage highlights the importance of conscientious, wise, humble leadership. As we saw in the chapter on Haggai and Zechariah, leadership is very important. And in contrast with the mute, lazy, self-serving guard dogs of ancient Israel, we can go right to the best example of leadership: Jesus Christ. When his disciples were clamoring for the greatest place of honor, Jesus told them: if you wish to be most honored as a leader, you have to humble yourself and serve others, "even as the Son of Man did not come to be served, but to serve, and to give his life as a ransom for many" (Mark 10:45). For lack of a good shepherd, the sheep will be scattered.

(Anything but) Abundant Life

The meat of the criticism in this passage applies to the whole community. It could be summarized as the myriad ways that we try to pursue abundant life, apart from following God and holding fast to his covenant. We worship other things; we worship pleasure; we use and take advantage of other people, instead of honoring the image of God in each person.

And it seems like many of us want to exhaust every other path to abundant life before coming back to YHWH. For those of you who are children and teenagers, and young people, take note here; look at examples all around you of people who are trying to find abundant life by trying all these different paths. Yes, God accepts those who ultimately seek him—remember the hope for foreigners and eunuchs that we discussed in the previous chapter. But you'll spare yourself a lot of sorrow and hardship if you make God your *first* and *only* pursuit, rather than your last resort. Jesus says, "Seek first the kingdom of God and his righteousness," and all the other good things that God wants for you will be given to you in addition (Matt 6:33).

Repentance

And finally, the good news that comes out of this passage is that despite all that Israel has done, despite all that we do to avoid returning to God, He accepts those who humble themselves, admit their sin and rebellion, and take refuge in him. The passage is bracketed by repentance: the foreigners and eunuchs who hold fast to YHWH and his covenant; and then—the subject of the next chapter—those who humble themselves and take refuge in him. And more good news is that he doesn't just erase our sins; he gives us positive ways that we can honor and serve him, and build up his kingdom. And coming up, we'll also see the great lengths to which God has gone, and *will go,* to save us—from enemies and danger, and from ourselves.

A Prayer

Father, we confess to you that, too often, we follow the paths that we've devised in our hearts, or the paths that our culture lays out for us, in pursuit of life and joy and happiness. And when we find that those paths don't lead to abundant life, we double down on them and try harder, going down those same paths. We thank you that despite all we've done, you've said that the path back to your ways is still open, and that if we turn around and return to you, you will accept us and help us to live in your ways. By the power of your Holy Spirit, change our hearts so that we would truly desire to live with you and your people, in your holy mountain. It's in Jesus's name we pray. Amen.

7

I Have Seen Their Ways, but I Will Heal Them (Isa 57:14–21)

We saw in Isa 56:1–8 that no one—not even those born outside the covenant, not those who have been mangled by the culture and its lies—is beyond the reach of YHWH's mercy and his covenant. Whatever circumstances you were born into, whatever horrible mistakes you have made, whatever other people have done to you, there is no sin that God cannot forgive and no scars that he cannot heal, for anyone who calls out to him in repentance and holds fast to him.

But the key catalyst for the forgiveness and healing that YHWH offers is repentance—we have to admit that we have need of God's forgiveness. So we saw in the last chapter (Isa 56:9—57:13) that sadly, the people of Israel in this period—like their ancestors before the exile—continued on in their rebellion. According to the prophet, they seemed intent on exhausting every other possible path looking for abundant life before turning to YHWH. YHWH condemns their idolatry, turning to other gods, and treating other human beings as disposable objects.

In this chapter, we look at the rest of Isa 57. As we work our way through these verses and continue on in this section of Isaiah, a portrait emerges that will probably hit close to home for each of us, if we're honest. The problem with personal, human determination to "be better" or to "repent and change ourselves" is that it always comes up short. What we really need is for God himself to step in and change our hearts so that we can actually turn to him and love him. For our own good, we need him to do what we can't do for ourselves, what seems impossible. But our God is the God of new creation, and he does the impossible!

SCRIPTURE: ISAIAH 57:14–21

> 14 And it shall be said,
> "Build up, build up, prepare the way,
> remove every obstruction from my people's way."
> 15 For thus says the One who is high and lifted up,
> who inhabits eternity, whose name is Holy:
> "I dwell in the high and holy place,
> and also with him who is of a contrite and lowly spirit,
> to revive the spirit of the lowly,
> and to revive the heart of the contrite.
> 16 For I will not contend forever,
> nor will I always be angry;
> for the spirit would grow faint before me,
> and the breath of life that I made.
> 17 Because of the iniquity of his unjust gain I was angry,
> I struck him; I hid my face and was angry,
> but he went on backsliding in the way of his own heart.
> 18 I have seen his ways, but I will heal him;
> I will lead him and restore comfort to him and his mourners,
> 19 creating the fruit of the lips.
> Peace, peace, to the far and to the near," says the LORD,
> "and I will heal him.
> 20 But the wicked are like the tossing sea;
> for it cannot be quiet,
> and its waters toss up mire and dirt.
> 21 There is no peace," says my God, "for the wicked."
> (Isa 57:14–21)

OBSERVATIONS

In the last chapter, we saw that verse 13 is sort of a transitional verse; the first part underscores the pointlessness of relying on idols for help, but the second part contains a promise: blessings and safety for those who take refuge in YHWH's presence, on his holy mountain. In this more hopeful subsection, the beginning and end are marked out by two "speech words":

14 "It will be said"
15 "The High and Exalted One says"
(What he says)
19c "Says YHWH"
21 "Says my God"

Aside from these phrases, YHWH is the one speaking throughout, as he was in the previous subsection.

Prepare the Road!

In verse 14, we have a striking image that we've seen previously several times in the book of Isaiah: "prepare the way." In Isa 40:3-4 we have a more descriptive visual picture painted for us:

> 3 A voice cries: "In the wilderness prepare the way of the LORD; make straight in the desert a highway for our God. 4 Every valley shall be lifted up, and every mountain and hill be made low; the uneven ground shall become level, and the rough places a plain." (Isa 40:3-4)

Whenever I hear this hopeful passage (which is quoted in the Gospels in connection to John the Baptist: Matt 3:1-3; Mark 1:2-3; Luke 3:1-6; John 1:23), I can picture many majestic mountains that I've been privileged to see in different parts of the world—Table Mountain in South Africa; winding roads up mountains to remote European villages in Italy, Poland, Slovakia, Austria—as well as several amazing and beautiful valleys. Another striking view is Denver, where the Great Plains meet the Rocky Mountains. You'll be driving west from Kansas on I-70, and it's just flat, flat, flat—and then suddenly, rising up out of the plain is this mountain range! But we don't even have to go that far. My adopted home state of Pennsylvania has its own mountains and valleys. Particularly amazing for me is driving east over the Allegheny River on I-80 and continuing through the mountains into the central part of the state.

Imagine a world without air travel and facing the prospect of crossing those mountains and valleys without the benefit of bridges and tunnels. Can you picture the Israelites who had been taken hundreds of miles away from their land, around a desert, across mountains, and enslaved in Babylon—how they would have looked at that terrain that stood between them and their homeland? Imagine standing at the top of one of those mountains, looking down at the valley and the river and then the steep ascent to the next mountain. And even if you're younger and a good hiker, imagine doing this with some babies, an elderly parent, and maybe some animals to herd along. To say that the path to freedom was daunting is an understatement—it was impossible.

But imagine that God takes the valleys and the mountains, like a rug or a blanket that's all rumply, and pulls that terrain straight so it's nice and level! Imagine God taking Pennsylvania up off the map by the Ohio border and the Delaware River, and pulling it out straight and flat so that I-80 doesn't have to go over those rivers and around those mountains. That's what this passage says YHWH is going to do. First, he's going to smooth the way for himself, effortlessly, in order to go through the wilderness to rescue his people. That's what Isa 40 is about. And then, what we read here in 57:14, like in 35:8–10, is that the highway will be completely smooth for his people as he leads them back to their land, to freedom! Instead of mighty rivers like the Euphrates and the Jordan across their path, blocking their way, there will be gentle streams, springs, and wells alongside the highway that will provide for them on the journey back to their land (Isa 35:8–10).

If you remember, this is what YHWH did for his people in their ancient past when they went out of Egypt! He met Moses on Mount Sinai, his holy mountain in the wilderness; he passed with Moses through the Sinai desert to Egypt; he brought them out of Egypt into the wilderness of Sinai, providing for them water in the desert; and eventually took them to the land he promised to give them. Already in this first verse, we have YHWH preparing to do seemingly impossible things, leveling mountains and valleys, in order to save his people in a way that is reminiscent of the exodus from Egypt.

God Most High, God with Us

In verse fifteen, we have so much packed into just six lines of poetry. There are two *kinds* of truths about God's nature, and each of them has an implication for how we respond to him. In the first two lines, we see that God is transcendent: he is high and exalted, eternal, and holy.

Let's just dwell on this for a minute—or even longer! One reason why we sin, why we choose to go our own way, is that we don't think of God as holy and glorious, as he truly is. If we really grasped his holiness, we would feel deeply our own lack of holiness. When the prophet Isaiah himself, probably a mostly-upstanding guy (a faithful prophet and a priest), saw YHWH's heavenly throne room in chapter 6, his first reaction was (my paraphrase of 6:5): "I'm toast—I'm done! I am a man of unclean lips, and I live among a people of unclean lips—and my eyes have seen the Lord of glory!"

But YHWH, the triune Creator God of the Bible, is not just transcendent. He is also *immanent*, meaning he chooses to be near to his creation, especially his human images. Here in the third and fourth lines of verse 15, he says, "I live in the high and holy place, *but also with* the one who is contrite and crushed in spirit" (emphasis mine). He is everywhere, *with* his people. In Isa 7:14, we hear the assuring word, *'immānû 'ēl*, "God is *with* us." In 41:10 he says, "Don't be afraid, because I am *with* you." In 43:2 he says, "When you pass through the waters, I will be *with* you."

Most of our faulty understandings of God have something to do with missing one of these two truths: God's transcendence and his immanence. One type of worldview sees God as so holy, so transcendent, so distant from his creation, that he's not accessible to us or doesn't care much what we do—he's the absentee God, or the unavailable God.

But another type of worldview is more pantheistic, thinking that God is not really personal and distinct from his creation—he's more like a life force, in and around and through everything, with us all the time in that sense. But the biblical God is distinct from and over his creation, intimately involved in the workings of his creation—this verse is one of many that captures both truths side by side![1]

God is with his people, but particularly with the lowly, the humble, and the disadvantaged—in fact, it says those who are "crushed in spirit." This expression is only used one other place in the Bible: Ps 34:18, "[YHWH] is near to the brokenhearted, and saves the crushed in spirit." This word for "crushed" is used elsewhere in Isaiah to describe what has happened to the poor under their bad leaders (3:15). YHWH has always

---

1. Numerous theologians have made this point, but a great explanation of this dynamic and the two extremes of this dilemma is found in the first chapter of Horton, *Christian Faith*, 35–47. Horton describes this using the image of "estrangement" and knowing the stranger (i.e., God), presented by Paul Tillich.

had a preference for living with the lowly and downtrodden—after all, he found the Israelites in their slavery and brought them out of Egypt into freedom.

"Crushed" is also what happens to the Suffering Servant in Isa 53:5, 10. This is the gospel, right here: the Word became flesh and came to be near to the crushed in spirit, and he himself was crushed for our transgressions.

How do we respond to this? Just as thinking about God's holiness and exaltedness should lead us to recognize our own sin, these lines tell us about where God likes to "hang out" when he chooses to be "with us," with his creation. He likes to be with those who are humble. And there are really two kinds of "humble." There are those who are *humbled*, those who are beaten down by the world and by others; and there are those who *humble themselves* and recognize their true position before God. Often, it is easier for those who have *been humbled*, been beaten down, to cry out to God; those of us who feel like we have other legs to stand on (money, position, respect, a nice list of good deeds) have a harder time humbling ourselves. This is why YHWH dwells with the lowly and contrite. When asked why he hung around with prostitutes, tax collectors, and sinners, Jesus said, "Those who are well have no need of a physician, but those who are sick" (Matt 9:12). The religious leaders who questioned him were just as spiritually sick as those others, but they were also blind and failed to grasp their own condition.

Accusation and Despair

YHWH resolves and promises to change the situation that has persisted with his people who are rebellious against him. There are echoes of Ps 103:9–10 which says that he will not always be angry and accusing them and that he will not treat them as their sins deserve. He sees that this path—them sinning and him punishing them for their sin—has led them to despair of living. And he doesn't want that.

He fears for the sake of the very "breath[s] of life that I made," using the same Hebrew word found in Gen 2:7, *nᵉšāmâ*, for the "breath" of life that YHWH breathed into the man's nostrils. YHWH gave humans this breath and made them in his image, and he doesn't want to lose them! There are numerous times in the story of Israel that YHWH could have scrapped his human images, human beings, because of their sin and started all over—but he chose not to. There's humanity in the garden of Eden, believing the serpent and eating the forbidden fruit. There's the great flood in the days of Noah (where it says in Gen 7:22 that the flood destroyed everything that had this "breath" in its nostrils). There were times when Israel was rebelling against God in the wilderness, when he said to Moses, "Stand back from them so I can zap them and start all over with you!" (I'm paraphrasing!) There was the exile to Babylon, which could have been a genocide, the end of the people of Judah. And now, after the return from exile, they are still sinful, but God still doesn't want to give up on them or for them to give up on life. And I *know* that this is what he wants for us also: he doesn't want our spirits to grow faint or be continually crushed and exhausted.

But "not accusing them" does *not* mean that he'll just relent and give up, ignore and accept their wrongdoing, giving a get out of jail free card. In verse 17, it says that the punishment was deserved. Because of their greed, YHWH has "hidden his face" from them—YHWH's "face shining upon" someone is a source of blessing (Num 6:24–26).[2]

What "no longer accusing them" means is that YHWH is going to take serious measures to deal with the bigger problem, healing and transforming their sinful nature, so that he won't have to struggle with them or accuse them anymore. Punishing might be what they deserve, but it hasn't succeeded in changing them.

Healing, Comfort, Praise, Peace

Verse 18 says that *healing* and *comfort* are actually what's necessary, not punishment. "Comfort" is, of course, a word that comes up a lot in Isaiah, especially in 40–55; pairing it with *'ābal*, "mourn," looks ahead to 61:2, he will "comfort all who mourn." The "mourners" are those who are torn up with grief about the sins of their people and their own sinfulness. But in verse 19, that mourning turns to praise and to peace: "Peace, peace to those far off and those who are near." Once YHWH has dealt with the sin problem by healing their sinful natures, they will *each* have peace with God.

Reconciliation with God makes reconciliation between humans possible. This verse is quoted in Eph 2:17. In Isaiah, "those who are far off" seem to be Judahites that are still in the east, in the land of Babylon

---

2. See also Isa 8:17; 45:15; 53:3(!); 54:8; 59:2; 64:7.

and Persia (remember the highway in the desert that would allow them to return!); "those who are near" could mean those who returned or who had always remained in the land. Paul uses "far and near" slightly differently in Eph 2:17: in Christ, peace is achieved between gentiles, who had been "far off" from God, and Jews, who had been "near" to YHWH by virtue of being his chosen people.

The Wicked

It might have been nice to end on that positive note, but the last two verses are there to give us a contrast with the humble and contrite: those who persist in their wickedness are tossed like waves on the sea and never know the peace that comes from being reconciled to God by repentance and faith. This imagery reminds us of verse 13: the wind and breath that blows away those who trust their idol collections. Looking ahead to the next chapter, even though Isa 58 does have a hopeful conclusion, it starts out a bit harsh on those who have false piety. That's just kind of the ups and downs of poetry. Remember that the chapter divisions are not original to the Bible—those were added at a later stage and are not considered inspired.

This conclusion here is a further confirmation that the healing that YHWH offers is for those who repent and turn to him—it's not enough to just "run out the clock" until he becomes weary of punishing them. There is no rest for the wicked who persist in their wickedness, but any wicked person who humbles himself and asks to be healed is no longer defined by that wickedness, as we saw in chapter 5.

REFLECTIONS

I will highlight three truths that we've seen in this passage and then describe three results of God's work in our lives.

Three Truths

The first truth is that God is high and holy, glorious, and exalted! Let's never forget it, and this why we come together each week to sing about the true God: his attributes, his character, his actions. Encountering

God's transcendence and his holiness should convict us of our sinfulness and remind us of our dependence upon him.

The second truth, that complements the first one, is that YHWH is immanent: he is with his people, and with those who are crushed and downtrodden, and those who have humbled themselves. This should lead us each day to humble ourselves. What does this look like? It starts with worship and prayer, I think. But then it manifests itself when we order our lives according to God's priorities, rather than our own; when we regard other people (made in God's image) as worthy of our time and our love and our respect. And it means that if we want to seek out God's presence, we need to go to the dark and difficult places and hang out with the people that God wants to hang out with. Our hearts should be moved with compassion for those who are close to God's heart: the poor, the sick, children who don't have parents or who don't have loving parents, people who have been beaten down by the world, and people whose lives are filled with true regret over their own mistakes, but think it's hopeless. God sends us as messengers of faith, hope, and love—those who have been crushed, hearing and responding to God in faith.

And that brings us to the third truth which is that God's presence comes to us in our need and does for us what we can't do for ourselves. He is a God of justice, but he is not eager to punish us forever. Rather, as he promises here in verse 18, he wants to heal us from our sinful nature so that we can actually have abundant life—fellowship with God and peace within this earthly life, and the promise of eternal resurrection life.

Three Results

And this passage shows us at least three results of our encounter with these truths. First, as we already said, God heals and comforts his people, those who are crushed, those who are humble, those who have humbled themselves. This is something we see over and over again in the Old Testament: God transforming our lives and doing for his people what we can't do for ourselves! He is the God who makes a path in the desert for his people when the way seems impossible. (Note: if you ever want to see an Old Testament professor absolutely lose it—pull out their hair, tear their clothes, and run around gnashing their teeth—say something to them about how the Old Testament is all about the works we're supposed to do to earn God's favor and the New Testament is all about God's grace!) The

Old Testament shows us clearly what we find filled out in God's plan in the New Testament: we are stuck in sinful nature, unable to please God, but God heals and transforms—he is the God of new creation!

So the first result is healing; the second result is praise! God does his transforming work, remaking us into what we were always intended to be, so that we can honor and praise him! This, as the Westminster Larger Catechism summarizes so well, is our chief purpose: to glorify God and enjoy him forever.[3]

So God's work of healing results in praise and also—the third result—peace! Once we've humbled ourselves and been forgiven, the result is a lasting peace between us and God. And this makes true peace between human beings possible. We'll see this developed more in the chapters ahead.

This message, that God dwells with the humble, if we take it to heart, will lead us to seek out the crushed and lowly, and lift them up in compassion because that means we are close to the heart of God (where God hangs out). And this links up with Isa 58: true, biblical worship that truly honors God *must* drive us to compassion for the lowly.

A Prayer

God in heaven, thank you that you have made yourself present with us in the person of Jesus Christ. Sometimes when we think about our sin and our fragility, we're tempted to despair. Thank you that you are gentle enough to be with us in our lowly state but also holy and powerful and strong to do for us and in us what needs to be done for our own good. Help us, as followers of Jesus, to walk humbly before you and to walk alongside the humble and oppressed. By the power of the Holy Spirit, help us to be messengers of your comfort and strength to those around us. In our healing, our repentance, our living before you, receive the glory! Amen.

---

3. Westminster Standard, "Larger Catechism," §1:1.

8

Then You Will Find Your Joy in YHWH (Isa 58)

The end of Isa 57 shows that humility is the catalyst for the healing and peace that YHWH wants for his people. Isaiah 58 shows us what that humility is supposed to look like in the life of God's people. The people of Israel—especially the elites—were embracing some of the outward rituals that are signs of humility, like fasting and sacrifices, but those rituals were not accompanied by tangible acts of love and justice.

Back in chapter 5, I mentioned the idea of ritual purity in connection to the foreigners and eunuchs, and I promised that we would engage this idea of ritual. That's a part of this chapter, and we will come back to it again in chapter 14. In this chapter, we will consider the purposes of rituals and ceremonies that God commands and see how they relate to other dimensions of God's word. In Isa 58, the outwardly humble rituals, like fasting, are not meaningful for the Israelites and for YHWH because the people are not *truly delighting* in YHWH. Instead, their rituals are tainted by self-love and pride; by a ritual*ism* that tried to manipulate God and other people with the *appearance* of holiness; and by their anxieties about building their own kingdoms, their own domains where they are in charge.

Of course, we all perform rituals in our daily and weekly lives, including gathering in church to sing, pray, listen to God's word, and celebrate the sacraments. The problem is not ritual or ceremony *per se*, but *ritualism*. When we consciously embrace the truths behind the rituals that God gives, and when we delight in God and his word, then the rituals are beautiful and joyful, and they reinforce the weightiness and importance of God's truth in our lives. And the rituals serve to remind us of the obedience that is the result of delighting in God.

SCRIPTURE: ISAIAH 58:1-14

1 "Cry aloud; do not hold back;
lift up your voice like a trumpet;
declare to my people their transgression,
to the house of Jacob their sins.
2 Yet they seek me daily
and delight to know my ways,
as if they were a nation that did righteousness
and did not forsake the judgment of their God;
they ask of me righteous judgments;
they delight to draw near to God.
3 Why have we fasted, and you see it not?
Why have we humbled ourselves, and you take no knowledge
of it?'
Behold, in the day of your fast you seek your own pleasure,
and oppress all your workers.
4 Behold, you fast only to quarrel and to fight
and to hit with a wicked fist.
Fasting like yours this day
will not make your voice to be heard on high.
5 Is such the fast that I choose,
a day for a person to humble himself?
Is it to bow down his head like a reed,
and to spread sackcloth and ashes under him?
Will you call this a fast,
and a day acceptable to the LORD?
6 "Is not this the fast that I choose:
to loose the bonds of wickedness,
to undo the straps of the yoke,
to let the oppressed go free,
and to break every yoke?
7 Is it not to share your bread with the hungry
and bring the homeless poor into your house;
when you see the naked, to cover him,
and not to hide yourself from your own flesh?

8 Then shall your light break forth like the dawn,
and your healing shall spring up speedily;
your righteousness shall go before you;
the glory of the LORD shall be your rear guard.
9 Then you shall call, and the LORD will answer;
you shall cry, and he will say, 'Here I am.'
If you take away the yoke from your midst,
the pointing of the finger, and speaking wickedness,
10 if you pour yourself out for the hungry
and satisfy the desire of the afflicted,
then shall your light rise in the darkness
and your gloom be as the noonday.
11 And the LORD will guide you continually
and satisfy your desire in scorched places
and make your bones strong;
and you shall be like a watered garden,
like a spring of water,
whose waters do not fail.
12 And your ancient ruins shall be rebuilt;
you shall raise up the foundations of many generations;
you shall be called the repairer of the breach,
the restorer of streets to dwell in.
13 "If you turn back your foot from the Sabbath,
from doing your pleasure on my holy day,
and call the Sabbath a delight
and the holy day of the LORD honorable;
if you honor it, not going your own ways,
or seeking your own pleasure, or talking idly;
14 then you shall take delight in the LORD,
and I will make you ride on the heights of the earth;
I will feed you with the heritage of Jacob your father,
for the mouth of the LORD has spoken." (Isa 58:1–14)

PROBLEMS

In this passage, there's a clear structure of problem → solution → result. Let's reflect on what exactly was the problem for the Israelites and think about whether there are parallels in our own time and culture.

In order to understand the problem, first we have to look at what seems to be going wrong and what's going right for the people. It appears that the people are at least making an attempt to seek YHWH, wanting his presence, wanting to hear from him. And they are engaging in the practice of fasting—refraining from eating for a set period of time, like a day—which demonstrates that they understand, at least to a degree, the need to humble themselves. So it sounds like they might be responding to the kind of prophetic message we saw in chapter 7: YHWH dwells with those who humble themselves (Isa 57:15).

There are several problems with their observances of fasting, though. I would say there are at least four problems.

Looking for a New Command but Missing the Old Command

First of all, it seems like they're fasting in the hopes of hearing something helpful from God that will lead their community back to flourishing, but they're overlooking the ways that God has already spoken in his word, the Torah of Moses. (We hear a lot these days about prophetic word and revelations, and yet, I always wonder whether we're fully exploring the riches of God's word before resorting to those supposed "revelations"?) Interestingly, the Torah, the five books of Moses, says nothing directly about fasting. It says that on the Day of Atonement, when the altar and sanctuary are purged of ritual uncleanness, the people are to "afflict themselves" (Lev 16:29), but it doesn't say precisely how. Since they weren't supposed to work that day, and beating or cutting themselves was forbidden (Deut 14:1–2), then pretty much the only remaining application was to abstain from food, bathing (see also "sackcloth and ashes, Isa 58:5), and marital relations. Other than on the Day of Atonement, some people might take vows to abstain from certain foods and drink for a time—for example, while fulfilling the *nāzîr* vow (Num 6:1–21).

But other than this, there are no fasts *required* in the Law. From other passages, it seems like fasting was an accepted part of the religious calendar and the cultural practice, especially when mourning someone's death or, in this case, mourning their sinfulness and asking YHWH for forgiveness.

Binding Yourself but Ignoring Those in Chains

So, *choosing* to fast was fine—maybe a good thing if done right. Something the Torah says a *lot* about, though, is doing justice in society and caring for the vulnerable! I could pick any number of examples, but here are just a few verses from the very first, simplest law code that YHWH gives Israel, the Covenant Code in Exod 20–23. Here's what 22:21–27 says:

> 21 "You shall not wrong a sojourner or oppress him, for you were sojourners in the land of Egypt. 22 You shall not mistreat any widow or fatherless child. 23 If you do mistreat them, and they cry out to me, I will surely hear their cry, 24 and my wrath will burn, and I will kill you with the sword, and your wives shall become widows and your children fatherless.
> 25 "If you lend money to any of my people with you who is poor, you shall not be like a moneylender to him, and you shall not exact interest from him. 26 If ever you take your neighbor's cloak in pledge, you shall return it to him before the sun goes down, 27 for that is his only covering, and it is his cloak for his body; in what else shall he sleep? And if he cries to me, I will hear, for I am compassionate. (Exod 22:21–27)

So the second problem is that they are doing the ritual of fasting while missing the more urgent matter: the people who are bound in unjust systems of oppression or cycles of poverty. The word for "fast" in Hebrew (*ṣôm*) may have an underlying connotation of "binding" or "tying up" (*ṣmm*).[1] So, in choosing to fast, you're voluntarily "binding yourself" from enjoying food so that your attention is drawn to weighty matters: mourning, humility, repentance, our human frailty and mortality. But if someone is *literally* bound with ropes, or bound by nakedness and hunger and debt, then addressing that person's needs is the more pressing matter. To sit by, fasting from food that *you* have, while *someone else* is starving is to lack the sense of urgency about what YHWH considers to be urgent.

Wrong Priorities

The reason why the elders of Israel miss this is the third problem: they're doing the ritual of fasting without the underlying reality that fasting symbolizes humility and repentance. We can tell that their hearts are not fully there because they're doing it wrong and without the right priorities. The word for "delight" occurs five times in this passage, and the ideal is that they would find their *delight* in YHWH and in his priorities; but then it

---

1. Thus, *ṣammîm*, "snare" (Job 5:5; 18:9); *ṣammâ*, "veil" (Isa 47:2).

says instead that they do what *they* please, according to *their* delight and desires.

If the elders and elites of Israel decided that a nationwide fast was necessary in order to humble themselves, confess sins, and seek YHWH's favor (like, say, in the time of Neh 8–9), what might a "national fast done right" have looked like? Well, it would certainly have been a day of rest for everyone including the workers because it's very difficult to labor when you haven't eaten food. But here in Isa 58, it says that the elites made their workers labor during a fast. The work itself seems to have been unnecessarily hard, exploiting the laborers with low pay or poor conditions.

Moreover, in an ideal "national fast done right," when the time would come to break the fast, the meat of the sacrifice of well-being would have been shared with the poor and with the priests and Levites, as well as the family of the wealthy landowner bringing the sacrifice. It would be an act of fellowship with God and with others. But here in Isa 58:4, it says their fasts end in selfishness, quarrelling, and fistfights.

RITUALISM AND MANIPULATION

And this brings us to the fourth problem: the elites of Israel want to think that they *delight* in YHWH, but they actually seem to be attempting to manipulate him with rituals. I'm going to observe some negative things about rituals, ceremony, and formality, which most Westerners would instinctively agree with, but then I want to say some things in favor of ritual, which will hopefully be a corrective for our misconceptions and bring us closer to understanding the biblical text.

Ceremony and Ritualism?

The terms "ritual" and "ceremony" have negative connotations for many people, especially Americans. In general, we have less formality than other societies do—when I worked in Eastern Europe, I observed that it was more common for students to dress up when going to class, especially the women but also the men. The American study-abroad students often came to class in jeans or sweatpants (which was fine with me because I often wore jeans myself—and not just once I got promoted!).

It is tempting for evangelical Protestants to scoff at Roman Catholics and Eastern Orthodox, with their robes, candles, incense, pre-written prayers, their emphasis on ceremony, and doing everything just right. Aren't they adding man-made laws to the gospel of freedom? Evangelicals might also caricature more liberal Protestant churches as leaning on ceremony—"smells and bells," incense, and robes—to compensate for lack of strict adherence to Scripture on moral and doctrinal matters.

Especially in a religious context, we can all think of examples of people who use ritual to manipulate others and to make themselves feel morally superior. And ritual also gives a feeling of comfort for some people—comfort in the rules, and maybe comfort in feeling as though we can manipulate God with our adherence to formulas of behavior. That seems like what is happening here in Isa 58, just like we see back in Isa 1: the people expect God to respond to their ritual of fasting by making them flourish once again, but he's not responding.

But, let's be honest here, evangelicals have worship rituals, too. They might not be written down formally. But services follow a pattern (that's called "liturgy"), our prayers follow a pattern, and our clergy tend to dress consistently in church—maybe we'd call it pseudocasual. I think for some churches, *insisting that we don't follow rituals* is its own form of ritual: pastors and worship leaders are expected to wear and do certain things that demonstrate that we're not stuffy and bound by rules. Can you imagine the uproar on Christian X (formerly known as Twitter) if Rick Warren or Chris Tomlin wore a suit in church?

Rituals: Not Gone, Just Replaced

North American society is less formal than in times past, and we tend to shy away from rituals. We dress less formally than we used to; we don't say "Mister" and "Miss" with last names much anymore. Because many people don't go to church, we don't have as much structure in our weekly schedules (notice references to the Sabbath in Isa 56:4, 6, and 58:13). We don't observe many rites of passage: baptism, confirmation, coming of age ceremonies, marriage, etc. Most of us don't spend much time in legal or governmental settings where formality is required. In terms of formal dress, only in certain contexts does special dress communicate status: the military, a courtroom, an academic ceremony, and occasionally a pastor, a crucifer, a choir member, or an acolyte in a church, depending on the tradition.

But our desire for ceremony isn't gone—it's just redirected. Just think about how many Americans still inexplicably follow the British royal family! (Didn't we send them packing two centuries ago?) At key moments in our lives, religious rituals have been replaced by secular ones. Instead of baptism and confirmation, we have "first day of day care" pictures and kindergarten graduations. Because we don't have "coming of age" rituals for young people, and many couples don't bother with marriage ceremonies, we replace them with other weighty actions that serve to announce our entrance into adult society or into a relationship—actions that might be destructive. Instead of a bar mitzvah or a quinceañera or a walkabout in the desert, a young person declares his or her entrance into adulthood with a first alcoholic drink or a first sexual encounter. Couples might get tattoos together or move in together or get a dog together to cement their relationship with a meaningful sign of commitment. "Rituals" aren't gone completely—we just make up our own rituals to try to add weightiness to our life events. Most of those rituals are things we choose to do to declare our own status, rather than consisting of a community declaring to us our status and how we belong. The endless self-definition and self-declaration becomes exhausting, but it's also destabilizing and anxiety-inducing.

And because the prevailing religion of our time is secular modernity and the god is scientific progress, we still have revered clergy in special garb—but the priests are academics in robes and scientists in lab coats. As we saw on full display all the errors during the COVID pandemic, wearing a lab coat and holding a beaker doesn't make you a scientist or a doctor.

Positive Ritual

Lest we fall into the trap of reading Isa 58 as God saying, "I gave you rituals to do, but I don't really care if you do them—it's your job to sift through my commandments and decide which ones are legitimate," let me say some positive things about ritual and ceremony, generally. Rituals have the power to *reflect* and *shape* our reality, by giving structure and meaning. When a ritual is done apart from the underlying reality, it's pointless. But when a ritual is done that truly reflects the reality, it is positive because it reinforces the significance of the reality.

In addition to my academic robe and sash that I received at the completion of graduate studies, I have a minister's robe that was given to me when I was ordained. It's black and has three velvet bars on each shoulder, indicating that I have a doctoral degree. I was also given a set of stoles—cloth sashes worn over the shoulders, behind the neck, and hanging down the front of the robe—that indicate the office of elder in my tradition (as contrasted with the stole of a deacon). The colors of the stoles represent different seasons and holy days in the liturgical year.

I wear this robe and stoles to minister on special occasions, like holidays, baptisms, or weddings. I used to wear my academic regalia when participating in commencement ceremonies at university. But even when I don't wear the robes, that reality of my calling and my qualifications is still true. Similarly, if someone without those qualifications were to put on my robes, that wouldn't make them a pastor or a professor. But the robes communicate something about the weightiness of the circumstance in which I am living out those vocations and remind me of the importance of living as a Christian minister even when I'm not in the pulpit or at church. Everything I'm doing when I'm not wearing a robe and "acting as a pastor" in church still affects my calling as a pastor, and vice-versa.

Likewise, there is a piece of paper somewhere in our files that shows that Corrie and I got married. There was a ceremony with vows and witnesses who agreed to hold us accountable, and rings were exchanged. Now, if we weren't living in harmony as husband and wife, the certificate or the rings wouldn't solve all our problems, but those symbols can serve as a *guide* or a *guardrail* to remind us of what it means to live as a married couple and to make it costly for us to not work towards reconciliation. (It's much more effective than simply getting a dog together—and not just because I'm not a fan of dogs!) Again, the rituals, ceremonies, and signs are not the thing itself, the reality, but good rituals and signs can reinforce and strengthen the reality and point us to the purposes of fulfilling that reality.

Back to Isa 58: the Israelites are showing by their behavior that they don't understand the point of fasting. And the real point of fasting should be expressing the desire to have fellowship with YHWH. Their current practice indicates that they don't truly delight in their God.

RITUALS OF SABBATH AND FASTING: JESUS'S TAKE

I've been commenting on rituals as a general concept; in this passage, fasting and Sabbath rest are the specific rituals in view. Thankfully, the ultimate authoritative Interpreter of Scripture—Jesus—has himself explained the purpose of these very two rituals! On several occasions described in the Gospels, Jesus comments on Sabbath-keeping and fasting. We will look at a few examples from the Gospel of Luke.

In Luke 13:10–17, Jesus encounters a woman who has been afflicted by an evil spirit, crippled by back trouble, for eighteen years. Jesus heals this woman—on the Sabbath. When pressed by the religious leaders to defend "working" on the Sabbath, Jesus responds, "Does not each of you on the Sabbath untie his ox or his donkey from the manger and lead it away to water it? And ought not this woman, a daughter of Abraham whom Satan bound for eighteen years, be loosed from this bond on the Sabbath day?" (13:15–16). In Luke 6:1–11, Jesus is walking with his disciples on the Sabbath, picking some heads of grain and eating as they walked (which might have been construed as harvesting the grain).[2] Jesus later heals a man on the Sabbath, as well. Jesus asks his opponents, "I ask you, is it lawful on the Sabbath to do good or to do harm, to save life or to destroy it?" (Luke 6:9). Jesus, as the Creator of both human beings and "the Lord of the Sabbath" (Luke 6:5), tells us that one purpose of the Sabbath is to set free, to give life and refreshment. For him to have come across these people in need of healing and to have said, "Sorry, I can't set you free today, but wait twelve hours and I'll do it then," would have betrayed the purpose of the Sabbath.

Jesus points us to the true significance of fasting, as well. In Luke 5:33–35, when asked why his disciples don't fast, Jesus spoke in this metaphor, "Can you make wedding guests fast while the bridegroom is with them? The days will come when the bridegroom is taken away from them, and then they will fast in those days" (5:34b–35). The fasting is for when the bridegroom is not present with those who are anticipating his arrival or return. But when the bridegroom—Jesus himself, Immanuel (cf. Isa 7:14), God-with-Us—is present, then we shouldn't fast; we should feast and rejoice! The fasting focuses our attention on what (or who) is absent and makes us long for that presence! Sincere fasting reflects our delight in the One who is absent and our desire to be with him.

---

2. Note that according to the Law, Jesus is not *stealing*. Deuteronomy 23:25 permits picking a few kernels of grain when passing through a neighbor's field but prohibits using a sickle—that would constitute harvesting your neighbor's grain, which would amount to theft. This is probably why Jesus and the disciples don't consider what they're doing "work." Harvesting vigorously enough to violate the Sabbath would also be stealing in this case!

ISAIAH 58: THE SOLUTION AND THE RESULT

So, coming back to Isa 58, the most important problem that we see was that the people (especially the elites) were not actually *delighting* in YHWH. If they had, they would have fasted correctly and actually paid attention to all of God's Law. The solution, we see, in verses 6, 7, and 10, is that they need to care about and delight in the justice that God delights in! This means caring for the poor, clothing the naked, feeding the hungry. Several times he mentions "the yoke of oppression," using a word (*môṭâ*, 58:6 [twice], 58:9) that is used in the Law in Lev 26:13 to describe the yoke that the Israelites were under in Egypt. YHWH says that he *broke* that yoke and stood them up straight, restoring their dignity! What are the structures in our society that keep people stuck in poverty and dependence, unable to hold their head up with dignity? What can we be doing out of love for God that can help people to break out of these shameful structures and patterns so that they can stand dignified as sons and daughters of God? These are the things that God wants us to be about.

God promises beautiful results. If you do these things, you will experience healing: "Your light will break forth like the dawn"; "righteousness"—remember, they were hoping for that before?—"shall go before you; the glory of [YHWH] shall be your rear guard," to protect them (58:8)! YHWH will be with them and will hear them when they call (58:9). And because they raised up the needy to a place of dignity, he will empower them to build up their community and its walls—and it's not just that they will accomplish things, they will also be honored with epithets and titles such as "Repairer of Broken Walls" and "Restorer of Streets" (58:12). I imagine memorial plaques being placed on streets to honor those who sponsored the repaving or improvements—not unlike the foreigners and eunuchs who hold fast to YHWH in 56:5! (In chapter 12, we'll go into more detail about names and epithets in examining Isa 60 and 62.)

In 58:13–14, similarly, the root cause of their failure to keep the Sabbath is that their priorities are not aligned with YHWH's glory. When YHWH created the world, he rested on the seventh day as Creator King, enjoying what he had made. To rest on the Sabbath is to honor YHWH's kingship. But working on the Sabbath amounts to striving to build up my own kingdom, not trusting YHWH to give me all that he wants to entrust to me. Refraining from working is to be content with and to enjoy YHWH's kingship—and to enjoy fellowship with him! That's why we gather on Sunday for worship, and YHWH is in our midst in a special way when we gather (Matt 18:20). The promised result is striking: "I will cause you to ride in triumph" and "feast on inheritance." If we rest from our strivings and honor YHWH as king, then he will give us all we need and more—much more than if we had kept working on the Sabbath to build our own kingdoms!

REFLECTIONS

Ritual and Reality

It bears repeating because many people reading this will be North American evangelicals (like me) and because it's my duty as a student of the Old Testament: *rituals are not inherently bad*. God gave us rituals to structure our lives. He gave us the weekly Sabbath and commanded us to observe it with worship, singing, prayer, fellowship. Often when we meet, we celebrate a ritual that Christ commanded: the Lord's Supper. On occasion, we perform another ritual that God commands for believers (and—most Christian traditions believe—for the children of believers): the ceremony of baptism.

The crucial point, though, is that rituals must *reflect* and *reinforce* the truth of God's word that is *already at work* in our lives, in the form of love for God and our neighbors. Otherwise, the rituals lose their meaning entirely. They may even give a false sense of security such that we think we're honoring God when we're not. That was the stumbling block for those who were fasting and sacrificing in Isa 58. If our adherence to rituals and ceremonies somehow distracts or pulls us away from loving God and loving others, or crowding it out of our attention, then we are definitely not performing God's rituals in a manner that is pleasing to him—or we're only following rituals that we made up for ourselves.

Jesus, Healing, and Priorities

In reading Isa 58, we feel a sense of the urgency of pursuing justice, as contrasted with the ritual of fasting. Does this mean we should not fast or perform any rituals until all injustice and poverty in society has been solved? Why are we gathered here when there are needy people out there? Does this mean we cannot rest on the Sabbath until everyone has the opportunity to rest?

We have to keep all of these actions in proper perspective. As always, Jesus's actions and attitudes are instructive for us. Think about all the people that Jesus healed from sickness or raised from the dead. Every single one of them eventually got sick and died again. And there were many other people that Jesus did not heal in his earthly ministry. So why did he heal some if he wasn't going to finish the global task?

In his earthly ministry at his first coming, Jesus healed, fed, and freed individual human beings not because they would never be sick or hungry again, but as a sign that the power of sin and death was about to be broken through his death and resurrection. At his second coming, he will raise to eternal life all those who have trusted in his salvation (1 Cor 15:20–28), and he will usher us into eternal Sabbath rest (Heb 4:1–11).

Regarding our fasting, our helping the poor, our worship, our Sabbath rest—if we do all these things sincerely, as best we can by the strength and means that God has entrusted to us—these are all anticipating the ultimate rescue, the ultimate justice, the ultimate healing, and the ultimate rest that God has promised to accomplish. When we rest, it's an act of faith that God will bring about his new creation, just as he made the first creation and rested on the Sabbath to enjoy the creation as its King.

As we seek God's will as individuals and as congregations in these increasingly difficult days, let's make sure that our worship and our rhythms and rituals of life reflect a true and deep delight in YHWH because of who he is and what he's done. And as we delight in God, we will find ourselves delighting in the things he delights in: mercy and justice.

A Prayer

Father, we confess that sometimes we find ourselves going through the motions of faith because they feel comfortable, because it's what we've always done, and because it feels like what we need to do in order for you to be pleased with us. Messiah Jesus, we thank you for the salvation that you have won for us and that there is nothing that we can do or need to do in order to earn your favor. But we wish to delight you and to take our delight in you. Holy Spirit, fill us with your power and your zeal, to not grow weary in serving others in the ways you care about: care for the poor and for justice. And let the rituals and rhythms of our lives be a true reflection of the work you are doing in and through us. In Jesus's name we pray. Amen.

9

His Own Arm Worked Salvation for Him (Isa 59:1–21; 63:1–6)

Sports commentators sometimes describe an athlete, in an exceptionally good performance, as having "carried the whole team on his back." By this they mean that the athlete—usually the star or the captain—took matters into his own hands, dug deep for all the strength he could muster, and did what it took to win the game for his team. Picture a powerful running back, just unstoppable—time after time lowering his shoulder, bowling over the linebackers into the secondary, refusing to be brought down, dragging would-be tacklers into the end zone with him for touchdown after touchdown. Or some would think of Michael Jordan—sick with the flu, on one famous occasion—taking the ball on almost every possession, double- and triple-teamed, and still just draining bucket after bucket!

The latter part of Isa 59 paints a similar portrait of YHWH. In order to rescue the creation and the people that he has made, he is going to take matters completely into his own hands. He straps on his armor to go to battle, but he is—to quote the old recruitment ad—an army of one.

Isaiah 59 is filled with very stark and vivid imagery in exposing human sinfulness and in describing YHWH coming to judge and save. It is a stark contrast to the hopeful, bright sections that follow it: Isa 60–62 is the central part of the bigger section (Isa 56–66). But before we can get to the hope, we have to plumb the depths of the problem, and that's what chapter 59 does.

But it's not just a matter of swallowing the bitter medicine—being convicted of our sins—in order to get to the sweet healing and grace. There is a progression within the passage that helps us to understand how human sin works in individuals, in societies, and across generations. There are connections to other Scriptures that are instructive. There is also a progression within the book of Isaiah, such that hearing this litany of condemnations in Isa 59 comes across differently than it does in Isa 1 or Isa 3. As we see alluded to in verse 19, YHWH's wrath has been building up for a long time and is about to burst forth in action. But that bursting forth is necessary to accomplish the justice that the world so desperately needs and the redemption for those who are God's people by faith.

The first six verses of Isa 63 have similar language to Isa 59:15b–19, so we'll consider these verses together with Isa 59. In fact, 63:5 is almost a verbatim repetition of 59:16. Having corresponding "YHWH as Warrior" sections immediately before and after Isa 60–62 creates a chiastic structure for the overall section.[1]

SCRIPTURE: ISAIAH 59:1–21 AND 63:1–6

> 1 Behold, the LORD's hand is not shortened, that it cannot save,
> or his ear dull, that it cannot hear;
> 2 but your iniquities have made a separation
> between you and your God,
> and your sins have hidden his face from you
> so that he does not hear.
> 3 For your hands are defiled with blood
> and your fingers with iniquity;
> your lips have spoken lies;
> your tongue mutters wickedness.
> 4 No one enters suit justly;
> no one goes to law honestly;
> they rely on empty pleas, they speak lies,
> they conceive mischief and give birth to iniquity.
> 5 They hatch adders' eggs;
> they weave the spider's web;
> he who eats their eggs dies,
> and from one that is crushed a viper is hatched.
> 6 Their webs will not serve as clothing;

---

1. Refer to table 3 back in chapter 3 for an adaptation of Goldingay's outline of Isa 56–66.

men will not cover themselves with what they make.
Their works are works of iniquity,
and deeds of violence are in their hands.
7 Their feet run to evil,
and they are swift to shed innocent blood;
their thoughts are thoughts of iniquity;
desolation and destruction are in their highways.
8 The way of peace they do not know,
and there is no justice in their paths;
they have made their roads crooked;
no one who treads on them knows peace.
9 Therefore justice is far from us,
and righteousness does not overtake us;
we hope for light, and behold, darkness,
and for brightness, but we walk in gloom.
10 We grope for the wall like the blind;
we grope like those who have no eyes;
we stumble at noon as in the twilight,
among those in full vigor we are like dead men.
11 We all growl like bears;
we moan and moan like doves;
we hope for justice, but there is none;
for salvation, but it is far from us.
12 For our transgressions are multiplied before you,
and our sins testify against us;
for our transgressions are with us,
and we know our iniquities:
13 transgressing, and denying the LORD,
and turning back from following our God,
speaking oppression and revolt,
conceiving and uttering from the heart lying words.
14 Justice is turned back,
and righteousness stands far away;
for truth has stumbled in the public squares,
and uprightness cannot enter.
15 Truth is lacking,
and he who departs from evil makes himself a prey.
The LORD saw it, and it displeased him
that there was no justice.
16 He saw that there was no man,
and wondered that there was no one to intercede;
then his own arm brought him salvation,
and his righteousness upheld him.
17 He put on righteousness as a breastplate,

and a helmet of salvation on his head;
he put on garments of vengeance for clothing,
and wrapped himself in zeal as a cloak.
18 According to their deeds, so will he repay,
wrath to his adversaries, repayment to his enemies;
to the coastlands he will render repayment.
19 So they shall fear the name of the LORD from the west,
and his glory from the rising of the sun;
for he will come like a rushing stream,
which the wind of the LORD drives.
20 "And a Redeemer will come to Zion,
to those in Jacob who turn from transgression," declares the LORD.
21 "And as for me, this is my covenant with them," says the LORD: "My Spirit that is upon you, and my words that I have put in your mouth, shall not depart out of your mouth, or out of the mouth of your offspring, or out of the mouth of your children's offspring," says the LORD, "from this time forth and forevermore." (Isa 59:1–21)

1 Who is this who comes from Edom,
in crimsoned garments from Bozrah,
he who is splendid in his apparel,
marching in the greatness of his strength?
"It is I, speaking in righteousness,
mighty to save."
2 Why is your apparel red,
and your garments like his who treads in the winepress?
3 "I have trodden the winepress alone,
and from the peoples no one was with me;
I trod them in my anger
and trampled them in my wrath;
their lifeblood spattered on my garments,
and stained all my apparel.
4 For the day of vengeance was in my heart,
and my year of redemption had come.
5 I looked, but there was no one to help;
I was appalled, but there was no one to uphold;
so my own arm brought me salvation,
and my wrath upheld me.
6 I trampled down the peoples in my anger;
I made them drunk in my wrath,
and I poured out their lifeblood on the earth."
(Isa 63:1–6)

BLOOD ON OUR HANDS

Powerful to Save

In 59:1, we hear what sounds like a hopeful start: YHWH's arm (literally, his hand) is not too short to save, and he is capable of hearing their cries for help. We've heard something similar, earlier in Isaiah. Back in 50:2, YHWH himself is speaking, and he asks rhetorically, "Why, when I called, was there no one to answer? Is my hand shortened, that it cannot redeem? Or have I no power to deliver?" Then he makes reference to drying up the sea and covering the sky with blackness, which are probably reminders of the wonders he did in defeating the gods of Egypt and bringing the Israelites out of slavery in ancient times—the exodus event.

In Isa 59, the prophet reminds us of YHWH's powerful salvation in the past and that he is capable of saving them again. And we'll see this in verse 15 onward. But before salvation, there's some business that has to be done. God's people, and really all of humanity and the nations, have to be confronted with their sinfulness, in all its grossness.

Litany of Errors

Verse 2 is an answer to verse 1 and sets us down this awful tour of the sins of humanity. YHWH is capable of hearing them, but he has hidden his face from them and can't bear to see how bad they've become. We've seen the "hidden face of God" image before, repeatedly in Isaiah, in contrast to the face of YHWH shining upon his people as a sign of his favor and blessing (see chapter 7, on Isa 57:17).

Verses 3 through 8 are where we get a description of the sins. There are a ton of points we could make about this "laundry list" of awfulness, but I want to focus on just a few.

First of all, there's an intermingling of categories of sin. One of the lines we pray in our prayers of confession is "Lord, we have sinned against you in thought, in word, and in deed—by the things we have done, and by the things we have left undone." Here in 59:3–8, we have it all: we have violence and active shedding of blood; we have deceitful and lying words; and preceding it all, we have thoughts, feelings, and plans ("conceiving trouble," "schemes," etc.). And there are sins of *commission*, things that they do, and sins of *omission*, things that they neglect, like doing and speaking up for justice. These types of sin are all mingled together in the passage, and this makes perfect sense because it's impossible to keep sin in a box, in a single category in our lives. As Jesus says, when calling the hypocritical religious leaders "snakes," "Out of the abundance of the heart, the mouth speaks" (Matt 12:34). So what you're thinking about and mulling over in your heart and mind will eventually flow over into your words and then ultimately into your actions.

Second, there's another connection to an earlier text in Isaiah. Back in the first chapter, YHWH says of a previous generation of Judahites, "When you spread out your hands, I will hide my eyes from you; even though you make many prayers, I will not listen; your hands are full of blood" (1:15). There's a double-meaning here because their hands could be covered in blood due to their pious act of sacrificing an animal to YHWH, but also covered in blood because of the violence that they committed against the poor and needy. In chapter 9, we saw that the rituals of prayer, fasting, and sacrifice are meaningless if they don't reflect the reality of a heart that delights in YHWH. So here in Isa 59:3, the "blood on their hands" could mean both violence *and* empty rituals.

Third, the overall sense we get from this description of sin in 59:3–8 is that sinfulness is coded into human nature. Just as spiders and snakes lay eggs that hatch into more spiders and snakes, what is corrupt gives birth to more corruption. There's a similar idea in 5:2–4: YHWH planted a vineyard, which is an image of his people, and he expected the vines to yield good grapes for wine—but they only yielded wild grapes. The problem with Israel is that the grape seeds are corrupt; it's the wrong kind of grape, so nothing can be done—genetically, they are irredeemable (that is, apart from an act of new creation!). In the New Testament, when Paul is pulling together evidence from the Old Testament about the utter depravity of all human beings, he quotes 59:7–8 in Rom 3:15–17. All humanity is corrupt, and that which is corrupt gives birth to more corruption.

Amok Time

In verses 9 through 15a, we see the darkness in society that results from this total corruption, when sin runs amok.

In 59:9, the "light" of YHWH's safety and his blessing, which was hoped for and promised in the previous sections of Isaiah (cf. 9:2[1]; 30:26; 42:16; 49:6; 58:8–10), is not forthcoming. In fact, there are a lot of parallels to Isa 42. In 59:10, we see the pathetic spiritual blindness of the people, like 42:6–7 and 16–18, along with 56:10.

And not only do they stumble around, blind and spiritually dead (59:10), they can't seem to get away from their many sins; they continue to dog them and drag behind them, like a ball and chain. There's a vivid picture here of sins and iniquities, rebellion and treachery, that is fully on display, like a scarlet letter that is obvious for everyone to see. A lot of us have private sins that we don't want anyone to know about—what if your recent browser history were printed on a T-shirt and you were forced to wear it around town, to church, to work, to school? What was private has now become evident to all. That's how sin works: it takes root in our minds and hearts and then comes out in our attitudes, words, and actions.

Finally, in 59:14–15a, we see a summary of the situation with these two concepts "justice and righteousness" completely absent, standing far off from this dumpster fire society.

From Denial Toward Acceptance

Before we move on and see what YHWH is going to do, I offer one more observation on 59:2–15. When we analyze who is speaking and who is being spoken to in these verses, we see an interesting progression. In 59:2–3, it starts out with "you," plural. It sounds as though YHWH or the prophet is accusing the people. Then in 59:4–8, it doesn't say who is speaking, but the subject shifts to "they." Then in 59:9–12, the subject is "we," that is, "all of us in Yehudian society." And in verses 13–15a, there's no "person" *per se*; those lines are about society, generally.

This progression may reflect a sort of acknowledgment: first YHWH (or the prophet) accuses the people; then the people acknowledge that "some people" or their leaders ("they") have led the nation astray; but it inevitably turns to "we," all of us. We can reflect on this in our own self-examination. Even though our first instinct is to blame other people for sin, when we start trying to untangle and assign blame, the finger ends up pointing back at ourselves, too.

YHWH, THE WARRIOR, SAVIOR, AND JUDGE

Sin is complex and deeply rooted. And these sins have taken root even among the people of Israel and Judah, whom YHWH had saved from slavery and to whom he'd given his good Law. He'd even lived alongside them, and nothing up to this point has been sufficient to convince or compel them to follow his ways, the ways that lead to light and life and flourishing and justice.

We feel a surprising moment of silence in the center of verse 16—it's as if YHWH looks around and finds that he seems to be alone in being utterly appalled by the lack of justice and righteousness. There's no one else stepping up to bring about justice (59:15b–16a).

So, as we noted at the start of the chapter, YHWH has to take matters completely into his own hands, strapping on his armor to go into battle alone. Interestingly, this passage is where Paul gets the imagery of the "armor of God" in Eph 6:10–20. The difference in Paul's metaphor is that we, the rebels who were called, rescued, given amnesty, and transformed by God's grace, get to put on armor and fight alongside God himself!

A Bloodthirsty God?

Isaiah 63:1–6 picks up the vivid imagery of YHWH putting on his armor and takes it to an even more vivid (and gory) conclusion. The passage is held together by references to things that—to put it awkwardly—partake in "redness":

- Edom (*'eḏôm*) is the southeastern neighbor of Yehud, their cousins descended from Esau, Jacob's twin (Gen 36:1). But the word for "red" garments in 63:2 is *'āḏōm*, from the same Hebrew root as Edom, meaning the reddish color of earth.[2]

- The "crimsoned garments" in 63:1 is a different word, *ḥᵃmûṣ*, which can also mean "reddish."

- The Warrior has garments stained by red wine (63:2b, 3) which is a metaphor for blood. "Drunkenness" with wrath of YHWH's judgment is mentioned in 63:6, parallel to Zion (and later, her enemies) drinking the cup of YHWH's wrath to the dregs in Isa 51:17, 21.

- "Lifeblood" (*nēṣaḥ*) of the Warrior's enemies has spattered on his garments and run out onto the ground (63:3, 6).

---

2. Esau received this nickname because of his reddish skin and hair but also because he demanded "red stew" (Gen 25:30). From this same root are also derived *'āḏām*, the name of the first human being (Gen 1:27; 2:5) and meaning "all humankind," and *'aḏāmâ*, meaning "ground" or "earth" (Gen 2:5).

The Edomites are repeatedly castigated in biblical texts for their co-operation with Babylon in the invasion of the region, failing to help their cousins. But Goldingay points out that the links to Edom and Bozrah in Isa 34:5–6 might indicate that this passage is intended to be universal in scope—all people of all nations who remain enemies of YHWH will become objects of his wrath.[3]

Some readers may find such violent, stereotypically masculine imagery of YHWH to be off-putting. It definitely doesn't feel like the kind of compassionate description of God that we find elsewhere in Scripture. But I believe that we *need* to believe in this God, and we need this vivid depiction of a warrior God.

First of all, we already have, even in the book of Isaiah itself, compassionate, feminine imagery used to describe YHWH—for example, in 49:15, YHWH cares for his people like a nursing mother who always has her baby on her mind. I don't think we need to go so far as to refer to God as "She" or "Divine Mother"—the Christian tradition always seems to have accepted the Bible's own masculine language to refer to God. The truth is that male and female humans are both created equally in God's image, and therefore masculine and feminine human qualities *both* reflect something about God's character. We have a God who is gracious and compassionate, but he is also angry at injustice—and when he sees that there is no one to act, he steps up.

Furthermore, when we see YHWH acting in this way in righteous anger, by himself, it underscores to us that we are, in our own sinful natures, born *on the wrong side* of this cosmic struggle, on the wrong side of God's justice. He acts alone because we are all rebels against him. By the time we get to this chapter in the book of Isaiah, we're forced to wonder if *anything* or *anyone* is capable of changing human nature; after all, despite the prophetic warnings of Isa 1–35 and the promises of future blessing in Isa 40–55, the people seem to be the same—no change, nothing is better.

---

3. "It corresponds to chapter 34 which also spoke of a day of vengeance (v. 4). If that denoted the punishment of Edom, it is here more explicit that, if Edom is being punished it is as a representative for peoples in general (v. 6)." Goldingay, *Isaiah*, 353.

The Evolving "Hero" of the Book of Isaiah: Three Facets of Jesus's Identity

But here's something interesting scholars have observed about how the book of Isaiah develops. When we think about the hero, the one who's at the center of the hopes and promises of salvation and redemption, the figure of David and the kings descended from David mostly *disappear* from view over the course of the book. In Isa 1–39, the hope is that there will be a human king, descended from David, who will have the Holy Spirit resting on him (11:2), and he'll rule with justice and mercy. Maybe initial readers in the prophet Isaiah's day would have thought that Hezekiah could have been this human king, but Isa 39 dashes that hope by reporting Hezekiah's key failure that led to the exile.[4]

But then in Isa 40–55, situated in the Babylonian exile (sixth century BC), David is only mentioned once and in passing (55:3). Instead, it focuses on this figure of the "servant of YHWH." Sometimes this figure is a bad servant, like blind Israel in chapter 42; sometimes it seems like the servant is the prophet himself. But eventually, the "Servant" figure evolves/unfolds into the "Suffering Servant" of Isa 52:13—53:12 who gives himself up on behalf of God's people. Now in Isa 56–66, David is not mentioned at all, but YHWH himself—the divine Warrior—is the central figure who will save his people. The "Servant" figure upon whom rests the Spirit of YHWH does return at the end of this chapter (59:21) but then more fully in Isa 61 (see chapter 11).

Looking back on this evolving focus in the book of Isaiah, we see that each of these central figures points us ahead to Jesus Christ, and each figure is one aspect of Jesus's identity. Jesus is the human king of Isa 1–39: stronger than David, more faithful than Hezekiah. Jesus is the Suffering Servant: the prophet who preaches alone to his people and eventually dies on their behalf (drinking the "cup" of YHWH's wrath on their behalf: Matt 26:39). And Jesus is also *YHWH himself*, this mighty warrior of chapter 59, who straps on his armor to do what it takes, acting alone, to save his people.

WHAT DOES SALVATION LOOK LIKE

So after all this sin, all this movement, all this build-up, what does YHWH's act of salvation look like?

---

4. See Giffone, "Toward a Better 'Hezekiah.'"

Judgment and Salvation

First, at long last, YHWH is going to save his people by judging the wicked. This is not a contradiction of his mercy. Throughout the Bible, YHWH holds back his judgment, giving a chance for as many people as possible to acknowledge their rebellion and change their ways. In the days of Noah, God waited over a hundred years before bringing about the flood that judged humanity for violence run amok. In Gen 15, YHWH says he'll delay saving the Israelites from slavery and bringing them into the land of Canaan because the sins of the Canaanites haven't yet filled up to the spillover point—he's waiting to see if they will repent. Throughout the book of Kings and beyond, he sent many prophets to urge the people of Israel and Judah to repent even though they deserved to be judged a lot sooner than they were.

But in the end, a god who claims to be holy and to care about justice and righteousness in the world and who *doesn't* eventually act to punish the wicked and rescue their victims is not a holy god at all. That god would be a fantasy that we would make up to assuage our personal guilt; a god who holds us to an inferior standard that we can sometimes meet (because we ourselves wrote the rules). As 59:19 says, the dam of God's patience is going to burst, and he will come suddenly, unexpectedly—it literally says, "A rushing stream, which the wind [Spirit] of the LORD drives." It's a flash flood combined with a hurricane-force wind! In the end, after he sweeps through, everyone will acknowledge and revere the name of YHWH and will see his glory and his power because he will win this victory (59:19).

But the good news in 59:20 is that there is redemption and amnesty for those who acknowledge YHWH as God! In Phil 2:5-11, that great christological hymn, we read that every knee will bow and every tongue will confess that Jesus Christ is Lord—in heaven and on earth and those under the earth—but for some, it will be too late for that confession to change their eternal fate.

Our parallel passage in 63:1-6 makes an even clearer connection between the wrath of God upon those who persist in rebellion, and the good news of redemption. YHWH the Warrior is characterized by "anger" (63:3, 6), "wrath" (63:3, 5, 6), and "vengeance" (63:4)—but also "splendor" and "strength," "righteousness" and "salvation" (63:1), "redemption" (63:4), and more "salvation" (63:5). When YHWH comes to finally make things right, there is no neat distinction between his acts of wrath and his acts of redemption; they are one and the same event. The only question is which side of the event will *you* be on?

Transformed by the Spirit

What assurances do we have that this redemption, this judgment for the rebels and rescue for those who are repentant, is going to be any better than the rescues from Egypt or from Babylon? In 59:21, YHWH is going to take extreme and certain measures this time to ensure that they will remain his people: a transformative work of the Spirit of YHWH.

There is a grammatical ambiguity in this verse that may point us ahead more clearly to the returning "Servant of YHWH" figure in 61:1. In 59:21, YHWH is the speaker, the "I/My/Me" figure. The "they/them" is the people: the offspring of the "you" figure. But who is the "you"? YHWH says, "My spirit which is *upon you,*" and the "you" in the traditional vowel pointed Hebrew text is masculine singular. This points us ahead to 61:1 in which a masculine figure says, "The Spirit of [YHWH] is *upon me*." However, without the vowel pointing (which is not considered original and inspired by Jews or Christians), the "you" in 59:21 could be feminine singular. This would match the "you" of the entirety of Isa 60 which is unambiguously feminine singular: Daughter Zion, the feminine personification of the city of Jerusalem (and the people of YHWH). This might fit a little better in 59:21 with the idea of "your offspring"—the offspring of Zion rather than the offspring of the Servant.

In short, the consonantal Hebrew text could read either "you," the Servant, or "you," Zion. Why does any of this matter? There is a small difference: Will YHWH's Spirit be upon the Servant, understood to be Jesus? Or will the Spirit be upon Zion, a type of the church?

But in the context of Isa 59, the meaning is not that different either way. YHWH's Spirit—the same word as the *wind* (*rûaḥ*) that came along with that rushing river of judgment (59:19)—will cause YHWH's words to "not depart out of [the] mouth" of his people (the offspring of the Servant or the offspring of Zion). This represents the "healing" that was hoped for and promised in 57:18–19 and 58:8. Whereas before our lips had spoken only lies (59:3–4), God transforms us and places his words in our hearts (Jer 31:33; Heb 8:10; 10:16) and on our lips (cf. Heb 13:15) so that we can remain within his covenant.

REFLECTIONS

There are certainly some *harsh* messages in Isa 59 and 63:1–6. But there's also an openness about it that can be oddly refreshing.

Denying Us Our Denial

The week I was working on this passage, I suddenly found myself in a rather dangerous driving situation. I was pulling out into traffic, and I completely forgot to check the traffic from one direction: the lane behind the person who was turning left from my right. Thankfully, there was no one coming from that direction, and I made it safely through. (The specifics aren't really that important.) The point is that *after* I had come through the dangerous situation unharmed, the more I reflected on it, the more freaked out I got even though the danger had already passed. And the more I thought about it, the more my mind went to the worst-case scenarios. *Could I even have survived such a crash? What would Corrie and the kids do without me? What if I'd been paralyzed, and they'd have had to take care of me forever?* Thus, my thoughts spiraled.

A passage like Isa 59 has a similar ability to cut through our apathy; the more we reflect on it, the seriousness of our situation (individual and social) becomes more vivid. We need to read passages like 59:2–15a to get us past our denial and our pride—it's a comprehensive, rock-bottom assessment of humanity. And this scathing condemnation encompasses human beings—ancient Israel and us today—who have *received* God's revelation about his glory and *understand* with head knowledge the consequences of "falling short of God's glory," and we sin anyway. It should be sobering.

Power and Transformation

But as bad as Israel was and as bad as we are, we get a striking picture of YHWH's strength and his power. He uses his power for justice *and* for love—love of the human beings he created, love of his creation. His arm is *not* too short to save, and his desire *is* to save and to put things to right.

Part of putting things right in the world is that YHWH's Spirit comes with power to transform us so that we become what he created us to be—instead of the disaster that we make following our own way.

There are two additional features to this redemption and transformation in this passage. YHWH's Holy Spirit transforms not only us in the present, but also God's "words will be on the lips of your children and the lips of their descendants . . . forever" (59:21). The redemption is lasting, and it's intergenerational. This redemption through God's Spirit is for you and for your children (cf. Acts 2:39).

The second "bonus" for Israel is that once YHWH acts for salvation, then the hopeful and universal vision of Isa 56 can be accomplished. Here in 59:20, he references "those in Jacob"—that is, YHWH's chosen family, Israel. But in Isa 60–62 and beyond, this vision expanded to include those who are repentant from among all the nations. And this is only fair because any Jews who are saved through this judgment are saved on the basis of faith, not by works or by membership in Israel (cf. Rom 3–4).

A Prayer

Father, when we're confronted with this list of sins—thoughts, words, actions that are displeasing to you—there's really no way we can deny that this is who we are apart from your mercy. So we confess to you, and we cry out to you: Hosanna! Lord save us! Save us from injustice, and save us from ourselves! We ask you, Holy Spirit, to do your work of new creation within us so that, instead of snakes and spiders hatching more snakes and spiders or bad grape seeds sprouting into bad vines, we would be people transformed, and that on our lips would be your word and your praises, forever. In Christ's name we pray. Amen.

10

Nations Shall Come to Your Light (Isa 60)

In Isa 56–58, we found that despite all YHWH has done to bring them back, and despite the purifying trial of the exile, the people continue to be morally disappointing (to put it diplomatically). In Isa 59, we saw the significance of YHWH as the divine warrior who acts alone to accomplish justice and to save his people. At the end of that chapter, his Spirit comes to replace the lies on the lips of his people with the true words of God, forever (59:21)—a sign of transformation!

We now move into this really hopeful, beautiful middle section of Isa 56–66 which is Isa 60–62 (see the chart of the chiastic structure of this section on page 41). There are many ways we could approach this section; I've chosen to focus on three main themes corresponding roughly to these three Isaiah chapters (but with some overlap): light (Isa 60); clothing and glory (Isa 61); and names (Isa 62). In each chapter, we'll see important ways that these images prefigure the events of the New Testament, including the work of Jesus and the inclusion of the gentiles in the family of YHWH.

Isaiah 60, with the theme of light, is an amazing answer to chapter 59 that describes how Israel stumbles about in darkness because of their sin. Isaiah 60 speaks about the nations coming to honor YHWH, the God of Israel, and to return Israel's sons and daughters to her.

Isaiah 60 is traditionally read on the holiday of Epiphany, which begins on January 6th in the Western church calendar, after the twelve days of Christmas. Sometimes in English we use the word "epiphany" to describe a sudden moment of inspiration or understanding. In Greek it literally means "appearing," but with the connotation of a glorious or miraculous appearance—usually sudden, sometimes of a god. And that is the sense in which we mean it in connection with the holiday: not a sudden inspiration but the appearance of God in bodily form.

The holiday of Epiphany in the Christian calendar marks the arrival of wise men from the east to visit Jesus when he was a baby (Matt 2:1–12). Sometimes it's called "Three Kings' Day." When we lived in a historically Catholic country, sometimes children would dress up as the three wise men and go door to door; there were other traditions involving foods and gifts. The holiday of Epiphany is special because it celebrates the first time that gentiles, people from outside Israel, honor Jesus as Israel's Messiah and the Lord of the world. This is very important, as we've already seen in Isa 56:1–8.

In this chapter, we will look at Isa 60 in context and then bring the passage into conversation with the story of the three wise men. It's easy to see why this passage is connected to Matt 2, when the three wise men follow a special star to see Jesus: "Nations shall come to your light, and kings to the brightness of your rising" (60:3); "They shall bring gold and frankincense" (60:6). The story about the wise men coming to see Jesus is rightly viewed as a fulfillment of this prediction in the book of Isaiah.

But there is a deeper connection here beyond a few borrowed phrases. The light is not just a special star in the sky but light that shines over all people. Two words for "glory" appear many times in this passage. The glory of YHWH, the God of Israel, is displayed through his people. Isaiah 60's powerful message is that the God of Israel—his glory and his work among his people—comes to be recognized by all nations. This is especially important for all of us who are not Jewish.

And we will see that this light and glory from God places before us a choice. We can either try to squish it down, try to darken it because we are afraid of what it will reveal. Or, hopefully, we can choose to embrace the light and the vocation of reflecting God's glory into the world.

SCRIPTURE: ISAIAH 60:1-22

After reading Isa 60, you may wish to read Matt 2:1–12 as well.

1 Arise, shine, for your light has come,
and the glory of the LORD has risen upon you.
2 For behold, darkness shall cover the earth,
and thick darkness the peoples;
but the LORD will arise upon you,
and his glory will be seen upon you.
3 And nations shall come to your light,
and kings to the brightness of your rising.
4 Lift up your eyes all around, and see;
they all gather together, they come to you;
your sons shall come from afar,
and your daughters shall be carried on the hip.
5 Then you shall see and be radiant;
your heart shall thrill and exult,
because the abundance of the sea shall be turned to you,
the wealth of the nations shall come to you.
6 A multitude of camels shall cover you,
the young camels of Midian and Ephah;
all those from Sheba shall come.
They shall bring gold and frankincense,
and shall bring good news, the praises of the LORD.
7 All the flocks of Kedar shall be gathered to you;
the rams of Nebaioth shall minister to you;
they shall come up with acceptance on my altar,
and I will beautify my beautiful house.
8 Who are these that fly like a cloud,
and like doves to their windows?
9 For the coastlands shall hope for me,
the ships of Tarshish first,
to bring your children from afar,
their silver and gold with them,
for the name of the LORD your God,
and for the Holy One of Israel,
because he has made you beautiful.
10 Foreigners shall build up your walls,
and their kings shall minister to you;
for in my wrath I struck you,
but in my favor I have had mercy on you.
11 Your gates shall be open continually;
day and night they shall not be shut,

that people may bring to you the wealth of the nations,
with their kings led in procession.
12 For the nation and kingdom
that will not serve you shall perish;
those nations shall be utterly laid waste.
13 The glory of Lebanon shall come to you,
the cypress, the plane, and the pine,
to beautify the place of my sanctuary,
and I will make the place of my feet glorious.
14 The sons of those who afflicted you
shall come bending low to you,
and all who despised you
shall bow down at your feet;
they shall call you the City of the LORD,
the Zion of the Holy One of Israel.
15 Whereas you have been forsaken and hated,
with no one passing through,
I will make you majestic forever,
a joy from age to age.
16 You shall suck the milk of nations;
you shall nurse at the breast of kings;
and you shall know that I, the LORD, am your Savior
and your Redeemer, the Mighty One of Jacob.
17 Instead of bronze I will bring gold,
and instead of iron I will bring silver;
instead of wood, bronze,
instead of stones, iron.
I will make your overseers peace
and your taskmasters righteousness.
18 Violence shall no more be heard in your land,
devastation or destruction within your borders;
you shall call your walls Salvation,
and your gates Praise.
19 The sun shall be no more
your light by day,
nor for brightness shall the moon
give you light;
but the LORD will be your everlasting light,
and your God will be your glory.
20 Your sun shall no more go down,
nor your moon withdraw itself;
for the LORD will be your everlasting light,
and your days of mourning shall be ended.
21 Your people shall all be righteous;

> they shall possess the land forever,
> the branch of my planting, the work of my hands,
> that I might be glorified.
> 22 The least one shall become a clan,
> and the smallest one a mighty nation;
> I am the LORD;
> in its time I will hasten it. (Isa 60:1–22)

LIGHT AND GLORY FOR ZION

When reading Isa 60, it's easy for Christian readers to hear the echoes of the wise men coming to visit Jesus. This is part of how we always read the Old Testament with at least two lenses. One lens focuses on the original context in which a text was written; the second lens is focused on how the text is fulfilled in Jesus and in the church.

Light Is Coming

The contrast of darkness and light is of course a very old and very common sort of image in literature. And of course in real life, light is important! In 60:2, the idea of "darkness covering the earth," pierced by light from YHWH rising over everything, is reminiscent of creation in Gen 1. The darkness represents chaos, evil, despair, oppression, sinfulness—and it covers all peoples.

But God's glory and his light are coming. Now when it says, "Your light has come," who is the "you" (60:1–3)? It is the light of Zion, Israel's holy city where God dwells on earth. What is the source of the light? It's very common in our day to think of ourselves as having some sort of light that comes from within, and some Christian traditions even speak of this. But here, Israel is not the source of its own light; their light shines from YHWH being in their midst. In 60:19–20, it says that the sun and moon will no longer be the source of light but rather YHWH "will be your everlasting light."

The Nations Are Coming

Imagine standing on the mountain of Zion, the holy hill of Jerusalem, and seeing the nations streaming toward you. What a sight this would be!

Would it be scary? Well, many times in Israel's story, including in their recent memory, the nations came with armies and surrounded Jerusalem to attack it. Other times the nations came with their goods and services, seeking to trade with Israel and bringing not only wealth but also the worship of other gods.

But in 60:4–7, the nations are attracted by Israel's light, which we've seen comes from God's glory in their midst. And with the nations come Israel's children: sons and daughters from afar. These are those children of YHWH's people who have gone astray or who have been held captive by other nations. Their masters will come carrying these sons and daughters near to Jerusalem, coming to the God of Israel!

And the nations come bearing gifts. In 60:5–7, notice the thrill and rejoicing of Israel to see the nations coming—rather than contempt and anger at unclean people approaching their holy city or terror at invaders coming to attack! This is a source of joy for God's people.

Second, note the wealth of the nations that is being brought to Israel. At first appearance, this seems like just a nice gesture, but it needs interpretation. Is it reparations for all that the nations have done to Israel? That could be part of it. Is it punishment of the nations? Possibly. But most importantly, the nations come to worship YHWH at his altar. They come from afar, proclaiming YHWH's praise (60:6), which is the same word that we saw in Isa 40–55 as being the "good news" or "gospel" announcement to Zion: "Your God reigns!" "Your God is becoming King!" (40:9; 41:27; 52:7). From far away, the nations have come to the knowledge that Zion's God is the true God and is worthy of their honor. This means that Zion is popular and worthy of honor not because of her behavior but because YHWH is in her midst, and she reflects his glory. The wealth of the nations will be brought to Zion because the Holy One of Israel has glorified her—actually, it's *his* glory that makes her shine!

Reversals

This chapter is marked by reversal or change: for YHWH, for the nations, and for Zion herself.

YHWH admits that in his wrath he punished his people (60:10). They deserved it; they had been very wicked, had worshiped other gods, and had even conducted human sacrifice. But his loyalty is still with his people, and he will have compassion on them and forgive them.

The nations are portrayed somewhat ambiguously. Are they voluntarily serving the God of Israel and his people? Or are they serving unwillingly under threat of punishment? Will some of them be punished? The answer is probably all three! The nations who oppressed Israel and had contempt for their God will recognize their error. But they have the opportunity to come willingly, to honor YHWH the God of Israel, without suffering punishment. This is the message of Ps 2: do homage to the Son or suffer his wrath if you continue in rebellion against him—blessed are all who take refuge in him!

The nations will help to rebuild Jerusalem's walls that had been torn down.[1] But notice that there will be walls and gates in this new Jerusalem, but the gates will never be closed, day and night. This is because the city is in no danger: YHWH is in her midst, so she will never be moved (cf. Ps 46). What then is the point of the nations rebuilding walls? This is for the honor and glory of God and shows that the nations are having a chance to participate in repairing what both Israel and the nations had destroyed through their sinfulness (the city and kingdom of God, which we talked a bit about in the previous chapter). So it's a gracious opportunity to demonstrate repentance and live out the forgiveness that YHWH has extended to them.

And finally, the reversals for Zion herself are striking. Her darkness becomes light (60:2, 20). Whereas she was formerly not beautiful, now she is considered beautiful (60:9). Gates that were shut will continually be open (60:11). Formerly she was afflicted and despised, forsaken and hated, with no visitors; but she becomes majestic, with those who afflicted her bowing down to her and honoring her (60:14–15). She even gets better gifts: more precious metals (60:17). Violence turns to peace (60:18). From a few small and insignificant individuals and families, she will become clans and a mighty nation (60:22).

YHWH Is There

YHWH is the speaker throughout this chapter. He calls himself the Savior and the Redeemer of his people in verse 16; in verse 17, he provides for them; and in verses 19–20, he is their everlasting light and their glory. The emphasis is on what *God* does, not on what his people need to do to

---

1. This is a hint to us that the text is possibly written before Nehemiah rebuilds the walls in the 440s.

receive it. We've already seen in Isa 56–59 just how bad human beings are, how turned away we are from God, and how much we need him to act on our behalf to save us—from our circumstances and from our own rebellious selves. We should be thankful that none of this depends on us to initiate or accomplish redemption.

THE THREE WISE MEN: FOLLOWING THE LIGHT

Let's consider now the story of the three wise men coming to visit and honor Jesus (Matt 2:1–12). There are of course the connections we saw earlier: "Kings will come to the brightness of your rising" and the bringing of gold and frankincense.

A King from the Countryside

These wise men who watch the skies for astrological signs have seen the star that they know, somehow, represents the birth of the king of the Jews. They travel from the east to Jerusalem, which would be the natural place to look for a Jewish king. Herod, who is not Jewish but is king of Judea under Roman rule, is disturbed by this threat to his kingship. But he summons the scribes who tell him that, according to Mic 5:2, the anointed king ("Messiah" or "Christ") would be born in Bethlehem of Judah. The wise men continue their journey following the star to Bethlehem where it comes to rest over the house where Jesus was staying. There, it says, they "rejoiced," as in Isa 60, and they gave him their gifts.

The king of the Jews is found in Bethlehem, not Jerusalem, in accordance with Mic 5, which is also speaking about the birthplace of King David. Jerusalem was David's royal capital that he conquered in 2 Sam 5, but his origins were in the humble town of Bethlehem. Jesus's birth in Bethlehem is a striking paradox, a subversion of expectations: the king is not born in a royal city but in a tiny provincial town in a stable.

Why from the East?

These important men come from the east, which probably means Mesopotamia—modern-day Iraq. Why is it significant that they came from Mesopotamia but not Rome (which was a major center of power), Greece, Egypt, Ethiopia, or Anatolia?

Mesopotamia is the place of *Abraham's* origins, where Israel comes from. But Mesopotamia is also the place where the nations of Assyria and Babylon used to enslave and oppress the people of Israel and Judah and where they mocked YHWH and his people!

Going back even further into the biblical story, the east (Mesopotamia) is the place of ancient civilization, including the cities that the ancient leader Nimrod built (Gen 10:8–12) as the different nations spread out after the great flood. In the biblical worldview, the east is sort of like Mordor in *The Lord of the Rings* mythology, and the ancient leader of the east, Nimrod, is a Sauron-like figure. Nimrod was the founder of the capital cities of the ancient civilizations of Babylon and Assyria—these two kingdoms that come to represent human violence and rebellion against the true God, YHWH. Nimrod founded the city of Babylon, which is also the site of the great tower that was a sign of human rebellion against the Creator God (Gen 11:1–9). Since ancient times, Jewish and Christian interpreters have understood Nimrod as a founder of these civilizations who led them in the way of arrogance, violence, tyranny, and evil.

But now in the time of Jesus, the east—the place that is the root of rebellion and human evil—is now producing rulers (at least a handful of them) who see the glory of Israel's God and king and come to worship him!

A Light to the Nations

Throughout the Old Testament, there is an important theme: people from *outside* Israel, God's people, recognizing the greatness of Israel's God—often seeing it even more clearly than Israel does! For example, Jethro, Moses's father-in-law, gives glory to YHWH after he saves Israel from slavery in Egypt. Rahab, the Canaanite prostitute, throws all of her trust on YHWH when the Israelites come to attack her city, Jericho. Ruth has more faith than her mother-in-law, Naomi, in the faithfulness of YHWH to his people.

This was YHWH's purpose all along in calling Israel to be his people: that his glory would shine in their midst and the nations would see and be attracted to it. Very often, Israel failed to live up to God's glory—as we all have sinned and fallen short of God's glory. None of us is worthy to carry forth God's glory into the world. In Isa 60, despite all that Israel, Judah, and Jerusalem had done to bring shame on God's name, God still displayed his glory through them. In Matt 2, despite all that the Jewish people (and all humanity) had done to dishonor the Creator God, he still chose to be born as a Jewish baby and to show his glory in the world through Jesus the Messiah.

REFLECTIONS

What are the implications of these truths for us?

Re-enchanted by God's Glory

First of all, we have to start by marveling at God's glory: who he is in himself and what he has done for us and for the world. I think we live in a time when there are more amazing things than ever before in human history, more for us to marvel at, at least in terms of technology and inventions. And even *if*, you might say, there's not as *much* good art being created, at least we can access the glorious artistic creations of the past and the present more readily. But amidst all this, we often forget the *source* of humanity's creativity and brilliance; we worship and serve the created thing rather than the Creator. And in some ways, looking at other human brilliance can allow us to deny God's glory and cope with our own natural tendency to glorify ourselves. But Isa 60 calls us to humility, to recognize that God is the source of anything good or glorious in us. This is not "our light" coming from us but rather it's the light that God has entrusted to us, the light that God shines through us!

The Warrior Savior Comes as a Baby

Next, we marvel at the work of the Father in planning salvation from start to finish. There was only darkness over the world before he said, "Let there be light!" There was only darkness of sin spread over each human heart after Adam and Eve's sin. The Father is still saying into the darkness, "Let the light of my glory shine!"

The work of God is the work of the Son, Jesus, come to earth as a baby. God has shown his glory in the world in the form of a baby! Isaiah 59: God himself comes to do battle to rescue his creation because he wants the job done right! He strapped on his sword to do battle; he put on his crown to be worshiped—but he became a baby and slept in a feeding trough for animals and grew up in a working-class family as a builder. He died a painful death, and that was his mighty victory over the powers that held his people hostage.

The work of God is the work of the Spirit in our hearts making us more like Jesus each day and moving the hearts of Jews and gentiles to be attracted by God's glory.

All Our Devotion

So what do we do after recognizing God's glory? I said at the beginning: this light and glory from God places before us a choice. We can either try to squish it down, try to darken it because we are afraid of what it will reveal. Or we can choose to embrace the light and the vocation of reflecting God's glory into the world. We have examples of both in Matt 2: Herod who saw the light as a threat to his power and tried to snuff it out; and the wise men who saw the light from far off and brought their treasures and their own selves to offer to Jesus, the Light that has come into the world.

And thinking beyond ourselves, is our church and are each of us—as individuals and families—shining the light of God's glory so that the nations—people outside—will stream here and seek God himself? Again, I want to stress the *surprise* that Israel seems to feel in Isa 60 when the nations are attracted to them and their God. Maybe we expect that people outside the church will only ever be hostile to the message of Christ, so we hesitate to share it. Or, maybe we think that they will be put off by how flawed *we* are as God's people. As much as we should be trying to love others and "be better people," strictly relying on our morality to "get people to like us" is going to fail because we will fail at it. Rather, our approach should be allowing God to receive glory as *he* makes us holy and glorious. Our role to play is to respond with joy to what God does in us and how he shines his light through us.

Finally, if you are not a believer in Jesus, come to this light! Come to this glorious God who loves you, who desires to make peace with you, and who wants to give you a life of flourishing. C. S. Lewis wrote: "I believe in Christianity as I believe that the Sun has risen, not only because I see it, but because by it I see everything else."[2] Just like the sunlight allows us to live in the world, so the light of Christ allows us to see everything else—ourselves, other people, the world—as it truly is so we can flourish

---

2. Lewis, *Weight of Glory*, 140.

in the truth. There really is no better day than today to admit your sin and rebellion against God, accept the free gift of forgiveness in Christ, to receive the gift of the Holy Spirit, and to pledge your only allegiance to the Holy One of Israel—the light of nations! May it be so.

A Prayer

Father, we thank you for the light that has come into the world: your Son, Jesus Christ. Thank you that his light has shone into our hearts, banishing the darkness. We confess that, too often, we suppress that light from you, or we don't think that the light is sufficiently bright to attract others around us. Spur in us, we pray, a fresh passion to see your glory go forth into the world. We ask that we might be the means by which others would see your glory and that the nations would run to you, their Hope. Amen.

11

He Has Clothed Me in Robes of Righteousness (Isa 61)

Within the hopeful middle section of Isa 56–66, chapters 60 and 62 are both addressed to a feminine singular "you." This "you" is Daughter Zion: the feminine personification of the city of Jerusalem, David's capital in ancient Israel. In English, we just have one pronoun for "you" that we use for one person or multiple people, male or female, whereas Hebrew has four different sets of forms for "you"![1] "Daughter Zion" is a poetic way of speaking about the city of Jerusalem, or the area of Judah/Yehud more broadly, and "her children" are the people. YHWH, the God of Israel, is sometimes described as her husband.

Isaiah 61 is tucked between these two chapters that are addressed to Daughter Zion, and so it is the center of the center, the climax of this final section of Isaiah. It's addressed to "you" plural, meaning the people of Judah. It has many themes and images that we've seen before, and so it ties many things together.

---

1. To add more complexity, some of the masculine and feminine singular forms are differentiated only by the vowel pointing that was added to the consonants to reflect the pronunciation known to the scribes. Usually, we rely on this pointing as a faithful conduit of the original meaning, but occasionally scholars will suggest that the consonants (which are the original authoritative Hebrew text) should be "re-pointed," which could alter the meaning slightly. For example, "you"/"your" singular with the same consonants could be understood as masculine *or* feminine depending on the pronunciation indicated by the pointing.

There are so many different ways to approach this chapter. Obviously, liberation is an important theme; we've already looked at this idea in detail back in chapter 8 (on Isa 58). So, I've chosen two other ideas to focus on. This passage describes the things that God does for his people with the metaphor of *clothing* or *things we put on our body* to adorn ourselves—we could expand the category a bit to include perfumes and nice textiles that we put on our beds and couches. We notice that there are quite a few different references to clothing and adornment in Isa 56–66; these are usually metaphors for glory—in particular, the glory that God gives his people.

The second angle of approach is to see how Jesus himself uses this passage to signal his first coming, his arrival to comfort his people, found in Luke chapter 4. Jesus's example opens up for us how we should interpret Isaiah's prophecies—and it's even more brilliant and beautiful than the prophet could have imagined. But it has a sharp message for us: the day of salvation, amnesty, forgiveness, and reconciliation is now—today—this moment between Jesus's first coming and his second coming. We need to embrace this and pledge our allegiance to Jesus because the day of vengeance is still to come.

SCRIPTURE: ISAIAH 61:1-11

> 1 The Spirit of the Lord GOD[2] is upon me,
> because the LORD has anointed me
> to bring good news to the poor;
> he has sent me to bind up the brokenhearted,
> to proclaim liberty to the captives,
> and the opening of the prison to those who are bound;
> 2 to proclaim the year of the LORD's favor,
> and the day of vengeance of our God;
> to comfort all who mourn;
> 3 to grant to those who mourn in Zion—
> to give them a beautiful headdress instead of ashes,
> the oil of gladness instead of mourning,
> the garment of praise instead of a faint spirit;
> that they may be called oaks of righteousness,
> the planting of the LORD, that he may be glorified.
> 4 They shall build up the ancient ruins;

---

2. On the construction "Lord GOD," see the footnote in chapter 5 on Isa 56:8.

they shall raise up the former devastations;
  they shall repair the ruined cities,
  the devastations of many generations.
  5 Strangers shall stand and tend your flocks;
  foreigners shall be your plowmen and vinedressers;
  6 but you shall be called the priests of the LORD;
  they shall speak of you as the ministers of our God;
  you shall eat the wealth of the nations,
  and in their glory you shall boast.
  7 Instead of your shame there shall be a double portion;
  instead of dishonor they shall rejoice in their lot;
  therefore in their land they shall possess a double portion;
  they shall have everlasting joy.
  8 For I the LORD love justice;
  I hate robbery and wrong;
  I will faithfully give them their recompense,
  and I will make an everlasting covenant with them.
  9 Their offspring shall be known among the nations,
  and their descendants in the midst of the peoples;
  all who see them shall acknowledge them,
  that they are an offspring the LORD has blessed.
  10 I will greatly rejoice in the LORD;
  my soul shall exult in my God,
  for he has clothed me with the garments of salvation;
  he has covered me with the robe of righteousness,
  as a bridegroom decks himself like a priest with a beautiful headdress,
  and as a bride adorns herself with her jewels.
  11 For as the earth brings forth its sprouts,
  and as a garden causes what is sown in it to sprout up,
  so the Lord GOD will cause righteousness and praise
  to sprout up before all the nations. (Isa 61:1–11)

WHEN THE SERVANT RULES THE WORLD

As we look at this text, we should look first at who seems to be doing the speaking. We already talked about who is being spoken *to*: in chapters 60 and 62, it's Daughter Zion; here in chapter 61, the addressees are "the people," presumably the people of Jerusalem, Judah, and Israel.

But who is speaking? It's a person that says, "YHWH's Spirit is upon me to do" these things. We saw this figure addressed briefly by YHWH in

59:21, pointing us ahead to 61:1 (see chapter 9). I've previously described the shift in focus throughout the book of Isaiah: the kings descended from David (Isa 1–39), the "Servant" figure (Isa 40–55), and YHWH himself as the warrior (Isa 56–66). Each of these literary figures points ahead to one aspect of Jesus's identity: a human king, a suffering prophet who dies for his people, and also YHWH himself.

In Isa 61:1–3 like in Isa 50 and 53—and without any reference to David—the focal character appears to be a human figure upon whom is the Spirit of Lord YHWH. This figure is a prophet: he is the messenger of the good news that Zion's God reigns (61:1; cf. 40:9; 52:7). Throughout Scripture, we see YHWH's Spirit coming upon prophets in power to speak his words to the people. The Isa 61 figure is also a king: he is called "anointed," which is what was done for kings *and* priests in ancient Israel.[3] In Isa 11, YHWH's Spirit is said to *rest upon* the king from the line of David, and he would accomplish justice in the world; in 42:1, we saw that YHWH's Spirit would *rest upon* the Gentle Servant who also seems to be a prophet (and possibly a king).

With hindsight, we can see that this is very clearly pointing to the figure of Jesus who would fulfill both the roles of Suffering Prophet and Davidic King in Israel. As we will see below, when Jesus reads this Scripture in the synagogue centuries later and says to the Jews gathered there, "Today this Scripture is fulfilled in your hearing," they are shocked and excited (initially) because they know *exactly* who he is claiming to be.

We have this prophet-servant-king figure upon whom is the Holy Spirit! The "good news" he proclaims is that YHWH reigns in Israel and on the earth (Isa 52:7)! YHWH was king at creation when everything was perfect, but humans rebelled and declared our own kingship. Thus, YHWH intervened to reestablish his kingship within a specific people group: Israel, the descendants of Abraham. But Israel rebelled and rejected him just as Adam and Eve had, and so they suffered under the Babylonians. Now the prophecy is telling us YHWH's kingship has had to be re-reestablished, but it will be permanent this time! What does this reestablished kingship (which, as we see further in Isaiah, will amount to a renewed creation) look like?

YHWH's kingship will mean liberation and freedom from slavery, captivity, and oppression. This has been a significant theme in previous chapters, especially Isa 58. Freedom means that the people will no

---

3. Intriguingly, the only other "anointed" figure in Isaiah is Cyrus of Persia (45:1).

longer be captive to the self-serving gods of the nations, no longer slaves to their own sinful natures. Structures of oppression will be dismantled; the norms and patterns that kept people in shame and suffering will have been broken. Human beings, made in God's image, will be free to pursue productivity and beauty.

YHWH's kingship will mean comfort for his people and vengeance on his enemies. We'll come back to this below and see what Jesus has to say about it. But here again, like we saw in Isa 59, there is no tension between God's mercy and his justice. There's a nice little flourish here, a play on words: the root word for "vengeance" in verse 2 is *nāqam*, but the word for comfort is *nāḥam*—just a one-letter difference in Hebrew. We find wordplays like this, one-letter differences, elsewhere in Isaiah.[4]

YHWH's kingship will mean darkness turns into light, and the blind will receive sight. This idea of "light" is a dominant theme of Isa 60; release from "darkness" is only mentioned in passing in 61:1. But it's worth noting because in Jesus's reading of Isa 61, he appears to add "blind receive sight," which is interesting. Prophecies of "light and sight for the blind" are found elsewhere in Isa 35:5; 42:7; and 58:8–10. Light is the first thing that God created in the present creation (Gen 1:3). If establishing YHWH's kingship is an act of *new creation*, it makes sense that those in darkness will be under his light.

There are two more themes that we will look at in the next chapter in connection to Isa 62. The first is the re-created *land*, given back to God's transformed people, and the rebuilding of the towns and cities. Here in 61:4–5, there is replanting of vineyards, farms, and gardens, and the cities of Israel and Judah are rebuilt again. When YHWH places his people in the land, freed and transformed, they will be able to work and enjoy fruitfulness as he designed them to. Another theme in the next chapter is *names*. When God re-creates, liberates, transforms, and blesses his people, we receive new names and titles to reflect our new identity and newly-given dignity.

CLOTHING AND GLORY

So now, I want to talk a bit about *clothes* in this passage and what they signify. We all know that *clothes* tell us about someone—whether they're

---

4. The most notable example is in Isa 5:7b: "And he hoped for justice (*mišpāṭ*), but behold, bloodshed (*mišpāḥ*); for righteousness (*ṣᵉdāqâ*), but behold, outcry (*ṣᵉʿāqâ*)."

male or female, maybe what kind of job they do, or at least what job or task they are in the middle of doing. Are they exercising? Mowing the lawn? Working on the car? Are they hosting a party? Are they going to a funeral or to a wedding? Clothing communicates something about who we are and what we do. And smells, too, are part of how other people perceive us and are closely related to clothes. When we've been working or exercising in clothes that are dirty, we might not smell so great, but when we dress up for a wedding, we put on cologne and perfume to present ourselves more pleasantly to others. It would be strange if we put on fancy clothes to attend a wedding but didn't shower and put on perfume with those nice clothes. Similarly, just putting on perfume when we've been out working in the garden doesn't really do anything to help our appearance!

Clothed Images

Before they rebelled, Adam and Eve, the first humans, were naked and unashamed because they were clothed in God's glory. When they rebelled, they felt their nakedness, and God gave them clothes to hide their shame and give them some dignity.

When the nations around Israel made the images of their gods out of wood and stone and metal, they would cover the images with hammered gold and silver and place gemstones for their eyes, for beauty. And they would put clothes on their gods and burn sweet incense around them. And they would put food in the mouths of the idols, as if the god was eating the food.[5]

But this was all a pathetic parody of what the true God, YHWH, does for his human images. YHWH made living human beings to reflect his image into the world, breathed his breath into our nostrils, and he clothed us with his glory. He doesn't need us to feed him (see Ps 50:11–12 and chapter 4); he feeds and clothes us and gives us eyes for seeing, ears for hearing, and mouths for speaking and eating. When he brought Israel out of Egypt, he didn't just feed them and give them water; he gave them the Egyptians' gold, silver, and fancy textiles and exotic animal skins (Exod 3:22; 11:2; 12:35–36; cf. Ezek 16:10) for the Israelites' enjoyment and so that they could build a beautiful tent for him where they could have fellowship.

5. Walker and Dick, "Induction of the Cult Image."

In Isa 61, clothing signals that in YHWH's new creation, joy and gladness have replaced mourning and shame. The people's sackcloth and ashes, which were a sign of mourning and poverty, are replaced by garments of praise and a crown of glory (61:3). Oil is for the purpose of soothing dry skin in the desert and also for anointing an honored person, like royalty or priests (61:6, "You shall be called the priests"; cf. Ps 133:2). Israel's shame is taken away and replaced with abundance, a double portion of blessing (61:7)—in contrast to 40:2 which states that they had received double punishment for their sins.[6] In 61:10, we have the imagery of a wedding. The prophet-servant-king himself is dressed like a groom on his wedding day, and his bride, the people, is wearing her marvelous jewels for the wedding.

The Proof Is in the Clothing

If you take a quick look through the chapters we've already studied, this image of "clothing, oils, and perfumes" as representing glory has been present throughout. In 57:8-9, Israel is criticized for worshiping other gods; and we have a picture of Israel as an unfaithful wife inviting other lovers to share her fancy bed, her oil, and perfumes—all these beautiful things that YHWH her husband gave her for beauty, enjoyment, and glory—and squandering them with other gods (Isa 57:6-8, 13; cf. Ezek 16:39; 23:26, 29; Hos 2:3, 8-13).

We see some passages that speak about the kinds of clothing that Israel tries to make for themselves, for their own glory. In 59:6, they are like spiders spinning webs, but the webs aren't silk for clothing—they're only good for catching prey. Their schemes don't bring them any glory. In 64:6, it says that all the good deeds they try to do to produce their own glory are as worthless and repulsive as "filthy rags," menstrual cloths (see chapter 13).

But the solution for Israel's plight is also described using clothing imagery. They have to humble themselves not just by fasting and wearing sackcloth and putting ashes on their heads but *actually doing in their lives what those rituals symbolize*—including putting actual clothes on those who are so poor that they have none (58:5-7). And when YHWH himself

---

6. Traditionally in Israelite society, the firstborn son is honored by receiving a double portion of his father's inheritance (Deut 21:17). Hannah, the favored but initially infertile wife of Elkanah, received a "double portion" from her husband out of his sympathy and love (1 Sam 1:4-5). See also Zech 9:12, "I will restore it to you double."

comes to accomplish salvation, as we saw in 59:17 and 63:1–3, he puts on clothing that is appropriate for battle—his armor—and he comes back from battle with his garments stained bright red with the blood of his enemies. Even God has the dirty clothes to show how hard he worked.

Finally, we can marvel at the beautiful clothing that YHWH has prepared for his transformed people. In Isa 60, maybe even more so than 61, we see gold and silver and YHWH adorning his new temple, the place where he lives among his people. YHWH's glory covers his people like a garment, covering their shame and giving them dignity (60:1–3). Ultimately, YHWH's people will *become* his glory, a crown of splendor (62:3).

God Laying Aside His Clothing

God originally wanted his people to reflect his glory into the world as his images. We see a further demonstration when we think about clothing and the life of Jesus, the Prophet-Servant-King that this passage predicts.

As God himself, the Second Person of the Trinity, Jesus was clothed eternally in his own glory. On one occasion, the transfiguration, three of his followers got just a glimpse of this unveiled heavenly glory—and it overwhelmed them! Thus, God the Son set aside this glory for a time. He came into the world as a naked baby, exposed and vulnerable, having to be covered up with strips of cloth—not lying on a fancy couch but in a feeding trough filled with scratchy straw, surrounded by smelly animals. During his earthly life, he didn't dress in a way that would make him look special or different from other working-class people in Judea (cf. Isa 53:2b).

When he took on the vocation of the Suffering Servant and was condemned to die, the Roman soldiers clothed him with a royal purple robe and a crown of thorns to mock him. When they nailed him to the cross, he was naked, fully exposed, fully vulnerable. They divided and cast lots for his clothing as he hung there (John 19:23–25; Ps 22:18). His moment of greatest glory was his moment of greatest shame.[7] But by the power of the Spirit upon him, he was raised from the dead (Rom 1:4) and glorified by his Father (Phil 2:9–11). He shed his bloody burial shroud (Luke 23:52; 24:12) and received a resurrected body and clean clothes.

Having ascended into heaven, he is now about the business of making sure the church, his bride, is clothed in beauty and glory that he himself gives us. After his resurrection, Jesus describes the sending of the

---

7. Hengel, *Crucifixion*, 87.

Holy Spirit as his people being "clothed with glory from on high" (24:49). The Spirit that is upon him clothes us, as well. And as his redeemed people, we are clothed in his righteousness, symbolized in the Scripture by clean clothes (Zech 3:3–5; see chapter 4) and white robes (Rev 3:5, 18). Christ gives us our glory.

JESUS: A TIME FOR COMFORT, A TIME FOR VENGEANCE

When is new creation and all that comes with it—light, sight, liberation, land, glory—going to happen? To understand, we have to return to "comfort" and "vengeance" in Isa 61:2 and see how Jesus interprets this Scripture at the beginning of his ministry (Luke 4:14–30).

When Jesus stands up to read this passage from Isaiah in the synagogue, he begins his interpretation by saying, "Today this Scripture has been fulfilled in your hearing" (Luke 4:21). If we look closely and compare Luke's quotation with the original Isa 61:1–2, we see that Jesus leaves something out. He ends with, "To proclaim the year of the Lord's favor," and leaves out "The day of the vengeance of our God." What is Jesus communicating by this omission? Now, in the first century when Jesus has come to the earth, is the time of amnesty and freedom, the year of the Lord's favor. For those who don't accept this amnesty now, there will be vengeance when he comes again.

From our perspective looking backward, we can comprehend that the Isa 61 prophecy was going to be fulfilled in separate stages even though the prophet might not have understood it. This is how God chose to show prophets the future. In chapter 3, I suggested that it's like seeing a two-dimensional image but not realizing that it has depth and distance. If you look at a painting of mountains, you can see them off in the distance, but it's difficult to tell just how far away they are without perspective—some might be close and others might be really far behind the other ones, but you can't tell. So it is with these visions in Isaiah; what the prophet saw as one day of both comfort and vengeance, God in his sovereign plan had destined for two moments in history: the moment of comfort at Christ's first coming and the moment of judgment at his second coming.

REFLECTIONS

Personally, I'm not very into clothes—sometimes my wife wishes I'd put a little more thought into what I wear. There is a whole area of biblical and ancient studies that focuses on clothing, dress, and textiles and what they signify. There are other angles from which we could study this passage, and clothing is just one of them. Clothing is one powerful symbol of our status before God and before other people—we didn't even go into other "clothing" metaphors in Isaiah, but there are many. Whether we're thinking about "food," "clothing," or the "land," or "names," these are different ways of talking about the redemption that YHWH has accomplished for us and how he is remaking and healing us as his images in the world.

Taking a step back, we have to remember that these prophecies are spoken to people who have already experienced YHWH's glory and his word and the earlier rescues from Egypt and from Babylon; and yet, here they are, as we saw in Isa 56–59, still mired in their sin and rebellion. But God himself, through his Prophet-Servant-King, is determined to reconcile with them, to reconcile with them like a husband who forgives his wife and takes her back, and to clothe them in his glory once again—like having a second wedding ceremony where the bride gets to wear white again (see the discussion of Isa 49, 51–52, and 54 in chapter 3)!

There's one more question to think about: Who gets to be part of this kingdom, this renewed creation where YHWH is king? When Jesus reads this passage in his hometown, some of his Jewish countrymen are excited and hopeful, but that quickly turns to indignation and anger because of unbelief. Jesus says to them that he expects them to have hardened hearts because even in ancient times, foreigners from outside Israel were often more receptive to the message of YHWH's kingship. The Jews are so angry that they try to kill him then and there, but he escapes and continues his mission (Luke 4:14–30).

Ultimately, he goes to the cross to die for Jews and gentiles together, to cover over the sin and shame of people from every race and tongue and language. At the cross, he is lifted up before the Jews and the Romans, and the Roman centurion says, "Truly this man was the Son of God!" (Mark 15:39). At the close of Isa 61 we read, "For as the earth brings forth its sprouts, and as a garden causes what is sown in it to sprout up, so the Lord [YHWH] will cause righteousness and praise to sprout up before all the nations" (61:11). The purpose of YHWH redeeming his people and reestablishing them in the land is that his praise would sprout and spring up among all nations and that righteousness as well would spread.

For those of us who have trusted in this God, who have believed in Jesus and received the Holy Spirit, these promises are for our benefit, too! With these promised "robes of righteousness" comes a vocation for us. God clothes us in Christ's righteousness not just so we can stay separate and unstained by the world but so that we can go humbly but confidently into the world to follow where our Savior has led us. He proclaimed liberty to captives, recovery of sight to the blind, and release to those in darkness. Just as he proclaimed this good news, so he also sent his disciples—and all their disciples after them. He has sent *us* into the world to proclaim good news: that YHWH is king, and this is the time of his favor before he comes again. If the Holy Spirit is upon and within us, then we must proclaim his kingdom to all.

A Prayer

Father, we confess that from ourselves, we have only shame to offer you, only sackcloth and ashes, only disgrace that is well-deserved. But we thank you that you have clothed us in the righteousness of your Son, Jesus, and filled us with your Spirit that is upon him. It's through your work that the eyes of the blind are opened, and captives are set free. And we pray that you would give us boldness to live in this amnesty and proclaim this good news to those in our lives who desperately need to hear it. In Jesus's name we pray. Amen.

12

A New Name That the Mouth of YHWH Will Bestow (Isa 62)

Names are important for our self-understanding and for our relationships with other people. Since our parents "made" each of us and start out with authority over us, they give us our names. Sometimes people shorten our names or give us nicknames, which we might like because it shows a familiarity, or we might not like it because it presumes a familiarity that isn't there. My brother, Michael, really does not like to be called "Mike," so if I hear someone call him "Mike," it tells me that they don't know him as well as they presume that they do! Sometimes nicknames have a story behind them—for my kids' youth pastor and his students, it's a big deal when someone is bestowed a nickname for use within the group.

When we looked at Isa 61, we started to ask: What does it look like when the good news is coming true that YHWH's kingship is being re-established in Israel and beyond? In this chapter, we'll look at two themes: the blessings of the land and the city; and names and "being called" by a name or a title—that is, being given a new identity. In order to fully understand what is being promised here in Isa 60 and 62, we'll have to range a little further beyond these chapters. As we keep seeing in the New Testament, Jesus himself gives us the key to understanding how these prophecies are fulfilled and how they're relevant for us.

SCRIPTURE: ISAIAH 62:1–12

1 For Zion's sake I will not keep silent,
and for Jerusalem's sake I will not be quiet,
until her righteousness goes forth as brightness,
and her salvation as a burning torch.
2 The nations shall see your righteousness,
and all the kings your glory,
and you shall be called by a new name
that the mouth of the LORD will give.
3 You shall be a crown of beauty in the hand of the LORD,
and a royal diadem in the hand of your God.
4 You shall no more be termed Forsaken,
and your land shall no more be termed Desolate,
but you shall be called My Delight Is in Her,
and your land Married;
for the LORD delights in you,
and your land shall be married.
5 For as a young man marries a young woman,
  so shall your sons marry you,
and as the bridegroom rejoices over the bride,
so shall your God rejoice over you.
6 On your walls, O Jerusalem,
I have set watchmen;
all the day and all the night
they shall never be silent.
You who put the LORD in remembrance,
take no rest,
7 and give him no rest
until he establishes Jerusalem
and makes it a praise in the earth.
8 The LORD has sworn by his right hand
and by his mighty arm:
"I will not again give your grain
to be food for your enemies,
and foreigners shall not drink your wine
for which you have labored;
9 but those who garner it shall eat it
and praise the LORD,
and those who gather it shall drink it
in the courts of my sanctuary."
10 Go through, go through the gates;
prepare the way for the people;

build up, build up the highway;
clear it of stones;
lift up a signal over the peoples.
11 Behold, the LORD has proclaimed
to the end of the earth:
Say to the daughter of Zion,
"Behold, your salvation comes;
behold, his reward is with him,
and his recompense before him."
12 And they shall be called The Holy People,
The Redeemed of the LORD;
and you shall be called Sought Out,
A City Not Forsaken. (Isa 62:1–12)

HYPERLINKS AND RENEWED THEMES

In chapter 62, there are quite a few allusions to earlier chapters of Isaiah: the sadness of Zion as a desolate mother in chapter 49 and "build up, build up, prepare the way" found in 40:3 and 57:14. We read in 11:10 that the Messiah from the line of David will "stand as a signal for the peoples" (a line we just heard in chapter 62). All the way back in chapter 1 verse 26, we find this hopeful promise that God gave Jerusalem, "You shall be called the city of righteousness, the faithful city," which sounds a bit like what we've just read.

As we hear these passages of hope and promise, it makes sense that God would describe what he's going to do using language that is familiar and that builds upon the images and concepts they've already seen in Isaiah. I hope that by now you're thinking of the Bible as a hyperlinked text with connections and shared language all over it.

BLESSINGS OF THE LAND AND THE CITY

In Isa 62, we see the blessing of *land* and the protection of a *city* being restored to the people. But how did they lose these blessings in the first place?

Back in Genesis when God first created human beings in his image, he placed them in a special garden that was for them but also said, "Be fruitful and multiply, and fill the earth and subdue [cultivate] it" (Gen 1:28). They were tasked to take full possession of God's inheritance and to make it beautiful and productive—flourishing is a great word to describe this. This task was not a punishment: it was assigned to them before they rebelled. Their subsequent rebellion made this job much more difficult. But God had a plan for redemption.

As a first step in this plan, God called Abraham and declared that his descendants would eventually be given the land of Canaan. This promise came to a moment of partial fulfillment in the time of Moses when YHWH offered Israel this land, but with important conditions. He says that the land of Canaan was defiled by the Canaanites' awful practices—worshiping other gods, human sacrifice, and other abominations—so the land was now vomiting out those people (Lev 18:25, 28; 20:22). But if the Israelites turned to those rebellious practices, then the land would vomit *them* out as well. If they obeyed YHWH's laws, the land would be fruitful (Deut 7:12–16; 28:1–14); but if they rebelled, all their cities and towns and fields would be under a curse, and they would work and never gain anything (Deut 28:15–68). The sky over their heads would be like bronze and the ground beneath them would become as hard as iron (Deut 28:23).[1] We know from the story of Israel and Judah in the Old Testament that these warnings weren't heeded, and these punishments came upon the people—their land spewed them out.

What becomes of these "land" prophecies in the New Testament? What we find consistently is that the promise to make Israel a special people that would live with YHWH and possess this strip of land in Canaan is fulfilled with a much broader scope.

In Rom 4:13, Paul is talking about Abraham and the promise that his descendants would be numerous and be blessed, and he makes this subtle shift—he refers to, "the promise to Abraham and his offspring [*sperma*] that he would be heir of the world [*kosmos*]." In Hebrew, there is ambiguity in the promise found in Genesis: God promised Abraham that he would give "this land" (e.g., Gen 15:7)—meaning the land of Canaan—but the word for "land" can also sometimes mean "the earth." Paul, under the inspiration of the Holy Spirit, interprets this as "the world"—there are different words in Greek that Paul could have chosen.[2] The eventual fulfillment of the promise that Abraham believed by faith was *not* that his physical descendants would possess a strip of land in the Middle East but that *one* descendant—Jesus the Messiah—would inherit the whole world

---

1. In Lev 26:19, the image is reversed: the sky will become iron and the earth bronze!
2. For example, instead of *kosmos*, he could have followed the Septuagint of Gen 15:7 and used *gē*, "earth."

and that anyone who has the faith that Abraham had will share in that inheritance!³

This is why Christians who place their focus on the politics of the Middle East and the modern State of Israel, the Jewish people, and various end-times charts and speculation are misguided. I am quite familiar with their arguments as I grew up with Jewish heritage in Messianic Jewish circles hearing these sorts of things in the Messianic congregations and conferences I attended.⁴ In John 4 when Jesus was talking to the Samaritan woman at the well, she asks him about the controversy of whether Mount Gerizim or Jerusalem is the correct place to worship God, and Jesus says that soon it's not going to matter at all—but the true worshipers will worship the Father in the Spirit and in truth (John 4:19–24). In Eph 2, the place where God dwells is among his people, the church—Jews and gentiles together. And in Rev 21–22, the new Jerusalem comes down from heaven to fill the earth, so whether Jews or Arabs or anyone else possesses the earthly "Jerusalem" at that point isn't going to matter at all.

So this means at least two things related to the land in Isa 62. First, in 62:8–9, we see this beautiful promise: YHWH swears that the people of Zion will themselves get to enjoy the fruit of their own fields and their own vineyards, that he'll protect them from enemies stealing their harvest. They will get to cultivate and enjoy what YHWH has given them just as Adam and Eve were supposed to do in the garden of Eden!

Second, we see this command in 62:10, "Raise a banner for the nations!" The nations stream to Jerusalem (cf. 2:2–4): a picture of people from every nation and tribe and tongue coming to be part of the community who believes in Jesus, YHWH's Anointed. The "city of God" is not presently a single city but rather the place where YHWH dwells—the church and, eventually, the new Jerusalem. What YHWH promises in Isaiah to do for Israel and Jerusalem, he does for us! The land is for us, and its fruit is for us as well—all given to us by God himself.

---

3. In Gal 3:15–18, Paul "clarifies" that the promise refers to Jesus based on the singular use of "seed/offspring" rather than "seeds," plural, which would be the people of Israel.

4. "Messianic Jew" describes someone of Jewish ethnicity or heritage who believes that Jesus is the Messiah (the Christ). Their beliefs are fundamentally Christian, but Messianic Jews often choose to worship in "culturally Jewish" ways and use less overtly-Christian language in their worship. Some Messianic Jews continue to follow Jewish liturgy and festivals and even keep kosher homes. See Willitts and Rudolph, *Messianic Judaism*.

WHAT'S IN A (NEW) NAME

The blessings for Zion are accompanied by new names—or maybe epithets, designations, or nicknames would be better terms. Many times in this chapter, we see something like, "You will be called" or even, as in 60:18, "Your walls and your gates will be called." This phrasing is not uncommon throughout Isaiah: cities and peoples and even individuals like the anointed Messiah get titles or designations/nicknames like this.[5] Why is this important? What's the difference between saying "You will be a holy people" and "You will be *called* 'A Holy People'"?

As I pointed out at the start of the chapter, names and nicknames are important signifiers of identity, relationship, and degrees of intimacy. In the Bible, naming is a sign of authority, and sometimes people receive new names at turning points in their lives. As a positive sign of his authority and his relationship with them, YHWH renames Abraham and Sarah (Gen 17:5, 15) and Jacob (Gen 32:27–28; 35:10). In the New Testament, Jesus gives Simon the new name "Peter" (Matt 16:18), and Joseph receives the nickname "Barnabas" (Acts 4:36).[6] By contrast, we see the mistake of the people at the tower of Babylon who tried to "make a name for [them]selves" (Gen 11:4). They wanted to be self-defining in a way that only YHWH can be; they wanted throw off his authority. In a more coercive way, Daniel and his three friends are renamed by their Babylonian captors: changing their names that make reference to the God of Israel into names that reference Babylonian gods (e.g., Azariah, "YHWH Helps," becomes Abednego, probably "Servant of Nabu").[7] The inverse of this is also the experience of some Christian converts who change their given names that contain names of pagan gods.[8]

These are all *downward* designations in that they come from an authority to someone *under* their authority. But names, titles, and epithets

---

5. Isa 1:26; 9:6; 19:18; 30:7; 47:1, 5; 56:5; 58:12; 60:18; 61:3, 6; 62:2–4, 12.

6. Contrary to popular belief, there is no evidence that Saul received an entirely new name upon his conversion (Acts 9). However, it is possible that he switched (Acts 13:9) to using his Roman name, "Paul," rather than his Jewish name to signal his call as an apostle to the gentiles. Thus, the switch would still indicate a turning point in Luke's account of Paul's life.

7. "Theophoric" is the term for a name that carries within it the name of a deity.

8. Adeboye (*Can a Christian Be Cursed*, 95–97) describes the practice of African Christians changing names/surnames that honour or refer to gods or occultism (e.g., the Yoruba names Ogungbemi, "god of iron protects me," and Awokoya, "occultism has relieved me of suffering") to more neutral or "Christian" names and the claims that subsequently negative trends/patterns in those individuals' lives were reversed.

can also function *upwardly*, signifying dignity and honor, and relationship and intimacy. I've experienced this a few times as new relationships and statuses in my life warranted new "titles" or names. I obviously became a father when my son was first born—but there was something special about the first time he called me "Dad." When I started serving as an ordained pastor in a church, being called "Pastor Benj" took some getting used to.

It's nice for a human leader or authority to receive this affirmation, but does our divine Authority want to receive titles and names? Yes, he does; in the Bible, YHWH sometimes allows humans to give him titles and epithets. He allowed the patriarchs to call him ’ēl šadday ("God of Mountains"; Gen 17:1; 35:11; 48:3), ’ēl ‘elyôn ("God Most High"; Gen 14:18–22), and ’ēl ‘ôlom ("God of Eternity"; Gen 21:33).[9] Hagar, the victimized Egyptian slave of Sarah, was the first person in the Bible to call God by a new name[10]—he allowed her to call him ’ēl rŏ’î, "The God Who Sees Me." Even when he revealed his special name, "YHWH," to Moses (Exod 6:2–8), he also gives some humans the privilege of adding honors to his name: "YHWH Who Heals You" (Exod 15:26), "YHWH Is My Banner" (Exod 17:15), "YHWH Who Provides" (Gen 22:14). YHWH doesn't do this because he needs the affirmation—rather, he wants humans to feel close to him.

In the New Testament, names are also important, starting with the "name of Jesus," which Phil 2:5–11 tells us is exalted over every other name (cf. Heb 1:4; Eph 1:21). In Eph 3:15, Paul says that Jesus's name is the name from which all other names receive their honor or worth because he is both the Creator and the Savior of a new human family that includes every tribe and tongue and nation. In Rev 3:12, we read that the name of God, the name of God's city, and the new name of Jesus will be written (in permanent marker!) on all those who belong to Jesus.[11] There is even a special name of Jesus that no one knows except himself; it's a part of his divine identity that is hidden from us as created beings because we can't fully comprehend him (Rev 19:12–13). As people who

---

9. If we take Exod 6:2–8 at face value, then all of the uses of "the LORD"/ "YHWH" in Gen 12–50 by the characters are anachronistic. I explore the significance of this fact in Giffone, *Storymaking*, 120–48.

10. Pointed out by Trible, *Texts of Terror*, 18, 28.

11. In the heavenly city (Rev 21:12, 24), the names of the twelve tribes are written on the gates, and the names of the twelve apostles are written on the foundation stones of the city. This likely represents all God's people, old and new covenant.

belong to Jesus, Christians receive a new name (Rev 2:17), and our names are written in the book of life (Rev 3:5; 20:15; etc.).[12]

Coming back around to the "new names" in Isa 62, we get a sense of their significance in the prophecy, and we understand that the names are a promise for us, as well. In 62:1, the prophet uses both of Jerusalem's traditional names—Zion and Jerusalem—but then in 62:2-3, he says that the city will receive a new name from YHWH. Zion had been rebellious and had engaged in spiritual adultery and had brought shame upon YHWH her God, her king, her husband. But the new name signifies a fresh start—new creation—so that she will be a shiny crown for YHWH to wear and be proud of and for the nations to see and marvel at.

Zion's new names in 62:4 are not attributes that she has in herself, but they describe her relationship to YHWH. The old names "Forsaken" (also in 62:12) and "Desolate" are descriptions of Zion back in Isa 49 (vv. 8, 14, 19); she certainly had reason to think that YHWH her husband had abandoned her. But now she gets to be called not just $be^{\,\prime}\hat{u}l\hat{a}$, "Married Woman," but $hep\d{s}\hat{\imath}$-$\d{b}ah$, which means "My Delight Is in Her." What beautiful names for a wife—YHWH delights in his people! He doesn't just want us to fall in line, keep the rules, and not cause trouble because he's almost at the end of his patience with us. He really enjoys fellowship with us and wants that to be the normal relationship between himself and each of us—a relationship of "delight." And we already saw the significance of this word "delight" back in Isa 58 when YHWH said that the people's fasting and Sabbath-keeping should reflect *their delight* in spending time with him and caring about the things he cares about (such as justice). To reflect that "delight" and that joy that he wants his people to have in him, YHWH also gives them some new epithets or titles that they can call him: "Your God," "Your Savior." (When we get to Isa 63, we'll see that YHWH has even another title he wants his people to call him: "Our Father.")

THE TRIUNE GOD IS THE SOLE ACTOR

A third point applies not just to Isa 62 but also to this central section that promises the redemption of God's people and the new creation that he will accomplish by his Spirit (Isa 60–62).

---

12. Contrast these examples with the "name of the beast" written on people (Rev 13) and the name of the whore of Babylon (Rev 17).

These new names that YHWH declares for Zion are pronounced over them at a time when they are certainly not living up to them in practice. "A Holy People" and "Highly Sought-After" (62:12) do *not* reflect the reality of the Persian-period community in Yehud.

By pronouncing these epithets, God in his grace is committing to redemption, to a process that will cause them to "live into" or "live up to" these names. God in his triune nature is at work in accomplishing this process.

Isaiah 62 seems to be a continuation of the speech begun in Isa 61, which is in the mouth of the Prophet-Servant-King figure. In the last chapter, we recognized that this figure is fulfilled in Jesus Christ. He says that he will continually advocate for Zion (62:1)—he's not going to shut up, not going to stop speaking on her behalf. For how long? The ESV says, "Until her righteousness goes forth." Another way of translating "righteousness" is *vindication*: it will be publicly recognized that Zion is *in the right*.

But how can we say that Zion is "in the right" when she's mostly been "in the wrong," a rebellious people? There's a paradox here that also applies to each of us personally who have trusted in Christ. Having been incorporated into Christ by faith, Christ's righteousness is accounted to us, so we are considered righteous before God the Father even though we are still sinners.[13] Then the power of the Holy Spirit works throughout our lives to make us more Christlike (Rom 8) so that in the final reckoning, we in fact will be righteous before God. Back to Zion: the prophet speaks up for Zion both because she *belongs* to YHWH and because Zion is going to be *made into* the righteous city that God intends for her to be. We see him in 62:7 telling the people to join him in *pestering* God the Father, "To give him no rest" until he makes Zion into what she's supposed to be. The prophet—none other than Jesus himself—protects Zion; Isaiah 62:6 says he appoints watchmen on her walls. And this is exactly what we see in the New Testament that Jesus does for his people: he sits at the right hand of the Father and advocates for his people (Rom 8:34; Heb 1:3, 13; 8:1; 10:12; 12:2; 1 John 2:1–2).

And all of this is accomplished by the power of the Holy Spirit who is sent from God the Father and is "upon" the Prophet-Servant-King as we saw in 61:1. God is the actor—in his three persons, the Trinity acts as one to accomplish salvation (cf. Eph 1:3–14).

---

13. As Martin Luther put it: *simul iustus et peccator* ("at the same time, righteous and sinner"). George, *Theology of the Reformers*, 72.

REFLECTIONS

Deep Truths

First of all, God himself is the actor throughout this section—he justifies the unjustifiable. And then, he sanctifies (makes holy) and glorifies his people. These are the steps that God takes on our behalf, powerfully and lovingly doing for us what we cannot do for ourselves.

Second, we just marvel at these poignant pictures of the blessings that YHWH lavishes upon his people. In previous chapters, we talked about the blessings of liberation and justice; clothing and glory; light; and comfort and favor while vengeance is postponed. In this chapter, we see the land and city restored for the protection and flourishing of people, and we see the blessing of names/epithets for dignity, honor, and intimacy!

Despite all the history between YHWH and Israel, despite all the water under the bridge, despite the hurt, he wants to be with them, wants to be identified with them as their God and they his people, and he wants to *delight* in them! And this is true for us as well: however long you've walked with God, whether you've walked away from God at times, he stands ready and willing to forgive you, to call you his son or daughter, and to be called "My God," "My Savior," "My Father," by *you*!

Our Response

How do we respond in faith and obedience to a passage like this? We notice that there aren't really too many "commands" or instructions in a section like this, and that is by design, I believe. Some passages are just meant to be truths that we let wash over us and transform us and that let us rest in them. But there are some responses that I think we should have.

Reading such a passage presents a great opportunity for us to confess our sins and turn to YHWH as we are told to do in Isa 56–59. Starting in the next chapter, we will look at a long prayer of confession (63:7–64:12), and then YHWH himself gives one long response that is Isa 65–66.

After confession, another task is to follow the example of the prophet: to pester God to do *in* and *through* us the things that he's promised! Remember 62:7? It says, "Give him no rest until he . . . makes [Jerusalem] the praise of the earth." This is not us *demanding* something that we deserve, but we eagerly *want* and *need* for God to keep the promises he voluntarily made (a prominent theme in Isa 63:7—64:12).

Finally, we can do what it says in 62:10: "Raise a banner for the nations." We should be inviting others to experience this joy, proclaiming the good news! As we round out the examination of the theme of names, we note that there's a twist coming up in a few chapters: YHWH says that his faithful servants from outside ethnic Israel "will be called by another name" (65:15). The purpose of having a special people, Israel, was always that YHWH would shine the light of his face upon people of every nation, tribe, and tongue. Let's declare that message with our words, our attitudes, and our deeds.

A Prayer

Lord, we praise you for your many blessings. We thank you that, despite all that we've done, you still wish to place your holy name upon us, and you still want us to call you the names and titles that you deserve. Let us delight in you as you delight in us. And let this forgiveness, this dignity, this joy that you've given us be so evident to those around us that they will ask us about the hope that we have. In Jesus's name we pray. Amen.

13

No One Strives to Take Hold of You (Isa 63:7—64:12)

For quite a long time, one of my favorite passages in the Bible has been the penitential prayer found in Isa 63:7—64:12.[1] It is a deeply emotional prayer for forgiveness and for God to act on behalf of his people to save them. It is also one of the places in the Old Testament that speaks of God as "Father" of his people—many Christians are under the mistaken impression that Jesus is the first to mention the possibility of praying to God as "Our Father" (Matt 6:9).

This prayer is a great model for us today. It is easy to fall into a rut in our prayers—we tend to ask God for things, and we thank him when he answers our previous prayers. There is nothing wrong with either of those elements. But prayer should also remind us of who God is, what he has done, and what he wants to change in our lives—not just what we want. That's why it is good for us to pray *from the Bible* the prayers that God has given us, especially the Psalms but also from the Prophets and the prayers we find recorded in the New Testament.

Isaiah 63:7—64:12 is a great example because the faithful prophet who articulates the prayer knows what his people need: they need God to change their hearts, and they need God to be near to them. The prayer is passionate and thoughtful, and it is based on God's promises to his people in ages past. It's also instructive and inspiring for us to think about

1. Isa 63:1–6 is covered in chapter 9 due to its parallels to Isa 59:15b–19.

how God answered this prayer, including in ways that his people "did not look for" (64:3).

Thus, the prayer is also good for congregations like those that I described back in chapter 4. As we look back on the history of what God has done through declining local congregations in past decades (even past centuries, for some), we long for those halcyon days and wish we had just a taste of those blessings that we used to enjoy. But as we pray to God for renewal, we have to desire not just the way that YHWH was with us "in the good old days" but to ask for his presence in whatever form that is best for us *right now* according to his wisdom, even in ways that might surprise us.

(This chapter [and the next two] incorporate some insights from an article that I wrote along with a former student of mine. In one of my courses on Isaiah, she wrote about some echoes of Isa 64 in the New Testament, and I thought it was worthy of further exploration; so, we ended up expanding the study to include Isa 63–66 and Mark's use of this language and themes in Mark 5.[2])

SCRIPTURE: ISAIAH 63:7—64:12

> 7 I will recount the steadfast love of the LORD,
> the praises of the LORD,
> according to all that the LORD has granted us,
> and the great goodness to the house of Israel
> that he has granted them according to his compassion,
> according to the abundance of his steadfast love.
> 8 For he said, "Surely they are my people,
> children who will not deal falsely."
> And he became their Savior.
> 9 In all their affliction he was afflicted,
> and the angel of his presence saved them;
> in his love and in his pity he redeemed them;
> he lifted them up and carried them all the days of old.
> 10 But they rebelled
> and grieved his Holy Spirit;
> therefore he turned to be their enemy,
> and himself fought against them.
> 11 Then he remembered the days of old,
> of Moses and his people.

---

2. Giffone and Wile, "Mark 5's Echoes."

Where is he who brought them up out of the sea
with the shepherds of his flock?
Where is he who put in the midst of them
his Holy Spirit,
12 who caused his glorious arm
to go at the right hand of Moses,
who divided the waters before them
to make for himself an everlasting name,
13 who led them through the depths?
Like a horse in the desert,
they did not stumble.
14 Like livestock that go down into the valley,
the Spirit of the LORD gave them rest.
So you led your people,
to make for yourself a glorious name.
15 Look down from heaven and see,
from your holy and beautiful habitation.
Where are your zeal and your might?
The stirring of your inner parts and your compassion
are held back from me.
16 For you are our Father,
though Abraham does not know us,
and Israel does not acknowledge us;
you, O LORD, are our Father,
our Redeemer from of old is your name.
17 O LORD, why do you make us wander from your ways
and harden our heart, so that we fear you not?
Return for the sake of your servants,
the tribes of your heritage.
18 Your holy people held possession for a little while;
our adversaries have trampled down your sanctuary.
19 We have become like those over whom you have never ruled,
like those who are not called by your name.
1 Oh that you would rend the heavens and come down,
that the mountains might quake at your presence—
2 as when fire kindles brushwood
and the fire causes water to boil—
to make your name known to your adversaries,
and that the nations might tremble at your presence!
3 When you did awesome things that we did not look for,
you came down, the mountains quaked at your presence.
4 From of old no one has heard
or perceived by the ear,
no eye has seen a God besides you,

who acts for those who wait for him.
5 You meet him who joyfully works righteousness,
those who remember you in your ways.
Behold, you were angry, and we sinned;
in our sins we have been a long time, and shall we be saved?
6 We have all become like one who is unclean,
and all our righteous deeds are like a polluted garment.
We all fade like a leaf,
and our iniquities, like the wind, take us away.
7 There is no one who calls upon your name,
who rouses himself to take hold of you;
for you have hidden your face from us,
and have made us melt in the hand of our iniquities.
8 But now, O LORD, you are our Father;
we are the clay, and you are our potter;
we are all the work of your hand.
9 Be not so terribly angry, O LORD,
and remember not iniquity forever.
Behold, please look, we are all your people.
10 Your holy cities have become a wilderness;
Zion has become a wilderness,
Jerusalem a desolation.
11 Our holy and beautiful house,
where our fathers praised you,
has been burned by fire,
and all our pleasant places have become ruins.
12 Will you restrain yourself at these things, O LORD?
Will you keep silent, and afflict us so terribly?
(Isa 63:7—64:12)[3]

THE HUMANS PRESENT THEIR CLOSING STATEMENT

The prayer in Isa 63:7—64:12 is the final prayer in the book: the final words spoken by humans to God. In Isa 65–66, we find God's response.

---

3. In the numbering of verses used in most editions of the Hebrew Bible, the verse that is numbered 64:1 in English versions is numbered as the second part of 63:19. This means that the Hebrew 64:1 is the English 64:2, etc., all the way up to the Hebrew 64:11, which corresponds to the English 64:12. Readers who are consulting a Hebrew Bible or a more technical commentary will notice the discrepancy. The contents of the verses are the same—only the numbering is different. In this book, I use the English numbering for verses and chapters.

These two sections sum up much of what we've seen in the book of Isaiah to this point.

Isaiah 63:7—64:12 belongs to the genre of *penitential prayer*. There are several examples of penitential prayers in the Old Testament including Ezra 9, Neh 1 and 9, Dan 9, and Ps 106. This is typically a prayer of confession prayed by a faithful individual or small representative group asking for forgiveness on behalf of a largely unfaithful people.

Mark Boda has helpfully described some of the common features of these prayers.[4] A penitential prayer is characterized by distress over sin and its consequences for the community, expressed with deep emotion. The prayer expresses a theological credo: the greatness and graciousness of YHWH. The prayer appeals to divine promises in requesting that YHWH "modify his disposition" (i.e., change his attitude) toward them. Sometimes the prayer mentions specific provisions in the Law that the community has broken and for which they deserve the punishment they've gotten. But the Law, especially its stories of YHWH's choosing his people and showing mercy to them, is also appealed to as path for covenant renewal in the strong hope that the community will be restored if they keep the Law.

In such prayers, the person praying the prayer is typically a righteous or faithful individual but counts himself/herself as part of the sinful group. Being the only person (or one of few) who cares about faithfulness to God and seeking to have a restored relationship to God can be lonely. In Isa 63:7—64:12, the prophet begins by saying, "I will recount the steadfast love of the LORD." But subsequently, he doesn't usually say "I" or "me"—it's almost always "we," "us." He says in 64:7, "No one calls on your name or strives to take hold of you," but of course *he*, the prophet, is faithful to call on God's name. But the only other time he speaks about himself is 63:15: "The stirring of your inner parts and your compassion are held back from *me*" (emphasis mine).[5] The point is that the prophet feels alone and isolated among his people; and he feels distant from God—because of his own sinfulness, but mainly because his people as a whole have rejected their God.

---

4. Boda, "Priceless Gain," 82–85.

5. The MT (Hebrew) says, "From me"; some translations, such as the NIV, follow the LXX (Greek) version, "From us."

Declaration of Dependence

The prayer repeatedly acknowledges God's authority and power. The prophet recalls the exodus from Egypt (63:10-12, 17). This is *the* spectacular, unique event that makes Israel special! In Deut 4:32-35, Moses marvels at what YHWH did for Israel: When has this ever happened before?! When has a people heard a god speaking to them from the midst of the fire and survived? When has a single god ever gone to rescue a people, for himself, from being enslaved by another people and another set of gods, with signs and wonders?!

Of course, modern nation-states consist of "the people" establishing themselves—this is what it means to live in a democracy. In the United States, we celebrate the ratification of The Declaration of Independence on July 4. When my family lived in Lithuania, we celebrated with the Lithuanians several holidays that marked the declaration or the reestablishment of statehood in the medieval period and in the modern era. Lithuania celebrates Statehood Day, July 6, when King Mindaugas was crowned in 1253. Then, after being under the Swedish and Russian empires, the day of Restoration of the State of Lithuania (February 16, 1918) was when Lithuania declared, "We are an independent people; we, not some overlords, will determine the laws and direction of our own nation." Then, after decades of Soviet occupation, March 11, 1990 is when they legally declared independence from the Soviet Union.

The rescue from Egypt is when YHWH declared to Israel, "You are *my* people, free to serve me and be close to me!" So YHWH declares his people's identity by saving them—they don't get to define themselves!

There's another statement of God's authority, which is the acknowledgment that YHWH is the potter, and they are the clay (64:8-9). This image connects Israel with the rest of humanity and shows God's authority over all people. The book of Isaiah has other examples of people who think that they are in control of their own lives when, really, God is in control. In Isa 10:15, we find the image of an ax (the king of Assyria) who thinks to itself, "*I* am the one responsible for cutting down trees!" when in reality it is the person *swinging* the ax (YHWH) that is in control. In Isa 29:16, the prophet criticizes the leaders of Israel who think that they can talk back to God: "Shall the potter be regarded as the clay, that the thing made should say of its maker, 'He did not make me'; or the thing formed say of him who formed it, 'He has no understanding'?" (29:16).

A third acknowledgment of God's authority and power is when the prophet says: "You are our Father!" (63:16; 64:8). The Father has the authority to direct his people and guide them, but they have resisted this. We will come back to this image of "Father."

Back in Our Sins

The prayer openly admits people's guilt. It talks about their past sins when they were struggling with God in the wilderness (63:10). And yet, God forgave them and brought them into the land at that time.

But now, they have fallen into a state of rebellion and hopelessness again. Part of this seems like the people's fault; their choices to abandon God and his ways (64:5–7): "No one . . . rouses himself to take hold of you." But part of this also is blamed on YHWH: "Why do you make us wander from your ways and harden our heart?" (63:17). Is God to blame, or are we to blame?

In the story of the exodus, we read in some places that Pharaoh hardened his own heart (Exod 8:15, 32; 9:34) to disobey YHWH and, in other places, that *YHWH* hardened Pharaoh's heart (Exod 4:21; 7:3; 9:12; 10:20, 27; 11:10; 14:4, 8). Both can be true simultaneously. Once we choose not to follow God, we become hardened in our hearts, and God simply lets us continue down that path. As Lewis puts it in *The Great Divorce*: "There are only two kinds of people in the end: those who say to God, 'Thy will be done,' and those to whom God says, 'Thy will be done.'"[6] And we reap the consequences.

And even those who try to repent and turn back to God find ourselves unable to please him. Isaiah 64:6 says that our righteous deeds are like "a polluted garment" (See "Clothing and Glory" in chapter 11); apart from God's forgiveness, our best attempts to please him are no good at all.

Won't You Come Back and Do Something?!

The third theme is that the prophet pleads with God that he would return and act! In Isa 63:11 and 15, he asks, "Where are you," and "Where is your zeal and your might?" In 63:15, he says, "Look down!" In 64:1, he says, "Come down and make your presence felt!" In contrast to Isa 49 and 62,

---

6. Lewis, *Signature Classics*, 506; emphasis in the original.

the prophet asks repeatedly in 63:15 and 64:9 and 12: You haven't forgotten us forever, have you?

And then we find this moving appeal to God's loyalty and love when the prophet says, "You are our Father!" (63:16). Many of us know what it is like to be alienated from or separated from our human fathers: the pain of knowing that this other person is responsible for your existence but has not loved you as he should, or you have not loved him—or both. Yet there is always a connection that cannot be severed, and that is what the prophet is appealing to; even though the people of Israel have become so bad that their ancestors Abraham or Jacob would disown them if they saw them today, YHWH is their Father who still loves them. At least, that is what the prophet is banking on!

YHWH'S ANSWER TO ISRAEL'S PROPHET

How does God answer the prophet's prayer? There are really two ways: his words in Isa 65–66 and in the gospel story.

If the prophet prays to God, "Why are you so distant? Why aren't you reaching out to us?" Isa 65 has God's answer: I *did* reach out to you, many times, but you did not answer! That is the subject of the next two chapters in this book.

But the gospel story provides God's ultimate answer to this prayer. In the New Testament, we see that, in Jesus, the God of Israel has in fact come back to his people. If we turn to the beginning of the Gospel of Mark, we see Jesus being baptized by John. In Mark 1:10, it says that the "heavens were torn open," and the Holy Spirit descended on Jesus. Matthew and Luke, who are likely using Mark's Gospel as a source for theirs, use the more neutral word *anoigō*, the heavens were "opened" (Matt 3:16; Luke 3:21). Mark uses the word *schizō*, "torn"—probably an intentional echo of Isa 64:1, the prophet asking YHWH to "tear open the heavens and come down."[7] And we hear the Father's words to Jesus: "You are my beloved Son." In this scene in Mark, we have the Father, the Son, and the Holy Spirit returning to Israel at last just as the prophet asked many centuries earlier. The "good news" mentioned in Mark 1:1 and 15 is the message of Isa 52:7 and 61:1; Zion's God is once again asserting his kingship.

As we read through the book of Mark, we find that not all of the Jewish people are receptive to YHWH's return. There are some who hold

---

7. Hays, *Gospels*, 17–18; Watts, *Isaiah's New Exodus*, 102–8, 176n203.

fast to YHWH (cf. Isa 56:4, 6; 64:7); they come to Jesus and follow him in faith. I want to explain one example of how this links up with Isaiah, explaining some parallels to Mark 5 that are outlined in the study mentioned previously.[8]

In Mark 5:25–34, we read a story of a woman who comes to Jesus in search of healing. She has had a medical condition called *menorrhagia*, constant or irregular menstrual bleeding, for twelve years. In addition to feeling weak and anemic all the time, she would be considered ritually impure according to the Mosaic law (Lev 15:19–30). She's unable to marry, unable to worship at the temple, and unable to have regular contact with her friends and family members.

One thing I didn't explain in the previous section is that the "polluted garment" mentioned in Isa 64:6 is actually the Hebrew word for "menstrual cloth"—not just repulsive but ritually impure as well. (In the next chapter, we'll explore more closely how ritual impurity works in the Old Testament.) Now the parallel between this Isaiah prayer and the woman's situation becomes more apparent. Despite her condition, she believes so strongly in Jesus's power that she says to herself, "If I can even just touch his garments, I'll be saved!" (Mark 5:28; cf. Isa 64:5). So she hides her face for fear of being recognized and then forces herself into the crowd that is pressing around Jesus. She "strives to take hold of him" even though his "face is hidden from her" (cf. Isa 64:7). When she touches Jesus, instead of ritual impurity transferring from her body to his—as would be expected—purity, healing, and new life flow from Jesus's body into hers.

Jesus feels power go out of him, and he says to those around him, "Who touched me?" After some confusion, the woman comes trembling before him (an echo of Isa 66:2, 5) and tells what she did and how she was healed. And even as the prophet in Isa 63 says, "You are our Father" (63:16), Jesus says to this woman, "Daughter, your faith has saved you"—she is the only person in the Gospels that Jesus calls "Daughter."

In our article, Sage and I argued that Mark is shaping this story to communicate that Jesus's actions constitute God's response to the prayer in Isa 63 and 64. We identified other echoes of this conclusion to Isaiah that can be found in Mark 5—I'll mention a few of these other parallels in the next chapter.[9]

---

8. Giffone and Wile, "Mark 5's Echoes."

9. Some of these parallels have previously been identified, but we (Giffone and Wile) discovered additional echoes. Furthermore, we observed that Matthew and Luke,

This is one woman who "strives to take hold of" YHWH incarnate, Jesus. But many of his people, the Jewish people, don't end up following him. And in fact, many people from outside the Jewish people, from other nations, *do* in fact hold fast to Jesus and become his faithful servants. And this is exactly what God predicted at the end of the book of Isaiah: people from many nations, tribes, and tongues would join his people by "holding fast" to him in faith.

REFLECTIONS

So what does all this mean for us—our hopes, our prayers, our relationship with God? First of all, I think that this prayer and others like it serve as a reminder that it's OK to pray from deep emotion and pain—in fact, that is when we should pray most. The Bible gives voice to all our emotions, not just joy and thanksgiving but also anger, sorrow, and isolation.

Second, our prayers should acknowledge who God is and be honest about how we stand before him with our sins and rebellion all about us. But our prayers should also recall God's faithfulness—not because *he* needs to be reminded but because we need to be reminded! We need to remember God's faithfulness to Israel in ages past; God's faithfulness to the church from the first century until today; and his faithfulness to each of us personally. Despite what you're going through right now, each of us can look to our past (and our present) and see ways that God has been faithful even when we haven't been faithful to him. These reminders, as part of our prayers, form the basis for hope that God will hear our prayers and act to redeem and rescue us.

And finally, our prayers should look to God's word showing us the way to holiness and hope! The prayers that God gives us contain reminders of his will that show us how he wants us to be, what he wants us to believe, and how he wants us to live. The Isa 63–64 prayer communicates God's desire that we would reflect his image into the world. We are his images: lovingly crafted like a potter with clay, God's Spirit breathed into our lungs, and walking and speaking in this world that God created. And the prayer also reminds us of the work of the Holy Spirit in softening and changing our hard hearts so we would be drawn back to our Father.

---

in their use of Mark's material, don't seem to have identified the concentration of Isaian echoes; the other evangelists change or rearrange Mark's stories in a way that obscures the Isa 63–66 connections.

God hears our prayers, and we can cry out to him. We can recognize his faithfulness to his people from ancient times until now and trust that he will hear us and give us what we need. He will forgive us if we humble ourselves before him because of what Jesus has done. He will come to us when we are in need—in fact, the Holy Spirit is already his abiding presence with us. As the prophet says, he will do "awesome things which we did not expect" (64:3).

A Prayer

Lord, as we recount your kindnesses to us today and to your people throughout all generations, we long to know you better—the God who saves and who delights to be with us. We know that our sin separates us from you and that our best attempts to make things right just make things worse. We give you thanks for not leaving us in our sins but instead rending the heavens and condescending to live among us. We pray that you would soften our hearts so that we would love you and follow your ways. And help us to cry out to you, especially in times of anger, sorrow, and despair, knowing that you hear us and are mighty to save. In Jesus's name we pray. Amen.

14

I Stretched Out My Hands All Day Long (Isa 65:1–15; 66:1–6)

In the last chapter, we looked at the prayer of confession in Isa 63:7—64:12. In that prayer, the faithful prophet recognizes his people's greatest need: they need God to change their hearts, and they need God to be near to them. In these two chapters, we look at YHWH's answer to this prayer of confession. Immediately after the prayer spoken in the prophet's voice, YHWH starts his reply in 65:1, and his words continue nearly uninterrupted until the end of the book (so, two full chapters). I've chosen to address portions of Isa 65–66 more thematically in this chapter and the next one.

In Isa 65–66, YHWH responds first with anger and sorrow at how his people have rejected him. But he also says that a small group within Israel have, in fact, remained loyal to him even when they have been mocked and excluded by their fellow Jews. And also, there are people from outside Israel, gentiles, who have reached out to the God of Israel in faith even though he was first reaching out to the Israelites. Believing Jews and gentiles together, God says, will form his new people, his new servants, who will live peacefully and securely in a "new heavens and new earth." We will also see some more connections to Mark 5 where we see that Jesus, as God incarnate, embodies the stance of openness to sinful people—Jews and gentiles—who reach out to him in faith.

SCRIPTURE: ISAIAH 65:1-15; 66:1-6

1 I was ready to be sought by those who did not ask for me;
I was ready to be found by those who did not seek me.
I said, "Here I am, here I am,"
to a nation that was not called by my name.
2 I spread out my hands all the day
to a rebellious people,
who walk in a way that is not good,
following their own devices;
3 a people who provoke me
to my face continually,
sacrificing in gardens
and making offerings on bricks;
4 who sit in tombs,
and spend the night in secret places;
who eat pig's flesh,
and broth of tainted meat is in their vessels;
5 who say, "Keep to yourself,
do not come near me, for I am too holy for you."
These are a smoke in my nostrils,
a fire that burns all the day.
6 Behold, it is written before me:
"I will not keep silent, but I will repay;
I will indeed repay into their lap
7 both your iniquities and your fathers' iniquities together,
says the LORD;
because they made offerings on the mountains
and insulted me on the hills,
I will measure into their lap
payment for their former deeds."
8 Thus says the LORD:
"As the new wine is found in the cluster,
and they say, 'Do not destroy it,
for there is a blessing in it,'
so I will do for my servants' sake,
and not destroy them all.
9 I will bring forth offspring from Jacob,
and from Judah possessors of my mountains;
my chosen shall possess it,
and my servants shall dwell there.
10 Sharon shall become a pasture for flocks,
and the Valley of Achor a place for herds to lie down,

for my people who have sought me.
11 But you who forsake the LORD,
who forget my holy mountain,
who set a table for Fortune
and fill cups of mixed wine for Destiny,
12 I will destine you to the sword,
and all of you shall bow down to the slaughter,
because, when I called, you did not answer;
when I spoke, you did not listen,
but you did what was evil in my eyes
and chose what I did not delight in."
13 Therefore thus says the Lord GOD:
"Behold, my servants shall eat,
but you shall be hungry;
behold, my servants shall drink,
but you shall be thirsty;
behold, my servants shall rejoice,
but you shall be put to shame;
14 behold, my servants shall sing for gladness of heart,
but you shall cry out for pain of heart
and shall wail for breaking of spirit.
15 You shall leave your name to my chosen for a curse,
and the Lord GOD will put you to death,
but his servants he will call by another name."
(Isa 65:1–15)

66:1 Thus says the LORD:
"Heaven is my throne,
and the earth is my footstool;
what is the house that you would build for me,
and what is the place of my rest?
2 All these things my hand has made,
and so all these things came to be,
declares the LORD.
But this is the one to whom I will look:
he who is humble and contrite in spirit
and trembles at my word.
3 "He who slaughters an ox is like one who kills a man;
he who sacrifices a lamb, like one who breaks a dog's neck;
he who presents a grain offering, like one who offers pig's blood;
he who makes a memorial offering of frankincense, like one who blesses an idol.
These have chosen their own ways,
and their soul delights in their abominations;

> 4 I also will choose harsh treatment for them
> and bring their fears upon them,
> because when I called, no one answered,
> when I spoke, they did not listen;
> but they did what was evil in my eyes
> and chose that in which I did not delight."
> 5 Hear the word of the LORD,
> you who tremble at his word:
> "Your brothers who hate you
> and cast you out for my name's sake
> have said, Let the LORD be glorified,
> that we may see your joy';
> but it is they who shall be put to shame.
> 6 "The sound of an uproar from the city!
> A sound from the temple!
> The sound of the LORD,
> rendering recompense to his enemies!" (Isa 66:1–6)

YHWH'S ANSWER IN THE PERSIAN PERIOD

These verses follow on the prophet's prayer of Isa 63:7—64:12, which is a penitential prayer—a prayer of confession prayed by a faithful individual asking for forgiveness on behalf of a largely unfaithful people. The prophet is alone and isolated among his people, and he feels distant from God because his people as a whole have rejected their God. The prayer openly admits the sin and guilt of the people. The people made choices to abandon God and his ways (64:5–7), and so God gave them over to the consequences of those choices. Thus, the prophet pleads with God that he would return and act: Come down (64:1)! You have not forgotten us forever, have you? (63:15, 64:9, 12). These are the final words spoken by humans to God.

In Isa 65–66, we find God's response. Notice that, as in 63:7, there's no introduction, no transition phrase that says, "This is what the LORD says." We see phrases like that in verses 8 and 13 and 25 even though it's clear from 65:1 that YHWH is the speaker. It's a subtle thing in poetry, but sometimes when the speaking voice changes abruptly, it can give a sense of urgency or immediacy. It also gives a sense of intimacy; YHWH is speaking directly to the people—the intermediary role of the prophet is minimized.

Reaching Out, Calling Out

In these passages, we observe prominent motifs of YHWH "calling out" and "reaching out" to his people, but unrequited/unreciprocated—as a whole, they have rejected him.

Have you ever greeted a toddler or a small child that you expected to hug you, and didn't? I've had this experience where I knelt down, held out my arms, and waited for my little niece to run to me to give me a big hug—but instead, she ran past my outstretched arms to someone else. Now, if this just happens once or twice, no sensible uncle would take this slight personally—kids are kids. But if, let's say, my niece were to ignore me like this multiple times in a row, I'd honestly feel a bit hurt and sad. Maybe I'd consult my brother or sister-in-law to see if I did something unwittingly that could be scaring my niece.

This is how God felt about Israel rejecting him, but even more so. He didn't just want them to conform to some rule or standard; he wanted to be close to them. He made himself available to them, he held out his arms all day long to them (65:2), but most ignored him. I think we know that this is not unique to ancient Israel. We can probably each think of people—including each of us, at times—who ignore God's arms that are reaching out to them (to us).

In the Isaiah texts, YHWH continues to describe this situation that has made him sad and angry. Some of these faithless Israelites have ignored YHWH (or even told him to go away!), and they've shown their disregard for him in physical actions. There are basically three attitudes: ignoring, rejecting, or manipulating. Some of the people ignore YHWH altogether. They choose to honor and burn incense to other gods, not seeking YHWH at all. Others reject YHWH. They actively tell YHWH and his prophets and servants to go away, showing their contempt for him: Keep away because I'm perfect as I am—don't come near me! (65:5). And still others are trying to worship YHWH through ritual without caring about actual moral obedience (66:3).

Ritual Impurity: A Picture of Moral Impurity

That takes us to the next observation: this passage uses the concepts of *ritual impurity* to explain the people's *moral* relationship to God. We've talked a little about rituals in this book. In chapter 5, when we looked at Isa 56:1–8, we saw that foreigners and eunuchs, who were considered outsiders, could be accepted by YHWH regardless of their irreparable ritual impurity as long as they held fast to his covenant and kept his Sabbaths. We also talked a bit about sacrificial rituals and fasting in chapter 8 (on Isa 58) in comparison to the obedience of caring for the poor and the downtrodden—the relationship between ceremony and the reality that it symbolizes. And in chapter 13, we saw a reference to "filthy rags" in 64:6 and the ritual impurity suffered by the woman whom Jesus healed in Mark 5.

In this section of Isa 65–66 that we've read, many ritually impure actions or objects are used as a metaphor for the moral sins that the people have committed. The ritual impurity laws are found in Lev 11–15 especially and then other passages in Leviticus, Numbers, and Deuteronomy.

The concept of ritual impurity is hard for us as modern people to understand. We tend to link the ideas of "impurity" or "uncleanness" with pollution that leads to sickness—like water that is tainted by a chemical or with bacteria. Or, based on a handful of passages, we might conceptualize "impurity" as "moral sin." Neither of these is quite correct. Rather, this has more to do with appropriateness for approaching sacred space. My professor, Gary Schnittjer, helpfully (and humorously) suggests a more appropriate term with less baggage than "unclean" or "impure": "The concept 'unclean' does not mean physically dirty but ceremonially polluted or ritually contaminated—perhaps 'ritually challenged' in politically-correct terms."[1]

These laws seem irrelevant to us for two reasons: they don't match up with modern scientific understandings of purity and impurity and because God explicitly says in the New Testament that they are no longer necessary for humans to follow. Christians approach God differently, "with boldness," through the finished work of Jesus Christ (Heb 10:19–25). So what is the ongoing significance of Old Testament ritual purity laws for Christian believers?

One explanation is that these ritual purity laws point us to something about God's Creator-ness and our creatureliness. Regardless of our moral right-standing before God, these Old Testament laws can continually remind us of our humanness and dependence upon God.

Historically, some of the laws were about health and well-being, such as prohibiting the Israelites from eating animals (such as pigs—cf.

---

1. Schnittjer, *Torah Story*, 329.

Isa 65:4; 66:3) that could have made them sick.[2] Another example would be: a new mother and a newborn child were ritually impure for several weeks. But this was a blessing for them because other people would mostly not touch them, and they wouldn't be obliged to attend public gatherings like worship. The "ritually impure" status didn't persist forever, but for some period of time the status protected mother and baby from being exposed to sickness (Lev 12). It was a valid excuse for a new mom to rest!

Some of the Law's exclusions were based on bodily fluids or physical contact that related to *death* and *new life*. For example, a woman was ritually impure during her period, which is a natural part of her God-given reproductive ability (Lev 15:19-30). Also, someone who touched a dead body, even to bury the body with respect, was ritually impure for seven days (Num 19:11-22; cf. 9:6-14). None of this relates to *morality*: a woman who had her period or a man who buried his grandfather's body had not *sinned* to displease God, but they were not permitted to enter sacred space to worship God—for a period of time.

Also, some excluded behaviors were associated with worship of other gods. For example—and this is mentioned in this passage—it was against ritual purity laws to eat meat of an animal that had been strangled or had had its neck broken (Isa 66:3). Some pagan rituals involved strangling animals for sacrifice so that the life essence of the animal would pass into the worshiper who consumed the blood. By contrast, the Israelites were commanded to slaughter their meat by letting the blood drain, both as a mercy to the animal that would die quickly and also so that the blood would return to YHWH who gave it by pouring out on the ground (Lev 17:10-14; Deut 12:20-27).

So, those are some reasons for the purity laws: protecting health and safety; guarding the uniqueness of YHWH as the giver and taker of all life; and avoiding practices that were too close to paganism.[3]

---

2. In Lev 11, most of the animals prohibited for meat are predators or carrion/detritus feeders. Eating such animals would expose the Israelites to diseased rotten flesh in the animals' stomachs. Also, the predators keep the ecosystem in balance: if all the owls and hawks were eaten, then mice and locusts would eat the crops of the land.

3. There is also an element of YHWH's fiat, however. Some purity laws appear to have no symbolism, health benefit, or association with the worship of other gods—the Israelites are just expected to obey YHWH in such matters because he is God. To build on an example described above, there is no obvious health reason why the mother of a newborn *daughter* should be ritually impure twice as long as the mother who gives birth to a *son* (Lev 12:1-5).

Here in Isa 64–66, we can see that *ritual impurity*, even though it does not *equate* to moral impurity, is used as a *metaphor* to describe the people's alienation from God due to their moral *sins*. As we noted in the last chapter, in 64:6, the prophet says that "all our righteous deeds are like a polluted garment," meaning menstrual cloth. In 65:4, YHWH criticizes the people for hanging out in graveyards among dead bodies and eating pork and eating unclean meats. These were all ritually impure acts. In 66:3, YHWH says that the rituals that the Israelites do to try to please him—sacrificing clean animals, grain offerings, incense—are disgusting to him, like ritually impure actions. Why, when the Israelites were sacrificing a nice lamb (a clean animal), would YHWH receive the sacrifice as if they were offering up a dog with a broken neck?

It's because their hearts are hardened. Because they had ignored YHWH and his laws for so long, anything they tried to do right in their own way of thinking turned out to be even more offensive to God. What a terrible, hopeless state to be in!

YHWH's True Servants Versus False Servants

So, what is YHWH to do? Is the situation fully hopeless? No, because YHWH is gracious and will judge between those who are his true servants and those who are not.

What do we see in this passage about those within Israel who have rebelled against him? YHWH reached out to them, but they did not respond or answer (65:1–2). They worshiped and burned incense for other gods (65:3, 5, 7). They mocked and excluded the small minority of faithful Israelites who were genuinely trying to follow God's way. In 66:5, YHWH addresses those who "tremble at his word," meaning they take his word seriously—it says that "your brothers . . . hate you and cast you out for my name's sake." The word for "cast out" here is a specific word for avoiding a woman who is experiencing ritual impurity during her menstruation—another connection back to 64:6. These rebellious Israelites don't see or care about how their actions and attitudes have made *them*, Israel as a whole, offensive to God. Overall, Israel has been rebellious and hostile to God despite him calling out to them and always reaching out to them.

But instead of giving up on Israel altogether, YHWH embraces his true servants. How do we know who are his true servants? Back in 64:7, he says that someone who would "call upon [YHWH's] name" or "rouse himself to take hold of [him]" would be a true servant—and we're reminded of the eunuchs and foreigners back in 56:3–7 who "bind themselves to YHWH" and "hold fast to his covenant."

Here in 65:8, he compares this faithful minority of Israelites to grapes! Have you ever picked up a cluster of grapes from the bag that got shoved to the back of the fridge for a few days? Usually, when you buy the grapes fresh, most of the grapes are good, and there might be just a couple of mushy ones in the middle. But if the grapes are a few days old, there might be more rotten or shriveled grapes in the bunch than good ones—you really have dig into the cluster to find a good one.

But what you *don't* do in that situation is simply throw the whole bunch away because of some rotten ones! Demetri Martin, the quirky comedian, calls grapes "the Fruit of Hope" because "with grapes, you always get another chance. If you have a gross apple or a peach, you're stuck with that gross piece of fruit. But if you have a gross grape, no problem—just move on to the next."[4] That is what YHWH is going to do with his people: he's going to sort out the good grapes within a mostly bad cluster of grapes. (At least it's better than the situation in Isa 5:1–4 in which YHWH's vineyard yields *only* unusable grapes.)

In 65:12–14, he refers to "my servants" who will be blessed, but the others will suffer because they did not listen when YHWH called. In 66:2 and 5, it says that these faithful ones "tremble at YHWH's word" and have a humble spirit. And in 65:15, we learn that these true servants will be "called by another name," something other than "Israel" or "Judah" (see "What's in a (New) Name" in chapter 12). This reaches its fulfillment in the church, the new covenant people of God, which includes Jews and gentiles.

YHWH'S ANSWER IN MARK 5

In the previous chapter, I mentioned several parallels to this overall section (Isa 63–66) in the New Testament and how Jesus's arrival and his words and actions are an answer to the prayer. I made reference to Jesus's baptism when the "heavens were torn open," alluding to Isa 64:1. The woman who was healed of a hemorrhaging issue in Mark 5:25–34 has a connection to 64:6 (also to 66:5; see above). My student, Sage, noticed

---

4. Miller, "Demetri Martin."

that parallel, and then we worked together on discovering several more parallels between Isa 63–66 and the other stories in Mark 5.[5]

The chapter begins with Jesus going to a gentile region and encountering a man possessed by many demons (Mark 5:1–20). It says that he lived among the tombs (5:3); when Jesus casts the demons out of the man, he sends them into a herd of pigs, and the pigs all rush off and drown themselves in the lake (5:11–13)! These details of the story remind us of Isa 65:4 where the rebels "spend the night among the graves" and "eat swine's flesh."

When Jesus returns to a Jewish area, he is approached by a synagogue ruler, Jairus, who falls down at Jesus's feet and begs him to come and heal his daughter (5:21–24, 35–43). Jesus is on the way to Jairus's house when the woman finds him in the crowd and touches his robe and is healed (5:25–34). After that delay, Jesus continues on to Jairus's house despite the news that the girl has died—but Jesus raises her from the dead by touching her hand.

All three of these people are at the end of their rope, and it seems like no one can rescue them! Each of them humbly bows before Jesus (Mark 5:6, 22, 33). In each case, there is some barrier of ritual impurity that symbolizes the desperate situation. For the demon-possessed man: he's a gentile and he hangs out with dead bodies in an area where they herd pigs. For the woman, it's her medical condition. Jairus's little girl is dead—it doesn't get more hopeless than that—and her corpse would be considered ritually impure.

Just like YHWH in Isa 65:2, Jesus holds out his hands to his people, preaching the kingdom of God to the Jews first but also to the gentiles. For the woman and the girl, Jesus heals by touching. Instead of ritual impurity transferring from these bodies to Jesus, purity, healing, and new life flow from Jesus's body into theirs. Among Jews and gentiles, there are many who ignore or disregard Jesus but also faithful ones who seek out Jesus and take hold of him. The gentile man who was saved from the demons begged to be allowed to follow Jesus, but Jesus sent him back to his hometown with a mission: "Go home to your friends and tell them how much the Lord has done for you, and how he has had mercy on you" (Mark 5:19).

We argue that Mark was keenly aware of these motifs in Isa 63–66 and shaped his stories in Mark 5 to show us how Jesus's words and actions constituted a fulfillment of God's purpose presented in the conclusion of Isaiah.

---

5. Giffone and Wile, "Mark 5's Echoes."

REFLECTIONS

We can't help but be struck by God's grace and mercy in this Isaiah passage and revel in it! As we've seen throughout this book, the story of God's love for Israel has meaning for us, too. We see God's mercy and love in each of our lives and in the stories of our local congregations despite the difficult situations we find ourselves in.

At the end of Rom 10, Paul reinterprets Isa 65:1–2 to contrast unbelieving Jews with gentiles who did not originally seek YHWH but have been permitted to seek him out and find him (Rom 10:19–21).[6] That's who we are if we respond in faith.

A Warning

But there's also a warning in this for us, which is one of Paul's main points in that section (Rom 9–11). Israel thought they were secure as God's people, that they didn't need to pursue holiness. They thought that they didn't need to worry about anything! Or, some of them saw YHWH as just like one of the gods the other nations worshiped: a source of power that they could access and manipulate for what they wanted, as needed.

This is a special warning for those of us who, like me, were/are raised in sincere Christian families. We should never take the grace of God for granted just because we've grown up having faith taught to us. I have plenty of friends raised in Christian families who, despite knowing the truth, have rejected it—just like the Israelites who grew up hearing stories of God's mercy for Israel and yet never held fast to his covenant for themselves. Each one of us who is raised with this blessing still needs to believe in Jesus for himself or herself. If you have been baptized (or dedicated to Christ) as a child but haven't publicly affirmed your faith in Christ before the church, identified yourself with Christ, and asked for the support and encouragement of the church in your Christian walk, then you should talk to your pastor about a good time to do that.

---

6. "This phase of the argument [in Rom 9:30–10:21] ends by recapitulating the paradox through Paul's remarkable misreading of Isa. 65:1–2: he splits the oracle down the middle, interpreting the first verse ('I have been found by those who did not seek me; I have become manifest to those who did not ask for me') innovatively as a reference to gentile Christians, and the second verse ('All day long I have stretched out my hands to a disobedient and contrary people'), quite properly, as a reference to Israel." Hays, *Letters of Paul*, 74–75.

Arms Open Wide

But we can conclude on a hopeful note. In Isa 63–64, the prophet prays to God, "Why are you so distant? Why aren't you reaching out to us?" Isaiah 65–66 has God's answer: I *did* reach out to you, many times, but you did not answer! (Most of you, anyway.) So, because you didn't answer, I will call *new* servants from among all peoples, nations, and tongues! The faithful few from among Israel will be joined with gentiles, and these together will be God's new people in the new heavens and new earth! (That's the next chapter of this book.)

In the Gospels, we see that Jesus's arms were open wide to those who would answer his call and take hold of him in faith. At the cross with his arms stretched out all day long in excruciating pain, he looked out at a rebellious and disobedient people—Jews and gentiles—and took upon himself the punishment for their sins, the sins of anyone who would repent.[7]

And his arms remain open, and his hands remain powerful to rescue us and loving and careful to shape us into the images that he created us to be—like a potter shapes the clay (cf. Isa 64:8). If you haven't done so yet, throw your faith and trust on Jesus! Or, if you have walked away from him, come back to Jesus! Confess your rebellion, your anger, your resentment, your self-love—and receive his forgiveness. Receive the Holy Spirit, who guided Israel in the wilderness (63:14) and is given to all who trust in Jesus. If we "tremble at [God's] word" and humble ourselves, the Lord will glorify himself, and all the nations will "see [our] joy" (66:5).

A Prayer

Lord, we recognize that you have been faithful in reaching out to us even though we turned our backs on you. But we thank you that you don't give up on your people, but you are in the process of making us into who you've designed us to be. Help us never to take your grace for granted but to acknowledge each day how much we need you. And let our joy in you be evident as we live our lives so that we would have opportunities to tell others about your mercy and grace. In Jesus's name. Amen.

---

7. Several of the church fathers made this connection between Isa 65:2 and Jesus's hands stretched out upon the cross, including Athanasius, *Apoll.* 38.2 and Theodoret of Cyr, *Commentary on Isaiah* 20.65.2 (Elliott, *Isaiah 40–66*, 265).

15

Rejoice Forever in That Which I Create (Isa 65:16–25; 66:7–24)

We've finally reached the conclusion of Isa 56–66 and of the book itself. And what a conclusion it is—we find both new heavens and new earth with such idyllic pictures of a wolf and a lamb playing together and the peace like a river; and on the other hand, fiery judgment and worms eating corpses! In fact, it's actually the common practice in Jewish synagogues when reading the ending of the book of Isaiah to read 66:23 aloud again after reading verse 24 so that "the worship of the one true God by his faithful has the last word."[1]

In the previous chapter, we talked about certain elements of Isa 65–66, the final answer by YHWH in the book of Isaiah. He says that he's been reaching out to Israel, his people, but many of them would not respond. We talked about how *ritual impurity* according to the law of Moses is used to picture this *moral rebellion* of the people against YHWH. But the flip side of this is that this opens the door for YHWH to create a "new people" made up of his faithful servants from every tribe and nation and tongue.

We're going to approach the remaining verses in these chapters through four questions: *What* is YHWH going to do? *Who* is he going to do it *for*? *When* is he going to do it? And, what does it mean for *us now*?

---

1. Childs, *Isaiah*, 546. This is also the synagogue practice (rereading the penultimate verse) when reading the books of Lamentations, Ecclesiastes, and the Twelve—see Salters, *Lamentations*, 375.

SCRIPTURE: ISAIAH 65:16-25; 66:7-24

16 So that he who blesses himself in the land
shall bless himself by the God of truth,
and he who takes an oath in the land
shall swear by the God of truth;
because the former troubles are forgotten
and are hidden from my eyes.
17 "For behold, I create new heavens
and a new earth,
and the former things shall not be remembered
or come into mind.
18 But be glad and rejoice forever
in that which I create;
for behold, I create Jerusalem to be a joy,
and her people to be a gladness.
19 I will rejoice in Jerusalem
and be glad in my people;
no more shall be heard in it the sound of weeping
and the cry of distress.
20 No more shall there be in it
an infant who lives but a few days,
or an old man who does not fill out his days,
for the young man shall die a hundred years old,
and the sinner a hundred years old shall be accursed.
21 They shall build houses and inhabit them;
they shall plant vineyards and eat their fruit.
22 They shall not build and another inhabit;
they shall not plant and another eat;
for like the days of a tree shall the days of my people be,
and my chosen shall long enjoy the work of their hands.
23 They shall not labor in vain
or bear children for calamity,
for they shall be the offspring of the blessed of the LORD,
and their descendants with them.
24 Before they call I will answer;
while they are yet speaking I will hear.
25 The wolf and the lamb shall graze together;
the lion shall eat straw like the ox,
and dust shall be the serpent's food.
They shall not hurt or destroy
in all my holy mountain,"
says the LORD. (Isa 65:16-25)

7 "Before she was in labor
she gave birth;
before her pain came upon her
she delivered a son.
8 Who has heard such a thing?
Who has seen such things?
Shall a land be born in one day?
Shall a nation be brought forth in one moment?
For as soon as Zion was in labor
she brought forth her children.
9 Shall I bring to the point of birth and not cause to bring forth?"
says the LORD;
"shall I, who cause to bring forth, shut the womb?"
says your God.
10 "Rejoice with Jerusalem, and be glad for her,
all you who love her;
rejoice with her in joy,
all you who mourn over her;
11 that you may nurse and be satisfied
from her consoling breast;
that you may drink deeply with delight
from her glorious abundance."
12 For thus says the LORD:
"Behold, I will extend peace to her like a river,
and the glory of the nations like an overflowing stream;
and you shall nurse, you shall be carried upon her hip,
and bounced upon her knees.
13 As one whom his mother comforts,
so I will comfort you;
you shall be comforted in Jerusalem.
14 You shall see, and your heart shall rejoice;
your bones shall flourish like the grass;
and the hand of the LORD shall be known to his servants,
and he shall show his indignation against his enemies.
15 "For behold, the LORD will come in fire,
and his chariots like the whirlwind,
to render his anger in fury,
and his rebuke with flames of fire.
16 For by fire will the LORD enter into judgment,
and by his sword, with all flesh;
and those slain by the LORD shall be many.
17 "Those who sanctify and purify themselves to go into the gardens, following one in the midst, eating pig's flesh and the

abomination and mice, shall come to an end together, declares the LORD.

18 "For I know their works and their thoughts, and the time is coming to gather all nations and tongues. And they shall come and shall see my glory, 19 and I will set a sign among them. And from them I will send survivors to the nations, to Tarshish, Pul, and Lud, who draw the bow, to Tubal and Javan, to the coastlands far away, that have not heard my fame or seen my glory. And they shall declare my glory among the nations. 20 And they shall bring all your brothers from all the nations as an offering to the LORD, on horses and in chariots and in litters and on mules and on dromedaries, to my holy mountain Jerusalem, says the LORD, just as the Israelites bring their grain offering in a clean vessel to the house of the LORD. 21 And some of them also I will take for priests and for Levites, says the LORD.

22 "For as the new heavens and the new earth
that I make
shall remain before me, says the LORD,
so shall your offspring and your name remain.
23 From new moon to new moon,
and from Sabbath to Sabbath,
all flesh shall come to worship before me,
declares the LORD.

24 "And they shall go out and look on the dead bodies of the men who have rebelled against me. For their worm shall not die, their fire shall not be quenched, and they shall be an abhorrence to all flesh." (Isa 66:7–24)

WHAT IS YHWH GOING TO DO?

Isaiah 65:16–25 talks about the new heavens and new earth; Isaiah 66:22 returns to this. Then, 66:7–9 talks about the power of YHWH to accomplish what he promised: to bring about the new birth of his new people. Isaiah 66:10–14a talks about the renewed city of God as a place of comfort. Isaiah 66:14b–17 shows us, though, the flip side of this comfort for God's people, which is harsh judgment for those who reject YHWH—Isaiah 66:24 goes along with this idea. And in 66:18–21 and 23, people from all nations gather to recognize YHWH for who he is and to worship him.

So, what is YHWH going to do?

New Creation

The most prominent motif in 65:16-25 is creation, especially *new creation* or *renewed creation*. We hear echoes of the first words of the Bible, Gen 1:1: "In the beginning God *created* the heavens and the earth" (emphasis mine). "Heavens and earth" are a *merism*, a way of speaking about all that exists in the created world. And the word here in Isaiah for "create" in verses 17 and 18 is *bārāʾ*, which is the word used in Gen 1 (and repeatedly in Isa 40–55; see chapter 3). There are more general Hebrew words for "make" or "do," but *bārāʾ* is only used to describe what God does: creating the world, human beings, and even doing miracles.

These terms are just the beginning. We see a beautiful picture of the reversal of the curses that YHWH made upon the first humans, Adam and Eve, when they rebelled against him in the garden of Eden. Before they sinned, Adam and Eve were given the vocation of cultivating the earth and making it fruitful. When they sinned, part of Adam's curse was that cultivation would now be extremely difficult: "By the sweat of your face" (Gen 3:17-19). In the new heavens and new earth, the land will be fruitful once again, and humans will get to enjoy the fruits of their work (65:20-23). The curse that was upon Eve, that she would give birth with painful and dangerous labor (Gen 3:16), is also alluded to: in 65:23, "They shall not . . . bear children for calamity"; and in 66:7-9, YHWH uses the image of himself as a sort of divine Midwife strengthening a woman in labor (Daughter Zion) to bring forth the birth of a new people (cf. 37:3). We also see a reference to the curse upon the serpent who deceived Eve: "Dust will be his food" (Isa 65:25; Gen 3:14).

We might think of it in this more nuanced way: the curse of fruitless work in the world is *reversed*; the curse of difficult childbirth is something that God *brings humanity through* and out to the other side; and the curse on the serpent, the enemy of God and his created images, is *fulfilled*.

There are implications for the rest of the created world, too. The references to the wolf and lamb and the lion and ox (65:25; cf. 11:6-9) remind us of the harmony of creation that existed before, as Paul puts it, it was "subjected to futility" because of human sin and mismanagement (Rom 8:20).

You might notice some strange or unexpected aspects of this picture of new heavens and new earth. It doesn't quite square with what we imagine heaven or "the resurrection to eternal life" would look like. It isn't clear that life is actually *eternal* in this vision. Isaiah 65:20 describes *long life* so that if someone dies at the age of a hundred, people will say, "That's a shame—he was so young!"[2] And 65:23 mentions "descendants"—so does this mean people will be marrying and given in marriage and having kids? I want to come back to this question below ("When?").

When we take the totality of Scripture, including Ezekiel and Revelation, a picture is gradually painted of new creation that restores some of what was lost from the "old creation" but is also *different*—it doesn't just turn back the clock to Gen 2. And this is the paradox in the book of Isaiah when it comes to "the former things," which it says will "no longer come to mind" in 65:16–17.

During the course of our lives, we experience painful things—sometimes, truly awful things. As we explored back in chapter 5 in relation to Isa 56:1–8, sometimes these are awful things that we have brought upon ourselves; sometimes these are awful things that others have done to us; sometimes they are things that we've done to others; and sometimes tragic things happen because the world is broken.

When we proclaim that God is "Savior" and "Redeemer," we are acknowledging that evil and suffering have existed both inside of us and outside of us and that God has overcome them. Each of us has our own story to tell of what God has redeemed us from. If our memories of those awful things were wiped away completely, then we would also not recall what YHWH has done, and we would not truly know him as Redeemer and Savior.

We find this paradox already embedded earlier in the book of Isaiah. In Isa 46:9, through the (exilic) prophet, YHWH says, "Remember the former things of old; for I am God, and there is no other; I am God, and there is none like me." In other words, *remember what God has done in the past as savior so that we can take hope that he is powerful to save us now*. But Second Isaiah also says in 43:18, "Remember not the former things, nor consider the things of old." In other words, *God is going to do something now that is even greater than his previous works and will make us forget our past troubles*. And even here in Isa 65, he says the former things will not be remembered or come to mind—but Israel's troubles *are written down* in the word of God, which will never pass away (40:6–7).

---

2. This may also be an allusion to the prediluvian (before the great flood) era when ancient figures are described as living hundreds of years. As a result of human violence, YHWH hinted that human lifespans would be shortened (Gen 6:3: "One hundred and twenty years"). Regardless of how one accounts for the long lifespans in Gen 5–11, the Isaiah text seems to harken back (in hope) to a pre-flood, pre-judgment era.

This means that somehow, as people of new creation who look ahead to the new heavens and new earth, we will be able to think back on our suffering and traumas *without tears or pain* in order to give God glory for all that he's done. Being reconciled to God and to each other can't mean forgetting what has happened, but it means that we're no longer defined or controlled by those stories of sin and suffering. Jesus's own body itself is a picture of this: after death, he rose from the dead with a re-created body, but he still had (has!) scars on his hands and feet and side from where he had been pierced as a sign that he had been "slain" in order to "ransom people for God from every tribe and language and people and nation" (Rev 5:6, 9; cf. John 20:24–29). He is scarred but healed, slain but alive—and the scars are a sign of his glorious redemption victory.

Reconciliation

Reconciliation is the renewal of relationship between YHWH and his people. And this is described in many ways, but one that sticks out to me is 65:24: "Before they call I will answer; while they are yet speaking I will hear."

Growing up, I heard this verse used as support for praying to God for some event that might have already happened—for example, even if it is now afternoon, I can still pray for someone else's surgery that has already happened at 9 a.m. because I don't know the results yet. Of course, God is outside of time, and so he can respond to prayers that he knows we will pray.

But this verse corresponds to 65:12 and 66:4, which use these same four verbs to describe YHWH's hurt and anger: "I *called*, but no one *answered*; I *spoke*, but no one *listened*" (emphasis mine).[3] So despite that past rejection, in this new creation, YHWH is so eager to reconcile with and relate to his people that he'll answer and listen before they can even say anything!

Genuine Worship

As part of this reconciliation, we will see renewed, genuine, heartfelt worship on the part of human beings. The genuineness of the worship

---

3. These four repeated words also provide a link to Mark 5:35–36; see Giffone and Wile, "Mark 5's Echoes."

is pictured, as we've seen before, using *ceremonial* or *ritual* purity as a metaphor: those who are truly YHWH's worshipers will bring their offerings in ceremonially clean vessels (66:20), but those who don't honor him will be like those who eat the flesh of unclean animals (66:17). Worship involves two things: people recognizing the glory of God (which will happen whether they are happy about it or not!) and people enjoying fellowship with God. Especially in 66:10–14a, we see God delighting in the joy of the people.

Judgment

Finally, the conclusion of YHWH's story of the world (the new heavens and new earth) does take place through judgment—including violent punishment for those who ultimately reject YHWH and rebel against him. Of course, we are all rebels deserving of judgment! But some he draws back to himself in humility and repentance. And the leader of heavenly and earthly rebels, the serpent of old (cf. Isa 27:1; Rev 12:9; 20:2) that I mentioned earlier: the curse upon the serpent is confirmed, and he will be judged with his followers. In Isa 66:17, there is a possibility that "the one in their midst, whom they follow" could be a reference to Satan, the chief rebel—but honestly, the Hebrew text is confusing, and not everyone agrees on that. But the point is that judgment is the necessary step, the culmination of God's mercy and his justice.

FOR WHOM?

We see numerous references to Jerusalem, Zion, and YHWH's "holy mountain," which are the same place. So, we could read this as speaking mainly about the people of Israel, Judah, and Jerusalem: God's old covenant chosen people. And yet, as we've seen before, the New Testament shows us how to interpret these prophecies not just as about a particular land or people but about the whole world. The reason why the New Testament writers, under the inspiration of the Holy Spirit, read the Old Testament in this fashion is in part *because of* passages like this one at the end of Isaiah. As the biblical story continues from Genesis, God created Israel, gave them their land, and established his temple in Jerusalem, as a reestablishment of the good creation (land) and the garden of Eden (temple). And so it makes sense that when Jerusalem is renewed and rebirthed, as we see here, that new life would actually spread from there to the whole world: to people of other nations, and to the creation itself—animals and plants. So, just like we saw in chapter 12, the focus is not a strip of land in the Middle East or a particular clan descended from Abraham; rather, YHWH will do for the world what he does for Israel.

Thus, the passage pictures the arrival of the nations from far away to worship the true God, YHWH, in Jerusalem. The specific nations that are mentioned in 66:19 are all very far away from Jerusalem in different directions, so it signifies the fame of YHWH going out into all the earth as it was known at that time—to the ends of the earth! This is a fulfillment of 2:2–4 and a restatement of other passages in Isaiah.[4]

But the twist on 2:2–4 is that the nations will bring the scattered Israelites and offer them as pleasing sacrifices (metaphorically!) to YHWH. This reminds us of the apostle Paul in Rom 15 saying that he has been given a particular mission: "The priestly service of the gospel of God, so that the offering of the Gentiles may be acceptable, sanctified by the Holy Spirit" (Rom 15:16). In Isaiah, the gentiles serve as worshipers and priests and Levites, and they bring the Jews as an offering. In Romans, Paul, the most Jewish of Jews (Phil 3:4–6), brings the gentiles as a pleasing sacrifice—an amazing picture!

Judgment *and* new creation happen both to Israel *and* to the nations. As mentioned before, the new creation also applies to the created order: animals and the plants of the land itself. This echoes Isa 25, and we see it also in Rev 21–22, Rom 8:18–23, and 1 Cor 15. Eternal life is *not* just for our souls in some disembodied existence as if we die and go to heaven, and that's simply the end of it. No, God created his world, and he's not rescuing us *out of* it—he is re-creating it.

WHEN?

When will these prophesied events occur? Different Christian traditions have diverging opinions on this point. The use in Isa 65–66 of the term "new heavens and new earth" makes it seem as though what comes next is the eternal state: the glorious resurrection. But in the actual description in 65:17–25, it seems as though people might die or be having children,

---

4. References to "the islands" acknowledging YHWH (Isa 11:11; 24:15; 41–42, several times; 51:1) and also "peace to those far and near" (57:19; 60).

which doesn't seem to square with what the New Testament says about the resurrection eternity (Matt 22:30; 1 Cor 15:50–57; Rev 21:4).

Therefore, some Christians think that Isa 65 describes instead a "silver age," not a "golden age" eternity. They would call this silver age the "millennial kingdom" (so called because of Rev 20:4–6) when—following a "rapture," a period of tribulation, and a battle between good and evil—Jesus will reign in Jerusalem over a Jewish kingdom for a literal thousand-year period. Along with a similar approach to reading Ezek 40–48, they believe there will be a rebuilt temple at which animal sacrifices will be offered but strictly as a memorial of Christ's new covenant sacrifice. During this millennial period, ethnic Jews will receive the blessings of being God's people, and the nations will enjoy the secondary blessings of world peace under Jesus's just reign—but people will still be born, marry, have kids, and (after living a long time) die during this period. Then after this age, there will be a final battle (Armageddon; cf. Rev 20:7–10), and *then* there will be the judgment leading into eternal life (or eternal punishment).

I think that this view—called "dispensational premillennialism"—reflects an overly literalistic reading of key texts in the Gospels, the Epistles to the Thessalonians, and the book of Revelation. Premillennialism was virtually unknown in the church from the Patristic era until the early nineteenth century; this does not mean that it's incorrect, but that should give its adherents pause.[5]

Rather, I think what's happening is that the prophet is describing the new creation in terms that connect to his immediate readers' situation in Persian-period Yehud—he's speaking about healing that reverses the worst aspects of their situation. They live as slaves; they can't follow God's word on their own strength; they suffer loss and fear; and they live with the guilt and scars of their past. The land doesn't work the way it should; lives of young and old are cut short; people aren't able to have fruitful, secure, and harmonious marriages; and Yehudians are at odds with the nations around them. *New creation*, the prophet says, changes all these and more. Though somewhat understated when compared to the fuller picture of new creation in the New Testament, the Isa 65 descriptions of these reversals do not point to a silver age that falls short of full renewal but rather to the golden age of eternity.

---

5. For a helpful comparison of different millennial views, consult Bock, *Three Views*.

When we ask the question, "When will God do these things," remember that, with prophecy, sometimes the text shows us one picture of things that will happen in several stages or eras. In chapters 3 and 11, I used the analogy of a two-dimensional picture of mountains in the distance—just by looking at a picture without depth, you can't tell how far away each of the mountains is.

The text itself points to this new creation happening in stages. Looking ahead from the Persian period, as we said, these are still hopes for the glorious future. But looking back from a New Testament perspective, we see types and shadows of what Jesus would eventually accomplish through his perfect life, his atoning death, and his glorious resurrection in the middle of time. In Isa 66:8, he asks rhetorically, "Can a country be born in a day, or a people in a single moment?" But Zech 3:9 says, anticipating the cross, "I will remove the iniquity of this land in a single day." In a sense, when Jesus went to the cross in excruciating pain, he "won" the victory over the serpent and ransomed a new people for himself from every nation (Rev 5:9)—a new people was birthed in a single day!

We are not yet all that we will be; many people have to be brought into this "new people . . . called by another name" (Isa 65:15; cf. John 10:16). People from all nations get to be priests and Levites before the God of Israel (Rev 1:6; 5:10). We experience rebirth to new life, spiritual life, that God gives (John 3:3–8); but then through a lifetime healing and sanctification process, the Holy Spirit makes us more into the new creation we are supposed to be. We experience the birth pangs (2 Cor 5:2) and suffering in this life, but God will finish his work of new birth in us (Phil 1:6). This is ultimately fulfilled in the new heavens and new earth: the redemption of our bodies and the whole cosmos.

REFLECTIONS

How do we look at this big story and this dramatic ending and connect it to our lives here in twenty-first-century North America (or wherever we may be)? What does it mean for us as part of local church bodies?

I'm continually struck by the depth, the tenacity, and the persistence of God's love for his people and his world. God wants to delight in us and have us rejoice in him. When we think about our situations as individuals and as local churches, we should remember our past—what he's done for us—to a degree, but we should also be forgetting the past and looking ahead in hope for the future that God will fulfill. No matter what is in our past, God will wipe away every tear.

In these chapters of Isaiah, YHWH speaks of judgment, re-creation, hope, love, and reconciliation using terms and images that would have made sense to ancient readers. How do we do our best to translate these images into our day, recognizing that we are on this side of Christ's death and resurrection?

It's incumbent upon us to pay attention and to ask: What are the places of rebellion, brokenness, death, slavery, and fruitlessness in our world and in our communities—and in our hearts? God has promised to make new creation happen, and we don't know what timetable that is for specific things. But it means that instead of sitting on our hands waiting for God to do it, we can begin to bring about new creation with our obedience, courage, humility, and action—fully confident that God will ultimately bring our efforts to bear fruit (see chapter 8 on Isa 58).

As we work to bring order and fruitfulness to the world, we should also be known as joyful and hopeful people—not as naïve Pollyannas ignoring anything that's bad in the world but as people of true hope and joy because we delight in God and have confidence in what he will do.

Last, but not least, our task as a church is to proclaim YHWH's glory among the nations. This means intentionally structuring our lives to "make new people of God," i.e., make disciples, incorporate new servants into God's people. This applies to "de-churched" people in our communities, as well—those who, like many in ancient Israel, were raised as part of God's people but have rebelled against him. Think about the imagery in Isaiah and in Romans: we should want to be priests and Levites bringing Israel and the nations to God and offering them up to God saying: *Here, Lord, take these broken but beloved images and do for them what you've done for us!*

And to that point: if you have reached the conclusion of this book and you have never thrown all of your faith and trust on Jesus for the forgiveness of your sin and rebellion and pledged to be his disciple, let today be the day! He is eager to forgive and to bless and to repair that relationship that's been broken between you and him. He will make you a new creation, and he will give you joy in this life and hope of eternal life with him. He will give you good things to do and good news to share so that the distant islands will "hear of his fame and see his glory" (66:19).

A Prayer

Lord, we thank you for these promises that you will make all things new—both in our sinful hearts and in this broken world. We ask that you would fill us with zeal and boldness, and creativity and compassion, to share this good news of Jesus Christ with those around us so that many would believe and rejoice in who you are and hope in what you will do. By the power of the Holy Spirit, we ask these things. Amen.

16

Isaiah 56–66 for Believers After Christendom

Isaiah 65–66 concludes hopefully with a statement of what YHWH will do for his people and for all nations. This is a conclusion not just for Isaiah as a whole but also of this smaller section, Isa 56–66, which is associated with the Persian period. It's worth comparing this conclusion to those of other Persian-period books.

For example, Chronicles ends its retelling of the monarchy of Israel (mainly Judah) with Cyrus's commissioning of the captive Judahites to return and rebuild the house of YHWH (2 Chr 36:22–23). This is a hopeful "future" that is already in the past for the Chronicler's readers. Malachi's conclusion has a future orientation towards judgment that is ominous but also hopeful—not unlike Isa 65–66 (Mal 4). On the other end of the spectrum, Ezra-Nehemiah (one book in the Hebrew canon) ends on a sad or pathetic note: despite the best efforts of the leaders in the Persian period, the people are returning to the sinful ways that led to the exile in the first place.[1] Nehemiah himself essentially says: God, remember that I did the best I could—but these people! (Neh 13:14, 22, 29–31).

Isaiah 56–66 is future-oriented—harsh in some places, but ultimately hopeful. In this epilogue, I provide some concluding reflections on the significance of Isa 56–66 and the Persian period for the life of the twenty-first-century Western church. Isaiah 56–66 as a whole and

---

1. Schnittjer, "Ezra-Nehemiah," 32–56.

as a "wrap-up" of the book of Isaiah presents us with three challenges or imperatives: saltiness, hospitality, and softheartedness. Another way to think about these three is our relationship to society, our relationship to those outside our society, and our relationship to God.

DECOUPLING OUR FAITH FROM CULTURE AND SOCIETY

Twenty-first-century believers need to recognize that it is time for a renegotiation of our relationship to Western culture, states, governments, and institutions that were founded and shaped by biblical truth but have drifted far from it. In this respect, faithful followers of YHWH today have much to learn from the examples of our ancient predecessors in Judah/Yehud.

Ancient Judah: Slow Decline, Then Rapid Decoupling

Under the kings of Israel and Judah, faithful YHWH followers observed in their society a long, slow decline from anything that would resemble YHWH's ideal as represented in the Torah. But then they experienced conquest by Mesopotamian powers (Assyria and Babylon), which represented a relatively sudden revolution in their relationship to culture, society, and power. As awful as it was to live under pagan oppression, there was at least no ambiguity about the antagonism between the temporal powers and the life of a YHWH follower.

It is possible that things were marginally more favorable after 539 BC, the Persian conquest of Babylon. The Bible speaks of the Persian kings' support for the rebuilding of the Jerusalem temple (Ezra 1–6). In recent decades, historians have become less certain of the classical presentation of Cyrus and the Persian rule as generally more tolerant and accepting of the religions of conquered peoples.[2] Living as a faithful YHWH follower under Persian pagans was not that different from living

---

2. Wiesehöfer (*Ancient Persia*, 42–55) argues that Cyrus may not have governed so differently from Xerxes (Cyrus's foil in the Greek imagination) after all. Grabbe's assessment of the Babylonian and Persian empires' attitudes toward local cults is somewhat more moderate than the theological presentation of the Hebrew Bible: "The religious policy of the Persians was not that different from the basic practice of the Assyrians and Babylonians before them." Grabbe, *History of the Jews*, 1:273; cf. 1:215–16.

under Babylonian pagans—your relationship to the world around you would have been difficult and antagonistic.

Is America the Twenty-First Century's Assyria?

The decline of Western culture away from its Christian roots has been slow and gradual rather than punctuated as in a sudden conquest. This perhaps has prevented many Christians, especially Americans, from seeing how post-Christian (even anti-Christian) our society has become.[3] Speaking as an American, American Christians (and Westerners generally) must come to grips with the fact that much of the rest of the world perceives America similarly to how ancient peoples perceived Assyria or Babylon. Whether this is a completely fair characterization is debatable, but it is hard to argue that the American elites' project of military and cultural hegemony in the twentieth and twenty-first centuries has some parallels to those of ancient empires. In my own adult lifetime (since 2001), American military and security forces have been involved in the Middle East, the Far East, and in Europe trying to protect "American interests"—but these interests are often those of international corporations or the elites' preferred ideologies concerning gender and sexuality. Regardless of what the average American or Westerner believes about the rightness of these projects, the American flag abroad represents drone strikes and rainbow flags—i.e., military threats (or actual force) and the use of soft power (media, academic culture, reputation, economic connections) to promote revisionary (nontraditional) views of gender and sexuality. Whereas we as a people and as a culture have perceived of ourselves as YHWH's instrument in the world to promote good and judge evil, we have forgotten that we ourselves will be judged if we descend into evil like every civilization before us.

While perhaps things are not so dire and dramatic for Americans living in all parts of America, this situation requires us to shift our perspective on the powers and institutions. We can no longer trust that they will generally act in accordance with our values and beliefs as we perhaps could have believed in, say, 1880 or 1960.

This means that we should look to texts in the Bible that reflect the sort of relationship to powers and institutions that we now face. While

---

3. Cultural critics making this case include: Dreher, *Live Not by Lies*; Renn, *Life in the Negative World*.

there is much to learn from texts that show us how to faithfully follow YHWH in a fully antagonistic period such as Babylonian rule, I have suggested that the Persian-period texts actually provide an even better guide for us: things are not as bad as they could be for followers of YHWH, but they are definitely not as good as they should be. Thus, Isa 56–66 and the struggles and problems reflected in this text can be useful for us in renegotiating this relationship with powers and institutions so that we can be faithful followers of the triune God, YHWH, in the twenty-first-century West.

THE SABBATH AND SALTINESS

I wish to highlight the surprising significance of the Sabbath in Isa 56–66 and what it means for the Christian sense of "saltiness" (Matt 5:13) in increasingly secular Western society. Jesus uses the metaphor of saltiness signifying difference, preservation, and flavor. How are we as Christians in the West supposed to stand out or be different from others in our society?

The Sabbath in Isaiah 56–66 and the Persian Period

In Isa 56–66, observance of the Sabbath—the seventh day of the week devoted to rest and worship—is a crucial sign of faithfulness to YHWH. Of the six references to the Sabbath in the book of Isaiah, five of them occur in Isa 56–66 (1:13; 56:2–6, three times; 58:13; 66:23). As we discussed back in chapters 5 and 8, Sabbath observance constitutes holding fast to YHWH and his covenant—as an act of faith, it can even overcome the default exclusions of eunuchs and foreigners (Isa 56:1–8). Lack of Sabbath-keeping was a cause of the exile (Jer 17:21–27; Ezek 20:12–24). In the Persian period, Nehemiah tried to lead a revival signified by closing the gates and preventing trade on the Sabbath day (9:14; 10:31–33; 13:15–22).

The Sabbath: Sacrificing Productivity, Sacrificing Social Standing

What did the Sabbath mean in the ancient world, and how is it important to us now?

We in the West live in exceptional times in human history in that most people do not live by subsistence work, a hand-to-mouth existence.

Compared to ancient societies, or to many emerging economies today, we are very rich. In ancient societies, and in very poor societies today, choosing not to work on one day out of seven was/is a significant act of faith in God's provision: Do I trust that if I forego productivity on one day, God will give me and my family "our daily bread" by making my other six days sufficiently productive? For some people in North America and Europe today, sacrificing productivity or trade on Sunday is a real sacrifice—I don't want to dismiss it, especially for people in service jobs.

But for many of us in a modern economy, "remembering the Sabbath day and keeping it holy" (Exod 20:8–11; Deut 5:12–15) is not so much sacrificing productivity but sacrificing activities and social opportunities—for us and for our children. It used to be easier to keep the Sabbath and not so much of a sacrifice. But it becomes harder and harder as Western society moves away from the norm of not having activities on Sunday.[4] It is difficult to tell your daughter that she can't participate in travel soccer at a higher competitive level because most of the games would require her and the family to miss church on Sunday. For many parents and families, that sacrifice of opportunity and social status is more difficult than a financial sacrifice of not earning money on Sunday.

The Sabbath as a Blessing and as a Sign of Faith

The Sabbath is important for Christians both for the objective benefits that it provides and for what it represents about the seriousness of our faith for our lives.

The Sabbath provides the objective benefits of rest. There is great concern in our society about overwork, mindfulness, work-life balance, anxiety, and depression. Setting aside a day to rest from our labors is a commonsense remedy.

Moreover, Sabbath observance allows worship of the triune God to be regular and to have its regular refreshing effect in our hearts and our minds even as our bodies receive rest.

As noted above, setting aside time for worship and rest represents an act of faith. Do I trust that God will provide for me what I am sacrificing

---

4. The early Christians began worshiping on Sunday ("the Lord's day"; Rev 1:10) because that was the day Jesus rose from the dead. Eventually, the significance and practices of the seventh-day Sabbath under the old covenant transferred to a first-day "Sabbath" for most Christians (except Seventh-Day Adventists).

in terms of social opportunities and provide for me what I need through attendance at worship?

I am not talking about a renewed legalism, laying upon Western Christians "a yoke . . . that neither our fathers nor we have been able to bear" (Acts 15:10). We are saved only through faith in Jesus Christ, not by Sabbath observance. I also do not wish to litigate details of how much yard work you should or should not do on Sunday, which I believe to be a matter of conscience. As we saw in chapter 8, the Sabbath is not intended as a burden or a formality (Isa 1:13) but rather as a gift and a delight (58:13). In Jewish tradition, because Sabbath observance is a right and an obligation for the poor and even for animals, it transforms even a poor person into "a prince of God."[5]

The Sabbath: Flexing Our "Muscles" of Faith and Resistance

The Sabbath is also an indicator of the ways that, as Christians, we either let ourselves drift along with the current of culture or swim against the culture. As our culture drifts further from Christian norms, differentiation of ourselves as Christ's disciples gets harder but becomes more important.

The Sabbath is a sign of our saltiness—if we become like the world and Sunday becomes just another day, we lose our distinctiveness. But if we keep the Sabbath despite the sacrifice it requires, we will be prepared to retain our distinctiveness in other ways.

As society changes, we will have to sacrifice opportunities and respectability. What if, for example, legislation were passed that compelled all medical schools to teach surgeons how to perform abortions and required all medical students to assist at least one abortion in their medical training?[6] Would this preclude faithful Christians from entering the medical profession? Would Christians be willing to exclude themselves from these "respectable" and lucrative professions for the sake of their faith? Would Christian medical students move overseas for comparable but less prestigious training that is more in line with their beliefs? Flexing our "faith muscles" in small, personal matters like the Sabbath will strengthen us to sacrifice greater things when obedience requires it.

---

5. Gordis, "Sabbath," 8.

6. Or, more likely than legislation might be changes in the standards of the bodies that accredit medical schools or license doctors.

NATIONS SHALL BRING THEIR LIGHT

As we decouple our faith from culture and society, we as Western Christians should look around at the nations of the world and view them differently. Here also, the text and the context of Isa 56–66 have a lot to say to us.

Christian Faith Is [What Remains of] "Our Light"

In chapter 10, we saw the picture in Isa 60 of the nations streaming to Jerusalem bringing their resources and themselves to worship Jerusalem's God, YHWH, and to honor Jerusalem. This happens even though Jerusalem/Judah herself has not been very deserving of honor. It is easy to see parallels in the waves of immigration from poorer countries to Western Europe and to North America. While I am not saying that America is "a Christian nation" or "God's Israel," much of what is good and successful about America and the West (which allows people to flourish) is the prevalence of Christianity and biblical truth applied in society. To the extent that the West is in decline, it is because we have moved away from those biblical foundations.

I am also not concerned with particular immigration policies—the fact is that immigrants want to come to the West, and many are here already. Much of what makes immigrants want to come here—freedom and prosperity—can be traced to our Christian roots.

So, "nations are coming to our light" even if our light is flickering and faltering. How should Western Christians treat them?

Learning from the Global Church

Christians can recognize that immigrants are often more traditional, with some values and norms that are more closely aligned with Christian values than our non-Christian, Western neighbors. Many immigrants are themselves Christians and can have a leavening influence on Western nations. Many Christian churches in urban or suburban areas have not experienced numerical decline simply due to immigrant communities replacing native-born attendees.

Moreover, these immigrants from the global church may have experience living in societies that are not sympathetic to Christian belief and practice; some of them even come from societies where they are persecuted for being Christians. My brothers and sisters at the South Asian seminary where I teach have a very different conception of their relationship to their governments (Islamic, or ostensibly secular but practically Hindu nationalist). They therefore have a lot to teach Western Christians—to modify Isa 60:3 and 5: "Nations will *bring their light*" and "The *spiritual wealth* of the nations shall come to you."

Investing in Our Own Future

Western Christians need to invest in the global church. This includes welcoming non-Westerners who come to our churches (again, irrespective of government policies) and also sending out missionaries into the world to fulfill the Great Commission.

One additional piece of this that Westerners are slow to recognize is that we in the West will need (or need now) missionaries from the global church to evangelize our societies. Thus, investment in the strength of the global church, including theological education, is an investment in our own future.[7]

All for the Glory of God—Not Just Pragmatism

Western Christians should view our opportunities to engage with foreigners on our shores, Christians and non-Christians, and to fulfill the Great Commission abroad as an objective good: the glory of God and the spread of the gospel. At the conclusion of chapter 5, I quoted Rev 5, which describes every nation, tribe, and tongue gathered around the throne glorifying "the Lamb who was slain." The inclusion of peoples from outside Israel is an essential theme of Isa 56–66 (especially 56, 60–62, and 65–66).

Reconciliation and unity of human beings in Christ across racial, ethnic, and language barriers brings glory to God. The work of the cross in reconciling peoples to one another across boundaries of difference (as individuals are reconciled to God through faith in Christ; Gal 3:26–29) is a testimony to the fallen spiritual powers that had held gentile individuals and peoples in bondage (Eph 3:10), but who are now "disarmed" (Col

---

7. Giffone, "(Ir)relevance of Biblical Scholarship?"

2:15). God is especially glorified when people come together to worship him across boundaries of difference (e.g., Rom 15:5–13).

EYES TO SEE, EARS TO HEAR: A WARNING (AND A COMMISSION) FOR US TODAY

In chapters 3 and 11, we saw that each prophet who wrote part of Isaiah picked up the mantle and ministry of the previous one and that Jesus, in identifying himself with the "Servant" of Isa 61:1–3 (Luke 4:16–21), picks up the mantle of all three (and fulfills the prophetic vocation even more fully). As we conclude this book, is there any sense in which this prophetic mantle passes to us as twenty-first-century followers of Jesus and his apostles? I believe there is.

The final quotation of the Old Testament recorded in the book of Acts, which is as far as the "story" goes within the New Testament, is Paul quoting Isa 6:9–10 to the Jewish descendants of Isaiah's original audience (Acts 28:25–28):

> The Holy Spirit was right in saying to your fathers through Isaiah the prophet: "Go to this people, and say, 'You will indeed hear but never understand, and you will indeed see but never perceive.' For this people's heart has grown dull, and with their ears they can barely hear, and their eyes they have closed; lest they should see with their eyes and hear with their ears and understand with their heart and turn, and I would heal them." Therefore let it be known to you that this salvation of God has been sent to the gentiles; they will listen. (Acts 28:25b–28)

Each evangelist has already recorded Jesus quoting this prophecy concerning the Jewish people as a whole in the context of the parable of the sower and seeds (Matt 13:13–15; Mark 4:12; Luke 8:10; see also John 12:39–40). Why does this passage of warning and judgment get so much attention in the New Testament? Why does the story of the New Testament leave off in this way?

At the risk of sounding very corny: the end of the book of Acts is not really an ending but just the beginning! It is the start of the spread of the gospel into all the world. Everyone who encounters the gospel message either receives it for what it is—the word of God—or is hardened to reject it, as in Jesus's parable.

Once we receive the word of God in this saving way, we have no choice but to spread the glory of the God who has saved us. As his reputation spreads into the whole world, everyone will confront this reality—"The LORD has bared his holy arm before the eyes of all the nations, and all the ends of the earth shall see the salvation of our God" (Isa 52:10).

One might even say that the prophetic messages of Isaiah have even greater force or imperative upon us today, given all that we know about the holiness of God, his love and faithfulness in the death and resurrection of Jesus Christ, and the giving of the Holy Spirit (as testified in the New Testament). If we harden our hearts, close our eyes, and cover our ears to God's summons to worship him and loyally serve him, then we have no excuse.

There is a very important difference between the situation of Isaiah ben Amoz's eighth-century audience of which YHWH spoke in Isa 6:9-10 and our situation today. Israel's eyes and ears were closed and their hearts hardened so as to create an opportunity for the nations to come into YHWH's people by faith. Paul explains this in Rom 11:7-27 and quotes both Isa 29:10 (Rom 11:7) to describe Israel's hardening and Isa 59:20 and 27:9 (Rom 11:26-27) to picture the restoration of both Israel and the nations by God's mercy and grace. The hearts of both ethnic Jews and people of all nations will be turned back to Israel's God.

This is accomplished by the "Spirit of YHWH" (11:2; 42:1; 48:16; 59:21; 61:1), the Holy Spirit that was poured out upon all flesh at Pentecost (Acts 2:17-18; Joel 2:28-29; Isa 44:3). By the power of that same Spirit, we can be confident as we proclaim this message from YHWH into the world: "My salvation is close at hand!" (Isa 56:1).

Bibliography

Adeboye, Godwin. *Can a Christian Be Cursed? An African Evangelical Response to the Problem of Curses.* Carlisle, UK: Langham, 2023.

Bock, Darrell L., ed. *Three Views on the Millennium and Beyond.* Grand Rapids: Zondervan, 1999.

Boda, Mark J. "The Priceless Gain of Penitence: From Communal Lament to Penitential Prayer in the 'Exilic' Liturgy of Israel." In *Lamentations in Ancient and Contemporary Cultural Contexts,* edited by Nancy C. Lee and Carleen Mandolfo, 81–101. Atlanta: SBL, 2008.

Chambers, Oswald. *The Quotable Oswald Chambers.* Compiled and edited by David McCasland. Ulrichsville, OH: Discovery House, 2008.

Childs, Brevard S. *Isaiah.* Old Testament Library. Louisville: Westminster John Knox, 2001.

———. *The Struggle to Understand Isaiah as Christian Scripture.* Grand Rapids: Eerdmans, 2004.

Dreher, Rod. *Live Not by Lies: A Manual for Christian Dissidents.* New York: Sentinel, 2020.

Elliott, Mark W., ed. *Isaiah 40-66.* Ancient Christian Commentary on Scripture. Downers Grove, IL: InterVarsity, 2007.

Fleming, Daniel E. *The Legacy of Israel in Judah's Bible: History, Politics, and the Reinscribing of Tradition.* New York: Cambridge University Press, 2012.

George, Timothy. *Theology of the Reformers,* Rev. ed. Nashville: Broadman & Holman, 2013.

Giffone, Benjamin D. "Can Theological Interpretation Soften the Protestant Problem of Old Testament Textual Plurality? Jeremiah as a Test Case." *European Journal of Theology* 29.2 (2020) 153–78.

———. *A House Divided: Technology, Worship, and Healing the Church After COVID.* St. Louis, MO: Libertarian Christian Institute, forthcoming 2025.

———. "The (Ir)relevance of Biblical Scholarship? A Challenge, and an Opportunity." *Scriptura* 120.1 (2021) 1–15.

———. *Storymaking, Textual Development, and Varying Cultic Centralizations: Gathering and Fitting Unhewn Stones.* FAT II/142. Tübingen: Mohr Siebeck, 2023.

———. "Toward a Better 'Hezekiah': The Literary Structuring of Isaiah 1–39." *Old Testament Essays* 36.2 (2023) 471–89.

Giffone, Benjamin D., and Sage E. Wile. "No One Strives to Take Hold of You: Mark 5's Echoes of Isaiah 63:7—66:17." *Neot* 57.2 (2023) 229–43. https://doi.org/10.1353/neo.2023.a943176.

Goldingay, John. *A Critical and Exegetical Commentary on Isaiah 56–66*. ICC. London: Bloomsbury, 2014.

———. *Isaiah*. Understanding the Bible Commentary Series. Grand Rapids: Baker, 2001.

———. "Isaiah 53 in the Pulpit." *Perspectives in Religious Studies* 35 (2008) 147–53.

———. *The Theology of the Book of Isaiah*. Downers Grove, IL: IVP Academic, 2014.

Goldingay, John, and David Payne. *A Critical and Exegetical Commentary on Isaiah 40–55*. 2 vols. ICC. London: T&T Clark, 2006.

Gordis, Robert. "The Sabbath—Cornerstone and Capstone of Jewish Life." *Judaism* 31.1 (1982) 6–11.

Grabbe, Lester L. *A History of the Jews and Judaism in the Second Temple Period*. Vol. 1 of *Yehud: A History of the Persian Province of Judah*. LSTS 47. London: T&T Clark, 2004.

Hays, J. Daniel. "Jeremiah, the Septuagint, the Dead Sea Scrolls and Inerrancy: Just What Exactly Do We Mean by the 'Original Autographs'?" In *Evangelicals and Scripture: Tradition, Authority, and Hermeneutics*, edited by Vincent Bacote, et al., 133–49. Downers Grove, IL: InterVarsity, 2004.

Hays, Richard B. *Echoes of Scripture in the Gospels*. Waco, TX: Baylor University Press, 2016.

———. *Echoes of Scripture in the Letters of Paul*. New Haven: Yale University Press, 1989.

Hengel, Martin. *Crucifixion in the Ancient World and the Folly of the Message of the Cross*. Philadelphia: Fortress, 1977.

Holter, Knut. *Second Isaiah's Idol-Fabrication Passages*. BBET 28. Frankfurt: Lang, 1995.

Horton, Michael. *The Christian Faith: A Systematic Theology for Pilgrims on the Way*. Grand Rapids: Zondervan, 2011.

Justin Martyr. *The Writings of Saint Justin Martyr*. Translated by Thomas B. Falls. Washington, DC: Catholic University of America Press, 1948.

Lewis, C. S. *The C. S. Lewis Signature Classics*. New York: HarperOne, 2017.

———. *The Weight of Glory*. New York: HarperCollins, 2000.

McConville, J. Gordon. *Exploring the Old Testament: A Guide to the Prophets*. Downers Grove, IL: IVP Academic, 2002.

———. *Isaiah*. BCOT. Grand Rapids: Baker Academic, 2023.

Miller, Paul, dir. "Demetri Martin." Season 8, episode 14 of *Comedy Central Presents*. Originally aired Mar. 19, 2004.

Mintz, Alan. *Hurban: Responses to Catastrophe in Hebrew Literature*. New York: Columbia University Press, 1984.

Philo. *On the Confusion of Tongues. On the Migration of Abraham. Who Is the Heir of Divine Things? On Mating with the Preliminary Studies*. Vol. 4. Translated by F. H. Colson and G. H. Whitaker. LCL. Cambridge, MA: Harvard University Press, 1932.

Poul, Alan, dir. "Main Justice." Season 3, episode 3 of *The Newsroom*. Originally aired Nov. 23, 2014.

Poythress, Vern S. *Biblical Typology: How the Old Testament Points to Christ, His Church, and the Consummation*. Wheaton, IL: Crossway, 2024.

Renn, Aaron M. *Life in the Negative World: Confronting Challenges in an Anti-Christian Culture*. Grand Rapids: Baker, 2024.

Salters, Robert B. *A Critical and Exegetical Commentary on Lamentations*. ICC. New York: T&T Clark, 2010.
Sandy, D. Brent. *Plowshares and Pruning Hooks: Rethinking the Language of Biblical Prophecy and Apocalyptic*. Downers Grove, IL: InterVarsity, 2002.
Sawyer, John F. A. *The Fifth Gospel: Isaiah in the History of Christianity*. New York: Cambridge University Press, 1996.
Schaff, Philip. *History of the Apostolic Church with a General Introduction to Church History*. Translated by Edward D. Yeomans. New York: Scribner, 1854.
Schnittjer, Gary E. "The Bad Ending of Ezra–Nehemiah." *BSac* 173.1 (2016) 32–56.
———. *Old Testament Use of Old Testament*. Grand Rapids: Zondervan, 2021.
———. *The Torah Story: An Apprenticeship on the Pentateuch*. Grand Rapids: Zondervan, 2006.
Shrier, Abigail. *Irreversible Damage: The Transgender Craze Seducing Our Daughters*. Washington, DC: Regnery, 2020.
Smith, Yancy. *The Mystery of Anointing: Hippolytus' Commentary on the Song of Songs in Social and Critical Contexts*. Gorgias Studies in Early Christianity and Patristics 62. Piscataway, NJ: Gorgias, 2015.
Soesbe, Susan M. *Bringing Mom Home: How Two Sisters Moved Their Mother Out of Assisted Living to Care for Her Under One Amazingly Large Roof*. Harleysville, PA: Rend, 2018.
Stanley, Andy. *Irresistible: Reclaiming the New that Jesus Unleashed for the World*. Grand Rapids: Zondervan, 2018.
Tolkien, J. R. R. *The Lord of the Rings*. New York: HarperCollins, 2021.
Trible, Phyllis. *Texts of Terror: Literary-Feminist Readings of Biblical Narratives*. OBT 13. Philadelphia: Fortress, 1984.
Tull Willey, Patricia. *Remember the Former Things: The Recollection of Previous Texts in Second Isaiah*. SBLDS 161. Atlanta: Scholars, 1997.
Van der Toorn, Karel. *Scribal Culture and the Making of the Hebrew Bible*. Cambridge: Harvard University Press, 2007.
Walker, Christopher, and Michael B. Dick. "The Induction of the Cult Image in Ancient Mesopotamia: The Mesopotamian *mis pî* Ritual." In *Born in Heaven, Made on Earth: The Making of the Cult Image in the Ancient Near East*, edited by Michael B. Dick, 55–122. Winona Lake, IN: Eisenbrauns, 1999.
Walton John H., and D. Brent Sandy. *The Lost World of Scripture: Ancient Literary Culture and Biblical Authority*. Downers Grove, IL: IVP Academic, 2013.
Watts, Rikki E. *Isaiah's New Exodus in Mark*. Grand Rapids: Baker Academic, 2000.
Westminster Standard. "Larger Catechism." https://thewestminsterstandard.org/westminster-larger-catechism/.
Wiesehöfer, Josef. *Ancient Persia from 550 BC to 650 AD*. Translated by Azizeh Azodi. New York: I. B. Tauris, 2001.
Willitts, Joel, and David J. Rudolph, eds. *Introduction to Messianic Judaism: Its Ecclesial Context and Biblical Foundations*. Grand Rapids: Zondervan, 2013.
Witherington, Ben, III. *Isaiah Old and New: Exegesis, Intertextuality, and Hermeneutics*. Minneapolis: Fortress, 2017.
Wright, N. T. *The Climax of the Covenant: Christ and the Law in Pauline Theology*. London: T&T Clark, 1991.
———. *The New Testament and the People of God*. Minneapolis: Fortress, 1992.

Subject Index

abortion, 72, 74, 84, 201
Abraham, 13, 20, 22, 50, 68n3, 70, 108, 134, 141, 152–154, 162, 167, 191
apocalyptic, 29–32
Assyria/Assyrian(s), 16–19, 21, 28, 32–35, 43, 50, 134, 165, 197–198
Augustine, 46–47

Babylon/Babylonian(s), 21–23, 29, 33–36, 38, 40–44, 51, 55, 61, 68, 70, 83, 92, 95, 120–121, 123, 134, 141, 147, 154, 156n12, 197–199
Boda, Mark J., 164
ceremonial law. *See* ritual purity.

Childs, Brevard S., ix, 3n1, 183n1
circumcision, 13, 68, 68n3
conflict, 49, 52, 55–56, 59–60, 62
covenant, 13, 46, 65, 67, 68, 69, 77, 80, 87–89, 103, 115, 123, 140, 164, 176, 179, 181, 190, 199, 200n4 ,
New Covenant, 13, 55, 68, 73, 155n11, 179, 192, 200n4
COVID-19 pandemic, 49, 56, 62, 106
Cyrus, 33, 36, 37, 39, 40, 42, 43, 51, 53, 141n3, 196–197

David, 12, 15, 21, 34–35, 39, 39n19, 44, 51, 54, 121, 133, 138, 141, 151
diaspora, 38, 52
divine images, 14, 36–37, 41, 75, 80, 83–84, 86–87, 89, 90–97, 120, 142–145, 147, 151–152, 169, 173, 182, 187, 194
division. *See* conflict.

economics, 5, 7, 27, 198, 200
Egypt/Egyptian(s), 9, 11, 14n7, 21–23, 28, 34, 38, 44, 50, 52, 55, 68n3, 92, 94, 103, 109, 116, 123, 133, 134, 143, 147, 155, 165
empire, 16, 20–23, 33–34, 43, 50–51, 58, 69–70, 165, 197–199
exile/exilic, 8, 29, 33–34, 36, 38–43, 46, 51–52, 55, 61–62, 68, 83–84, 89, 95, 121, 126, 131, 188, 196, 199

Father, God as,, 39, 44, 61, 67, 73, 75, 135, 145, 153, 156–158, 160–163, 166–169,
foreigners. *See* gentiles.

gender, 2, 5, 49, 198
gentiles, 9, 20, 45, 55, 68–69, 74, 75, 77, 127, 130–137, 147–148, 155, 159 169, 171, 178–181, 183, 186, 191, 193, 195–205
Giffone, Benjamin D., 28n5, 29n6, 34n10, 52n1, 62n4, 81n1, 121n4, 155n9, 168, 180n5, 189n3, 203n7
Goldingay, John, ix, 38n16, 39–40, 41, 43n23, 46n27, 66n2, 113n1, 120

Hays, Richard B., ix–x, 167n7, 181n6

Hippolytus, 14n7
human sacrifice, 84–85, 131, 152

idol. *See* divine images.
image of God. *See* divine images.
images of gods. *See* divine images.
imago Dei. *See* divine images.

Jacob, 20, 22, 36, 37, 46, 50, 100–101, 115, 119, 125, 129, 154, 167, 172,
justice, 27, 30, 35, 44, 54, 66–67, 81, 97, 102–104, 109–111, 113, 116–122, 124, 141–142, 156, 158, 198
Justin Martyr, 13

Lewis, C.S., 136, 166
Luther, Martin, 157n13

McConville, J. Gordon, ix, 25, 41
migration, 66, 202–204
military, 84, 105, 198–199
Mosaic law, 9, 12, 21, 39, 67–70, 102–103, 108–109, 152, 155, 164, 168, 175–178, 183

new creation, 30–31, 44, 65, 76–77, 90, 98, 111, 117, 125, 142, 144, 146, 156, 187–189, 191–194
North American church, 4, 10, 47, 50, 58, 65, 71, 82, 104–105, 110, 127, 161, 196–205

occult, 85, 154n8

Persia/Persian(s), 7, 20–23, 33, 36, 38–40, 42, 43, 48, 50–54, 59, 62, 78, 96, 141n3, 157, 174, 192–193, 196–199
Philo, 14n7

poetry, 3, 11n3, 24–28, 31–32, 82, 86, 92, 96, 138, 174
predictive prophecy, 3, 11, 29–32, 38, 40–42, 44–45, 51, 127, 146, 169, 193

re-creation. *See* new creation.
re-enchantment, 6, 135
repentance, 38, 62, 67, 74–77, 81n1, 86, 88, 89, 96, 98, 103, 122–125, 132, 166, 182, 190
ritual purity, 10, 60, 61, 67, 70, 93, 99, 102, 104–108, 110, 117, 144, 167–169, 175–178, 180, 183, 190

Sabbath, 39, 67, 69, 105, 107–111, 156, 176, 199–201
sacrificial system, 53–54, 66–67, 80, 99, 104, 110, 117, 176–178, 192
Sandy, D. Brent, 25, 28, 30n7
Schnittjer, Gary E., ix, 39n18, 68n3, 176, 196n1
sexuality, 5, 69–76, 82, 84, 106, 198
Spirit of the LORD. *See* Spirit of YHWH.
Spirit of YHWH, 39, 44, 121–126, 139–141, 156, 162, 169, 205

technology, 4, 5, 10, 82, 84, 85, 135
transgender(ism), 5, 70–71, 75, 198
typology, 9–20, 31, 73n5, 123, 193

violence, 2, 10, 69, 72, 74, 81, 84, 116–117, 119–120, 122, 132, 134, 145

Western church. *See* North American church.
Wright, N.T., ix–x, 38n17

Zion, 26, 33, 36–37, 42n22, 115, 119, 123, 129–132, 138–141, 150–157, 163, 167, 185, 187, 190

Scripture Index

HEBREW BIBLE

Genesis

1–11	20
1	36, 130, 187
1:1	187
1:2	44
1:3	142
1:27	119n2
1:28	151
2	72, 188
2:5	119n2
2:7	36, 94
3:14	187
3:16	187
3:17–19	38, 187
5–11	188n2
6:3	188n2
7:22	95
10:8–12	134
10:21	22
10:24–25	22
11:1–9	134
11:4	154
11:14–17	22
12–50	21, 155n9
14:18–22	155
15	122
15:7	152, 152n2
17:1	155
17:5	154
17:15	154
19	68n3
21:33	155
22:14	155
25:30	119n2
29:35	22
32:27–28	154
32:28	22
35:10	22, 154
35:11	155
36:1	119
38	14
48:3	155

Exodus

3:22	143
4:21	166
6:2–8	155, 155n9
7:3	166
8:15	166
8:32	166
9:12	166
9:34	166
10:20	166
10:27	166
11:2	143
11:10	166
12:35–36	143
14:4	166
14:8	166
15:26	155

Exodus (continued)

17:15	155
20–23	103
20:8–11	200
22:21–27	103
32–34	12

Leviticus

11–15	176
11	177n2
12	177
12:1–5	177n3
15:19–30	168, 177
16:29	102
17:10–14	177
18:25	152
18:28	152
20:22	152
21:17–23	69
26:13	109
26:19	152n1

Numbers

6:1–21	102
6:24–26	95
9:6–14	177
19:11–22	177
24:24	22

Deuteronomy

4:32–35	165
5:12–15	200
6:16	16, 76
7	68
7:12–16	152
12:20–27	177
14:1–2	102
18:18–20	12
21:17	144n6
23	68
23:1	69
23:3–6	68n3
23:7–8	68n3
23:25	108n2
28:1–14	152
28:23	152
28:15–68	152

1 Samuel

1:4–5	144n6
16:18	12
17:46	81

2 Samuel

5	133
7:2	54

1 Kings

12	22
1 Kings 11—2 Kings 17	24

2 Kings

6:1–7	13
17:31	84
18:13–20:19	28–29, 32, 33
20	33
21:6	84
24:14	52

Isaiah

1–55	43, 66
1–39	35, 39, 44, 121, 141
1–35	34–35, 120
1–12	32, 35
1–5	28, 32, 45
1	17, 105, 113
1:4	35, 44
1:8–9	35
1:13	199, 201
1:15	117
1:21	35
1:26–27	35
1:26	151, 154
2:2–4	45, 153, 191
2:2	86
3	17, 113
3:15	93
4:2–6	62n5
4:2–4	34
4:2	35

4:3	35	10:19–22	35
5–6	17	10:20–22	44
5	34	10:20	35, 44
5:1–4	179	10:24	45
5:2–4	117	11	34, 141
5:7	35, 142	11:1	62n5
5:11–12	82	11:2–3	45
5:12	82n2	11:2	44, 81, 121, 205
5:16	35	11:4	35
5:19	35, 44	11:6–9	187
5:22	82n2	11:9	86
5:24	35, 44	11:10	45, 151
5:29	35	11:11	35, 44, 191
6	17, 28, 32, 44	11:16	35, 44, 45
6:1	43	12:1–6	35
6:3	35	12:6	35, 44
6:5	93	13–39	35
6:8–13	45	13–27	28, 32
6:9–13	35	13–23	45
6:9–10	37, 204, 205	13–14	34
7:1–2	16	14	34
7:3–9	16	14:22	35
7:3	17, 19, 35	14:30	35
7:4	45	15:9	35
7:10–11	16	16:5	35
7:12	16	16:14	35
7:14–16	10, 16–19	17:3	35
7:14	17–19, 37, 93, 108	17:6	35
7:15–20	34	17:7	35, 44
7:17–20	16	19–20	34, 44
7:22	35	19:18	154
7–10	32, 43	20	27, 34
7–8	16–19, 28, 34, 44	21:9	34
8:1–4	17–18	21:17	35
8:3	18	22:13	82n2
8:4–8	34	23:13	34
8:7–8	16	24–27	30
8:8	18	24–25	34
8:12	45	24:6	35
8:16–18	45	24:7–11	82n2
8:16	28	24:12	35
9–12	28	24:15	191
9:2–7	34	25	191
9:2	45, 117	25:6	82
9:6	154	25:9	v, xii
9:7	35	26–27	31
10	34, 45	26:1–6	35
10:15	44, 165	26:7	45

Isaiah (continued)

Reference	Page
26:9	35
27:1–5	35
27:1	190
27:2	82
27:9	205
27:13	86
28–35	28, 32
28–33	44
28:1	82n2
28:5	35, 44
28:6	44
28:7	82n2
28:9–13	46
28:11	41
28:14–15	85
28:17	35
29:9	82
29:10	205
29:11–14	45
29:13	45
29:16	45, 165
29:19	35, 44
30–31	34
30:1–5	34
30:7	154
30:11–12	35, 44
30:15	35, 44
30:16–17	34
30:17	35
30:26	117
31:1–3	34
31:1	35, 44
32:1	35
32:15	44
32:16	35
33:5	35
33:6	45
34–35	30
34:16—35:2	44
34:5–6	120
35	31, 45
35:4	45
35:5	142
35:8–10	92
36–39	28–29, 32–34
36–37	33, 34, 43
36	44
36:6	34
36:9	34
37	34
37:3	187
37:4	35, 44
37:6	45
37:22–29	35
37:23	35, 44
37:30	82
37:31–32	35, 44
38	33
38:6	33
38:9–20	33, 35
39	29, 34, 44, 121
39:6	35
39:8	34
40–66	29, 35, 41, 44
40–55	29, 33, 35, 36, 37, 39, 41, 73n5, 83, 95, 120, 121, 131, 141, 187
40:1–9	45
40:1	36
40:2	36, 46, 144
40:3–4	91–92
40:3	36, 41, 151
40:6–7	188
40:6	46
40:9	45, 46, 131, 141
40:18–20	36
40:24	86
40:26–28	36
41–42	191
41:10–14	45
41:10	93
41:14	35, 44
41:16	35, 44
41:18–19	36
41:20	35, 36, 44
41:21–29	36, 41
41:25	36
41:27	131
41:6–7	36
41:8–10	37
42	118, 121
42:1–9	45
42:1–4	37
42:1	44, 141, 205

42:5	36	46:3	44
42:6–7	118	46:4	36
42:7	142	46:7	36
42:16–20	36	46:9	188
42:16–18	118	47	37, 45
42:16	45, 117	47:1	154
42:17	36	47:2	103n1
42:19–20	37	47:4	35, 44
43:1	36, 45	47:5	154
43:2	93	48:7	36
43:3	35, 44	48:16	44, 205
43:5	45	48:17	35, 44
43:7	36	48:20	37
43:8–10	37	49	151, 166–167
43:8–9	36	49:1–7	37
43:11–13	36	49:5	36
43:14	35, 44	49:6	117
43:15	36	49:7	35
43:16	45	49:7	44
43:18	188	49:8	156
43:19–20	36	49:11	45
43:21	36	49:13	36
43:26	35	49:14–26	37
44–45	43	49:14	156
44:1–2	37	49:15	120
44:2	36, 45	49:18	37
44:3	44, 205	49:19–22	37
44:9–20	36, 86	49:19	156
44:17	35, 36	49:21	35
44:18–20	36	49:25–26	44
44:20	36	49:26	82n2
44:21	36	50	141
44:21–26	37	50:1	37
44:24	36	50:1–3	37
45	44	50:2	36, 116
45:1–13	42	50:4–11	37
45:1	39, 40, 141	50:8	35
45:4	37	50:10	45
45:7–9	36	51:1	59n3, 191
45:9–10	45	51:3	36
45:11–12	36	51:5	35
45:11	35, 44	51:7	45
45:18	36	51:11	36
45:20	35, 36	51:12	36, 45
46	45	51:17—52:3	37
46:11	36	51:17	37, 82, 119
46:1–7	36	51:18–20	37
46:3	35	51:21—52:3	82n2

Isaiah (continued)

51:21	82, 119
51:22–23	37
52:1	37
52:3	44
52:3–5	37
52:7–10	44
52:7	46, 131, 141, 167
52:9	36
52:10	205
52:13—53:12	37, 38, 73n5, 121
53	41, 141
53:2	145
53:5	94
53:10	73, 94
54	37
54:1–3	37
54:4	45
54:5	35, 44
54:6–8	37
54:7–10	55
54:11	36
54:14	45
54:17	35
55	38
55:1–2	38
55:1	82
55:3–5	38
55:3	39, 121
55:5	35, 44
55:6–7	38
55:8–11	38
55:12–13	38
56–59	133, 147, 158
56	62, 125, 203
56:1–8	40, 45, 59, 64–77, 89, 127, 188, 199
56:1	35, 205
56:2–6	199
56:2	67
56:3–7	179
56:3–4	69
56:4	105, 168
56:5	42, 73, 109, 154
56:6	105, 168
56:7	69, 86
56:9—59:8	40
56:9—57:13	78–89
56:9–12	81–82
56:10–11	81
56:10	118
56:12	82
57	66
57:1–2	82–83
57:3–13	83–86
57:3	83
57:4	84
57:5–9	84
57:6–8	144
57:8–9	144
57:10–13	86
57:11	45
57:13	96
57:14–21	89–98
57:14	45, 91–92, 151
57:15	92–94, 102
57:16–17	94–95
57:17	116
57:18–19	95–96, 123
57:18	97
57:19	191
57:20–21	96
58	66, 86, 96, 99–111, 139, 141, 156, 176, 194
58:1	46
58:2	35
58:5–7	144
58:5	102
58:6	109
58:7	109
58:8–10	117, 142
58:8	109, 123
58:9	109
58:10	109
58:12	109, 154
58:13–14	109
58:13	105, 199, 201
59	44, 45, 112–125, 126, 135, 142
59:1	116
59:2	116
59:2–15	118, 124
59:2–3	118
59:3–8	116–117

59:3-4	123	61	121, 126, 138-148, 149, 157
59:3	117		
59:4-8	118	61:1-3	39, 46, 141, 204
59:4	35	61:1-2	46, 146
59:6	144	61:1	44, 66n1, 123, 141, 142, 167, 205
59:7-8	117		
59:9-15	40, 117-118	61:2	95, 142, 146
59:9-12	118	61:3	144, 154
59:9	35, 45, 117	61:4-5	142
59:10	118	61:6	144, 154
59:13-15	118	61:7	144
59:14-15	118	61:10	144
59:14	35	61:11	66n1, 147
59:15-21	39, 40, 67	62	109, 126, 140, 142, 149-159, 166-167
59:15-16	119		
59:16	119	62:1	156, 157
59:17	145	62:2-4	154
59:19	45, 113, 122, 123	62:2-3	156
59:20	122, 125, 205	62:3	145
59:21	121, 123, 125, 126, 141, 205	62:4	156
		62:6	42, 157
59:21—60:2	44	62:7	157, 158
60-62	40, 67-68, 125, 126, 156, 203	62:8-9	153
		62:10	45, 153
60-61	62	62:12	154, 156, 157
60	45, 109, 123, 126-137, 140, 142, 145, 149, 191, 202	63-66	161, 179, 180
		63	156
		63:1-6	40, 67, 112-125, 160n1
60:1-3	130, 145		
60:1-2	26	63:1-3	145
60:2	130, 132	63:1	119, 122
60:3	127, 203	63:2	119, 122
60:4-7	131	63:3	119, 122
60:4	26	63:4	122
60:5-7	131	63:5	122
60:5	203	63:6	119, 122
60:6	127, 131	63:7—64:12	40, 158-170, 174, 182
60:9	26, 35, 44, 132	63:7-19	67
60:10	131	63:7	174
60:11	132	63:10-14	44
60:14-15	132	63:10-12	165
60:14	35, 44	63:10	166
60:16	132	63:11	166
60:17	132	63:14	182
60:18	132, 154	63:15—64:12	42
60:19-20	130, 132	63:15-19	39
60:20	132	63:15	164, 166, 167, 174
60:22	132	63:16	44, 166-168

Isaiah (continued)

63:17	45, 165, 166
64–66	67, 178
64:1	166, 174, 179
64:3	47, 161, 170
64:5–7	166, 174
64:5	168
64:6	144, 166, 168, 176, 178, 179
64:7	164, 168, 178
64:8–9	165
64:8	45, 166, 182
64:9	167, 174
64:12	167, 174
65–66	31, 45, 62, 167, 174, 182, 183, 191, 195, 203
65:1—66:16	40
65	167, 188
65:1–15	171–182
65:1–2	41, 178, 181
65:1	174
65:2	175, 180, 182
65:3	178
65:4	177, 178, 180
65:5	175, 178
65:7	178
65:8	44, 174, 179
65:12–14	179
65:12	189
65:13	66n1, 174
65:15	66n1, 159 179, 193
65:16–25	183–195
65:16–17	188
65:17–25	191
65:17–18	187
65:20–23	187
65:20	187
65:21	82
65:23	187, 188
65:24	189
65:25	174, 187
66:1–6	171–182
66:2	168, 179
66:3	175, 177, 178
66:4	189
66:5	168, 178, 179, 182
66:7–24	183–195
66:7–9	186, 187
66:8	193
66:10–14	186, 190
66:14–17	186
66:17–24	40
66:17	190
66:18–21	186
66:19	35, 191, 194
66:20	190
66:21	69
66:22	186
66:23	183, 186, 199
66:24	183, 186

Jeremiah

7:30–34	84
16:16–18	36
17:21–27	199
18–19	84
19	27
23:5	62n5
29:1–14	51
29:11	8
30–33	51
31:33	123
33:15	62n5
36:4–32	28
45:1–5	28

Ezekiel

3–4	27
3	81
16	83
16:10	143
16:39	144
20:12–14	199
23	83
23:26	144
23:29	144
33	81
39:4	81
40–48	51, 192
43–45	38

Scripture Index

Hosea
1–3	83
2:3	144
2:8–13	144
11:1	11, 19

Joel
2:28–29	205

Micah
5	133
5:2	133

Haggai
1–2	38, 42
1:1–11	52–55
1:12–15	55

Zechariah
3:1–10	60–62
3:3–5	146
3:9	61, 193
9:12	144n6
11:13	41

Malachi
3:1	38
3:10	58
4	196

Psalms
1:4–6	86
2	132
22:18	145
34:18	93
46	132
50:12–15	54, 143
103:9–10	94
106	164
133:2	144

Job
5:5	103n1
18:9	103n1

Proverbs
1:2	81
1:20–33	14n7
2:5–6	81
15:14	81

Ruth
2	66
2:1	12

Song of Songs
1:2	14n7
1:13	14n7

Lamentations
1:2	36n15
1:9	36n15
1:16–17	36n15
1:21	36n15
2:13	36n15

Daniel
1	70, 154
7–12	29
9	164

Ezra
1–6	42, 197
4–5	54
5:2	55
6:13–22	55
6:21	55
9	164

Nehemiah
1	164
2–7	42
8–9	104
9	39, 164
9:14	199
10:31–33	199
13:14	196

Nehemiah (continued)

13:15–22	199
13:22	196
13:29–31	196

2 Chronicles

36:22–23	196

NEW TESTAMENT

Matthew

1:12–13	62
1:20	8
1:22–23	17–19
2:1–12	127, 128, 133–135, 136
2:15	11
3:1–3	91
3:3	41
3:16	167
4:1–11	17
5–7	12
5:13	199
6:9	160
6:33	62, 87
7:28–29	12
8:17	41
9:12	94
12:34	117
13:13–15	204
16:18	154
18:20	110
22:30	192
26:39	121
27:5	8
27:9	41

Mark

1:1	167
1:2–3	91
1:10	167
1:15	167
4:12	204
5:1–43	179–180
5:25–34	168, 179
5:28	168
5:35–36	189n3
10:45	87
15:39	147

Luke

3:1–6	91
3:21	167
3:27	62
4:14–30	146, 147
4:16–21	46, 204
4:21	146
5:33–35	108
6:1–11	108
6:5	108
6:9	108
8:10	204
10:37	8
13:10–17	108
13:15–16	108
23:52	145
24:12	145

John

1:23	91
3:3–8	193
4:19–24	153
10:16	193
12:39–40	204
13:27	8
19:23–25	145
20:24–29	189

Acts

2:17–18	205
2:39	125
4:36	154
8	41
8:1–3	74
9	154n6
9:1–2	74
13:9	154n6
15:10	201
28:25–28	204

Romans

1:4	145
3–4	125
3:15–17	117
4	13
4:13	152
5:14	12
6:1–7	76
8	157
8:18–23	191
8:20	187
8:34	157
9–11	181
9:30–10:21	181n6
10:19–21	181
10:20–21	41
11:7	205
11:7–27	205
11:26–27	205
15:5–13	204
15:16	191

1 Corinthians

6:9–11	74–75
10:1–13	13
10:1	9
10:6	9
10:11	9
14:21	41
15	191
15:20–28	111
15:50–57	192

2 Corinthians

5:2	193

Galatians

3:15–18	153n3
3:26–29	203

Ephesians

1:3–14	157
1:21	155
2:11–22	55, 153
2:17	95–96
2:19–22	69
3:10	203
3:15	155
4:15	75
6:10–20	119

Philippians

1:6	193
2:5–11	122, 155
2:9–11	145
3:4–6	191

Colossians

2:15	203–204

1 Timothy

1:13	74

2 Timothy

3:16	27

Hebrews

1:3	157
1:4	155
1:13	157
3:1–6	12
4:1–11	111
4:14–5:10	12
8:1	157
8:1–6	12
8:10	123
10:12	157
10:16	123
10:19–25	176
12:2	157
13:8	14
13:15	123

1 John

2:1–2	157

Revelation

1:6	193
1:10	200n4

Revelation (continued)

2:17	156
3:5	146, 156
3:12	155
3:18	146
5:6	189
5:9–14	77, 203
5:9	189, 193
5:10	193
12:9	190
13	156n12
17	156n12
19:12–13	155
20:2	190
20:4–6	192
20:7–10	192
20:15	156
21–22	153, 191
21:4	192
21:12	155n11
21:24	155n11

www.ingramcontent.com/pod-product-compliance
Lightning Source LLC
Chambersburg PA
CBHW062018220426
43662CB00010B/1384